UNLEASHING
CHANGE

UNLEASHING CHANGE

A Study of Organizational Renewal in Government

Steven Kelman

BROOKINGS INSTITUTION PRESS
Washington, D.C.

Copyright © 2005
THE BROOKINGS INSTITUTION
1775 Massachusetts Avenue, N.W., Washington, D.C. 20036
www.brookings.edu

Library of Congress Cataloging-in-Publication data

Kelman, Steven.
    Unleashing change : a study of organizational renewal in government / Steven Kelman.
        p.   cm.
    Summary: "Drawing on the experience of procurement reform in the Reinventing Government initiative of the 1990s, as well as organization theory and psychology, this book presents a comprehensive approach to improving performance in big public sector organizations that addresses both theory and practice"—Provided by publisher.
    Includes bibliographical references and index.
    ISBN-13: 978-0-8157-4899-1 (isbn-13, paper : alk. paper)
    ISBN-10: 0-8157-4899-X (isbn-10, paper : alk. paper)
    1. Organizational change. 2. Public administration. 3. Government purchasing.
4. Administrative agencies—Reorganization. 5. Government productivity.   I. Title.
    JF1525.O73K45   2005
    352.3'67—dc22   2005009621

9 8 7 6 5 4 3 2 1
The paper used in this publication meets minimum requirements of the American National Standard for Information Sciences—Permanence of Paper for Printed Library Materials: ANSI Z39.48-1992.

Typeset in Sabon

Composition by Kulamer Publishing Services
Potomac, Maryland

Printed by R. R. Donnelley
Harrisonburg, Virginia

For Shelley, Jody, and Leora

Contents

Acknowledgments

I have worked a long time researching and writing this book, and have accumulated many debts of gratitude to acknowledge. The first is to the 1,593 procurement professionals and 272 procurement employees, supervisors, and managers in eighteen buying offices in the federal government who graciously participated in the two surveys that provide the empirical material for this study. I also owe a huge debt of thanks to the senior headquarters–level contracting officials in a number of government organizations, both military and civilian, who agreed to facilitate my access to these buying offices, and to the directors of contracting in each of these buying offices, who agreed to let me undertake this research at their offices. Nobody who was approached refused my request for help. My commitment to provide them and their offices with anonymity prevents me from mentioning their names, but they know who they are, and I am very grateful to them. Our country is lucky to have a corps of dedicated contracting professionals committed to serving the public good.

My second debt of gratitude is to the various research assistants who over the years have provided invaluable help with this study. Troy Perry helped conduct the In-Person Interviews at many of the buying offices. Iris Yan, Junni Zhang, Ruoxi Tang, and Chris Hans aided me with the data analysis, including helping with many specific problems. Ruoxi and Chris, in particular, helped with many tough problems and gave of their time without complaint during vacations and odd hours of the day and night, even when they had conflicting requirements to do their own work.

A number of Kennedy School colleagues generously answered various questions about data analysis issues. In particular, Alberto Abadie, Chris Avery, Suzanne Cooper, Sue Dynarski, and Rob Jensen assisted with many data analysis and econometric problems I would otherwise have been unable to solve. I also received help with repeated questions from Keith Allred, Nancy Katz, David King, David Lazer, and Jim Stock.

Dan Carpenter, Richard Hackman, Larry Jones, Rod Kramer, Hal Rainey, Fred Thompson, and James Q. Wilson all kindly agreed to read and provide comments on an earlier, much longer, and considerably less-accessible version of this manuscript. Four anonymous Brookings reviewers provided useful comments that helped me improve this manuscript, as did Chris Kelaher from Brookings, who was accommodating to my wishes to publish a book that was more quantitatively empirical than a typical Brookings management study, while wisely encouraging me to make the manuscript as readable as possible. My assistant Greg Dorchak helped me with the tedious task of getting footnotes in order and in many other ways. Katherine Kimball provided expert copyediting.

The Center for Public Leadership at the Kennedy School and Accenture provided funding for this research, including funding for my research assistants. This study would have been impossible without their help. I would like to thank Steve Rohleder at Accenture and Barbara Kellerman at the Center for Public Leadership for their belief in this project.

Finally, my family has been very understanding during a long period when I was preoccupied with writing and thinking about this project. My dedication of the book to them is a small way to express my thankfulness.

CHAPTER 1

Introduction: Organizational Change and Improving the Performance of Government

Government does not perform as well as it should. Some of government's bad reputation is unfair. As Thomas Hobbes has noted, in *Leviathan,* government makes human cooperation possible by defining the rules of the game and protecting cooperators from predators. Without such government efforts, even marketplace relationships, sometimes erroneously seen as "natural" and independent of government, would have a difficult time getting established. One need look no further than Russia in the years after communism collapsed, when government was weak; at societies such as Nigeria for many years after independence, where government simply was a means used by the powerful to rob the people; at the breakdown of basic social peace in societies torn by civil war; or at the immediate and instinctive look to government for protection in the aftermath of the September 11, 2001, terrorist attacks on the United States to realize that human flourishing requires the social environment effective government creates. In the memorable phrase of Oliver Wendell Holmes, "Taxes are the price I pay for civilization." At this basic but crucial level, government has worked well. Government activities have also reduced pollution, extended life expectancy of the poor, and lowered crime rates.[1]

The fact remains, however, that government often underachieves. This applies most obviously to some of the biggest, hardest activities it undertakes—reducing poverty, battling drug addiction, educating disadvantaged children, or fielding new weapons systems on time and on budget. It also applies, however, to more mundane tasks, such as managing customer interactions in licensing drivers and applying the latest technology to air traffic control. Opinion data suggest that dissatisfaction with government performance reflects the view that programs are poorly managed more than opposition to the tasks government undertakes; in one poll, 54 percent of respondents agreed that government should be made "more effective through better management," whereas only 8 percent felt that government should be made smaller by cutting programs.[2]

The gap between aspiration and reality suggests a need for government to change. Change, of course, does not automatically produce improvement. However, if government is not performing as well as it should, government organizations clearly need some kinds of change (whatever the right kinds turn out to be) to improve performance. Therefore, anyone who cares about how well government works needs to care about how change in government organizations might occur.

This volume is a study of large government organizations that have succeeded, in response to a change effort initiated at the top of the system, in significantly changing the way they do business on the front lines of the system, where change efforts typically collapse. The organizations are those that buy products and services for the government; the change was called "procurement reform." I seek to explain how change was possible and to provide advice for leaders wishing to promote change on the front lines of organizations.

The approach taken by this study is unusual. Procurement reform was part of a larger initiative to "reinvent government" initiated during Bill Clinton's presidency (and shepherded by Vice President Al Gore). In 1990, as a professor of public management at Harvard's Kennedy School of Government, I published a book titled *Procurement and Public Management: The Fear of Discretion and the Quality of Government Performance*.[3] The book criticized how procurement was managed and proposed reforms. Based on this, the Clinton administration appointed me to a position in charge, along with another political appointee in the Defense Department, of reinventing government efforts for procurement—and hence of the change effort examined here. (My title was administrator of the Office of Federal Procurement Policy in the Office of Management and Budget, making me the government's senior procurement policy official.) I served from 1993 through 1997 and then returned to Harvard.

That I was centrally involved in this effort creates both problems and opportunities for the project of the present volume. It calls into question my ability dispassionately to evaluate the substantive accomplishments of reform (one reason I do not try to do so). But my work provided me with both unusual access to procurement organizations and a good position from which to develop research hypotheses.

Most of this book analyzes data from surveys of contracting employees conducted for this research. Those surveyed are people who actually buy goods and services; none worked for me. The analysis is social science, with every possible effort made to keep my personal involvement limited to insights on what questions to ask. But in some sections I present a first-person narrative of how I tried to encourage change from my perch. As a career academic and part-time practitioner, I hope to provide theoretical insights for scholars and practical prescriptions for practitioners and thus make a modest contribution to bridging the great divide separating organizational research and management practice.[4]

Procurement and Procurement Reform

Government buys everything from office supplies to computers to fighter aircraft, along with studies of the costs of proposed regulations and assistance with debt collection for delinquent student loans. In all, the federal government spends about $320 billion a year, close to 40 percent of federal discretionary spending, buying goods and services.[5] With the growth of outsourcing, contracting has become an increasingly important method by which government operates.[6] The organizations in charge of purchasing are buying offices, consisting of functional specialists in contracting, that purchase on behalf of end users, generally those working on an agency's substantive activities.

The specific change sought by procurement reform was to reduce bureaucracy—to diminish the role of rules, hierarchy, and specialization in the design of the system—in favor of a system both streamlined and more oriented toward accomplishing agency missions. Five years after it started, reform had produced significant changes in the attitudes and behavior of people on the front lines. In the survey of frontline procurement employees constituting the major data source for this study, the mean attitude toward procurement reform on a 100-point "feeling thermometer," where 100 represented the strongest possible support for reform, 0 strongest opposition, and 50 a neutral attitude, was 69.1. Seventy percent of respondents gave a score over 50. In the same survey, respondents were asked, "In terms of the way you do your job every day, how much impact has acquisition reform had?" The four response alternatives (answers were coded on a scale of 1 to 4) ranged from reform having "significantly changed the way I do my job" to its having had "no impact on the way I do my job." The mean response was 1.81, that is, higher than "some impact." The Brookings Institution, in a fifth-year report card on reinventing government, gave procurement reform its only full A grade.[7]

Before reform, buying offices were generally sluggish and oriented toward controlling the program customers on whose behalf they bought more than toward furthering the agency missions procurement was supposed to serve. As a result of the changes, the system became more mission oriented. Buying offices became faster. They focused more on serving program customers. They paid more attention to quality in choosing suppliers. Newly empowered, many developed novel ways to structure contractual relationships.

Procurement reform was exemplified by the new way the Defense Department bought food for soldiers. For many years, the military had used government specifications ("milspecs") in buying everything from ketchup to chocolate-chip cookie mix, purchasing from the lowest bidder meeting the specification. These milspecs—about twenty pages long for cookie mix, providing detailed instructions on ingredients and baking requirements—were objects of derision; knowledge of the finer points of cookie baking was hardly a core competency of the Defense Department.[8] The specification told how to make cookies but included no performance requirement that a cookie so produced would be one soldiers would want to eat. Finally, there was almost always something in the milspecs that did not correspond with how commercial producers manufactured the item, so the Defense Department ended up purchasing mostly from suppliers who did not sell in the commercial marketplace but had come into existence specifically to supply military needs. Large supplies were kept in government warehouses (suppliers generally lacked any distribution system of their own), and items for which there was little demand might stay in warehouses for years.

As part of reform, the military initiated a new way to buy food, whereby it contracted with commercial distributors that offered electronic catalogues of food items to mess sergeants, who placed orders and received daily delivery. This was normal practice for large meal providers to the private sector. However, its normalness was what was new: government was trying to act in a way that made good business sense.

Similarly, almost a decade after large corporate buyers began, during the 1980s, to use site licenses to buy software rather than buying individually shrink-wrapped software (as individual consumers did), most government organizations were still buying shrink-wrapped software. In the late 1990s, as reform took hold, the gap between adoption of another buying innovation in corporate America—use of online auctions to buy products—and its first use in government was less than a year.

The Challenge of Organizational Change

The subject of this book is neither (to any significant extent) the merits and demerits of bureaucracy as an organizational form nor whether reform substantively improved the procurement system. Instead, this is a book about how organizational change is possible.

In some senses, of course, organizations change all the time. Employees and managers come and go, new procedures get written, new products or services are introduced. Where organizational change becomes difficult is where it requires modification of embedded individual behavior patterns or ways the organization has been structured. Then change becomes hard—very hard. "People resist change," the saying goes.

Yet, to paraphrase Galileo from a very different context, the procurement system moved. As surely as organizational change is hard, it also sometimes succeeds. Change is easier when it involves adding an innovation to existing practice than when it involves, as with the effort to reduce bureaucracy in procurement, altering existing practice. Nonetheless, numerous accounts have chronicled successes of American companies rising to the challenge of global competition, including large, older firms such as IBM and General Electric, in significant measure through changes to existing practices. Moreover, although the phenomenon has received considerably less attention because, by media consensus, government success is not newsworthy, a number of accounts provide examples of successful change in government.[9] Many of these changes have made organizations less bureaucratic. So the fundamental question becomes, what explains the difference between success and failure?

Starting with the premise that people resist change, most prescriptive literature on how successfully to achieve change emphasizes two tactics.

The first emphasizes inducing attitude change—that is, convincing people that their resistance is mistaken and that they should embrace a new approach. The second proposes the use of "shock and awe"—overwhelming the reluctant with the necessity of change, despite their inclinations to preserve the status quo, or establishing powerful rewards and penalties tied to behavior change.

The central contention of this book is that the conventional explanation—that people resist change—is often oversimplified and misleading, and that common change strategies growing out of this view are therefore incomplete as well. Furthermore, the very hold that the conventional view has over our thinking about organizational change itself makes change more difficult. Instead, this book argues, there is often a constituency for change as well as for the status quo. Changing big government organizations may turn out to be easier than meets the eye. Here I argue that there are two little-discussed paths for successful organizational change: what may be called "activating the discontented" can be a path to successful change initiation, and what may be called "change feeding on itself" can be a path to successful change consolidation. Often, change need not be cajoled or coerced. Instead, it can be unleashed.

Arguments for why change is hard turn out to be not so much wrong as incomplete. Many organizations and individuals do become attached to how they have behaved in the past. But the view that people resist change ignores that social arrangements often create discontent as well as satisfaction. Those who are discontented with established arrangements form a constituency for change. Furthermore, some people, as a general matter, actually enjoy change because they like trying new things—like those who are early adopters of new gadgets. Such people create an additional constituency for change.

In the case of the traditional procurement system, the major source of dissatisfaction was unhappiness over lack of job autonomy produced by the heavy overlay of rules and sign-offs in the system. In addition, there were other sources of dissatisfaction. The spread of total quality management, and the "customer" concept associated with it, heightened concerns about tensions between procurement people and the end users on whose behalf procurement people were buying. The system's growing bureaucracy increased job burden and stress. Finally, some challenged the preoccupation of the traditional system with process over results, favoring a new ideology centered around gaining better value for the government. A significant proportion of frontline employees felt one or more of these sources of dissatisfaction, though not all those who were dissatisfied would have classified themselves as critics of the existing system, since they may also have felt countervailing reasons to support the status quo.

Thus the organizational status quo is often controversial. It has supporters, but it also has critics. Rather than saying that "people resist change," then, it is more appropriate to see initiation of a change process as setting in motion a political struggle inside the organization.

In this view, when leaders at the top proclaim change, supporters at the bottom are given an opportunity to initiate change they already seek. They start doing what they had wanted to do even before the change was announced. Through their actions, top leaders in effect intervene in the politics of the front lines. People who, absent a signal from above, would have nursed their grievances and gone about their jobs in the old way are encouraged to rise up. Intervention from top leadership also makes local change advocates stronger politically than otherwise. This can allow a change effort to gain a foothold.

Prochange forces, however, are seldom a majority when a change process begins. They were a minority in the case of procurement reform. How then can change eventually gather majority support? Good experiences with reform helped persuade people involved in the procurement system, of course, and it is hard to imagine any change that delivered a stream of negative results being sustained. However, the consolidation of change does not occur simply because change provides benefits. Support for change can feed on itself. The mere initiation of a change process and the mere length of time that the change goes on themselves generate forces that increase support for change. Change can feed on itself—or, to use social science language, positive feedback can occur—because a movement in one direction sets in motion forces producing further movement in the same direction. In other words, once a change process has been started, positive feedback, and not just the actual benefits of the change, make it easier for change to get consolidated.

Change can feed on itself in two ways. First, positive feedback mechanisms can expand change support indirectly by increasing the extent to which a person has good experience with change, independent of features of the experience itself. The good experience, in turn, works to increase support for change. To take one example, some people possess certain personality traits that incline them toward success at whatever they try. People driven to succeed at their jobs, for example, will work hard to succeed at whatever they are asked to do; if asked to try a new way of doing business, they will work hard to do it well. This increases the chances a person will have a good experience in trying the change, and good experience promotes support.

Second, positive feedback mechanisms can directly increase support for the change with the mere passage of time, independent of the impact of good experiences. For example, psychologists have established the existence of what has been called the "mere exposure effect," by which is meant the positive impact of simple repeated exposure on a person's attitudes toward something. Before a change effort has begun, mere exposure is an obstacle to successful change, since it increases support for established practices, independent of their benefits. However, once a change has gone on long enough, the mere-exposure film begins running backwards. Now, new behaviors that have been tried often enough begin to benefit. The same factors that had made it hard for change to gain a foothold, independent of the benefits of the status quo, begin to promote support for new attitudes, independent of their benefits.

The most important message that emerges from this account of procurement reform on the front lines of government is a hopeful one. There is more potential for successful frontline change in large organizations, including large government organizations, than is generally thought to exist. Successful change to existing organizational practice, in this view, does not occur more often for two simple reasons. First, leaders try introducing such changes too seldom in the first place (although new leaders frequently do seek to add new policies or programs to existing ones, rather than seek to change existing behavior in the organization, particularly at the working level). They may never try because they are convinced of the conventional view that "people resist change" and that it is too difficult to achieve change. Ironically, then, belief in the conventional wisdom that people resist change thus helps produce the results the conventional wisdom predicts.

Second, leaders do not persist long enough in change efforts they do launch. Psychologically, it is easy to get bored with something one has worked on for a few months, to move on to something else that is more exciting. Beyond that, an important difference between procurement reform and many other change efforts in government is that the top leaders of the effort had no other responsibilities. Other top leaders have operating organizations to run. This makes it difficult for them to devote large blocks of time over sustained periods to organizational change. The odds are high that something will "come up" to occupy one's attention other than a change effort the leader might have originally launched.

Hesitant leaders thus short-circuit both major elements of a hopeful view of the potential for successful frontline change. If leaders do not try to initiate change, supporters cannot be unleashed. If leaders do not persist, the operation of positive feedback to expand change support does not have time to occur. So the message to leaders who believe a change program has the potential to improve the performance of the organization they lead is a simple one: "Do it!"

CHAPTER 2

The Traditional Procurement System and the Difficulties of Change

Procurement reform sought to reduce bureaucracy in the procurement system. The traditional procurement system was bureaucratic in the sense this word is used in organization theory to describe a form of organizational structure. Max Weber's renowned essay enumerates five features of bureaucratic organization.[1] For my purposes here, these may be collapsed into three: extensive use of rules, hierarchy, and specialization.[2]

Rules lay out in advance what an employee is to do in a particular situation. "If faced with x, do y" is the basic structure of a rule. Employees do not need to work their way through the situation to figure out what to do; it has already been worked out. Rules may be informal as well as formal ("the way we do things here").

Hierarchy exists for situations that are not covered by rules. When hierarchy comes into play, employees at the working level must get approval from levels higher than their own ("buck a decision up" for approval or "sign off" on a decision) before undertaking an action. Hierarchy thus removes decisionmaking from the hands of the front lines, just as rules do. (Hierarchy may also be used for checking up on the behavior of lower organizational units.)

Specialization divides work into smaller chunks. This can occur within one organizational unit, as with the division of labor on an assembly line. It generally involves establishing separate suborganiza-

tions, often semi-independent of one another, specializing in some function. (These are often called "stovepipes.") Nonbureaucratic organizations emphasize discretion over rules (making decisions based on judgment about the most appropriate response to a situation), empowerment
over hierarchy (permitting those at working levels to make decisions),
and cross-functional teams over specialization.

The traditional procurement system was filled with rules, regulating
both government officials and contractors.[3] Most rules regulating government officials involved the process by which it was decided who
would be awarded a contract. The basic rule was that procurements be
publicly advertised so that any potential bidder could learn about the
buy and have an opportunity to bid ("full and open competition").[4] But
that was just the beginning:

—Contractors were not allowed to speak one-on-one with government officials while the government was preparing a procurement.
Communication between government and industry typically occurred in
formal meetings open to all potential bidders and in written communi-
cations, which were public information.

—In the bid solicitation, the government was required to specify precisely what it wanted (so bidders bid on the same thing). Specifications
could not ask for more than the agency's "minimum needs." The solicitation was required to express criteria, such as price or technical performance, for evaluating bids, and the relative weights different criteria
would be given in evaluation (for example, "price is the most important
factor, followed by technical approach and management plan, which are
of approximately equal weight"); many agencies gave exact numerical
weights for various factors.

—The past performance of bidders on earlier contracts could not be
used as an evaluation criterion. In some kinds of buys, government was
required to buy from the lowest bidder, and even when this was not
required, there was often an informal practice of awarding a contract to
the lowest bidder.

In response to solicitations, bidders prepared written proposals,
explaining how they planned to meet the requirements and their price
(or labor rates). Written proposals would often be hundreds or thousands of pages long (occasionally tens of thousands), sometimes delivered to the government by forklift truck. The reason was that the government generally could use only material in proposals to evaluate
bidders. The process was widely seen as an essay-writing contest. Pro-

posals were often written by professional proposal writers, seldom the same people who would work on the contract once it had been awarded. Each section of each proposal was point-scored, with documentation of reasons. After contract award, a disappointed bidder could file a protest, challenging the government's decision.

Rules regulated contractors as well. Certain costs could not be charged under cost-based contracts. (A simple example would be the prohibition against charging entertainment costs.) Complex rules governed accounting for indirect costs (for example, the cost of maintaining corporate headquarters). There were also rules requiring contractors to provide detailed information about their underlying costs to government before (and as a basis for) contract award. This procedure was initially designed to provide assistance to the government in negotiating sole-source contracts, but government gradually began to demand such data for all but the most straightforward products. Contractors typically needed to develop special accounting systems to comply.

Many of the system's rules were set forth in the nineteen-hundred-page *Federal Acquisition Regulation* as well as in agency supplements. The Defense Department supplement was more than eighteen hundred pages, and each military service had service-specific supplements. Many common practices—such as buying from the low bidder or giving no consideration to a supplier's past performance when awarding new contracts—were not part of the regulations but rather informal rules that nonetheless got followed. These reflected the spirit of a system that tried to reduce discretion as much as possible. For example, buying from the low bidder involved less discretion than making a trade-off between price and quality; not allowing past performance to influence contract award removed another area requiring judgment.

The traditional system also had significant internal hierarchy, as well as specialization that separated buying offices from the program offices for which products and services were being bought. Program offices, including those involving mission activities such as tank battalions or the National Weather Service, and functional offices, such as those managing information technology, are end users of what the procurement system buys. Procurement developed over time as a separate specialized function, with procurement offices responsible for managing the process. Generally, a reasonably sized program unit would have a dedicated buying office managing its procurement. Thus the Tank and Automotive Command of the U.S. Army and the Internal Revenue Service had their own buying offices. Buying offices reported to a headquarters organization. Both the *Federal Acquisition Regulation* and various departmental or local supplements laid out the many situations in which procurement decisions could not be made without higher-level approvals (and typically established different levels of approval for different dollar values involved in decisions, starting with levels inside a buying office and often including requirements for approvals from levels above the buying office itself). The headquarters procurement organization also frequently reviewed activities of local buying offices, primarily to check for compliance with regulations.

Responsibility for government-wide procurement policy is vested with the Office of Federal Procurement Policy in the Office of Management and Budget. The procurement policy administrator, the position I held, is a presidential appointee. In the decades preceding procurement reform, the congressional committees in charge of procurement policy had created much of the system's increasing bureaucracy.[5] Program managers in the Defense Department chafed under the system's bureaucracy. Because of the importance of weapons acquisition, they often got the support of senior Defense leadership for proposals to reduce bureaucracy.

Reasons for and Problems with Bureaucracy

The word *bureaucracy,* derived from the French word "bureau" (meaning desk or office), had a modest beginning.[6] However, it has had a tumultuous fate. In popular discourse, *bureaucracy* has come to be a vituperation, usually referring to people and organizations devoted more to red tape, "going by the book," and pencil pushing than to achieving results. Calls to reduce bureaucracy in organizations have become common during the past several decades. This trend blossomed in the 1980s as both practitioners and scholars asked what business firms needed to do to become more competitive in light of globalization, deregulation, changes in consumer preferences, and technological change. Out of these concerns grew an enormous practitioner-oriented literature criticizing bureaucracy for inhibiting excellent organizational performance.[7] For example, Tom Peters, a leading "guru" management writer, states, "The campaigns against bureaucracy must become strategic priorities of the first order" and reports approvingly that the "$1.9 billion retailer Nordstrom got by with a one-sentence policy manual:

'Use your own best judgment at all times.'"[8] In the early 1990s the spirit of this literature entered analysis of government.[9]

Procurement reform sought to reduce rules, hierarchy, and specialization, not to eliminate them. There were often good reasons for rules (and for hierarchy and specialization) in the traditional system, and significant elements of rules, hierarchy, and specialization remained after reform. Rules can help produce good decisions that help an organization do its substantive job better. If an organization has learned that certain approaches to dealing with recurring situations work, it can use rules to codify and transmit such information.[10] Why reinvent the wheel? To take a procurement example, why require each contracting officer to rediscover the virtues of competition?

However, rules (as well as hierarchy and specialization) in government are frequently justified on other grounds. They often grow out of a focus on abuse rather than substantive achievement. Believing good news is no news, and generally finding ongoing activities of government organizations arcane and boring, Congress and the media typically become interested in these activities only in connection with scandal. This, in turn, creates a focus on reducing abuse so as to minimize scandal. Rules are seen as necessary control mechanisms to reduce abuse because people in the system are distrusted: if people are left to their own devices, abuse will be common.

This was very much the case for the traditional procurement system. The system focused on control of abuse—particularly favoritism, corruption, and cheating—by government officials or contractors, rather than on accomplishing the substantive purpose of supporting agency missions. Officials free to make decisions unconstrained by rules, it was feared, might display favoritism or corruption.[11] They might take the easy way out and not bother to undertake efforts to protect the government, such as holding robust competitions for contract awards. Since they were not "spending their own money," program officials might ask for products or services that were too fancy and hence too expensive. Contractors might overcharge the government.

Frequently, practices justified only on the ground that they reduced abuse were applied at the cost of sacrificing good decisions under normal circumstances. For example, the prohibition against using information about a contractor's performance on previous contracts when deciding from whom to buy produced predictably bad results because it cut off the nexus, common to everyday experience, between how well a company has treated us in the past and whether we continue to do business with it in the future. In everyday life, if we have a bad experience at an auto repair shop, we usually will not patronize it again. With past performance missing from the contractor selection process, bidders chronically overpromised before contracts were awarded (since awards were made based only on promises about the future, not on evidence from the past), and once a contract had been signed, performance was often poor (since there was little link between past performance and getting future business).[12] The prohibition against using past performance could never have been justified as a rule that generally produced good decisions. Thus the rules misdirected the behavior of the many to stop the abuses of a few.

The same applies to the rule preventing one-on-one meetings with potential bidders while the government was planning a procurement. The only justification for the rule was distrust of government officials who might unfairly give information to one potential bidder that had not been given to others or might "cook" a solicitation to favor one bidder. However, this prohibition deprived the government of valuable feedback on whether the requirements the government was considering made sense, since in group meetings competitors avoided telling the government anything of interest, lest they reveal information about their bidding strategy to competitors. The rule contradicted commercial purchasing practice, which regards vendors as invaluable sources of information in early stages of a buy. The government's poor information was exploited by bidders who realized that doing what the government asked for in its solicitation would not produce the results the government intended: many firms adopted a strategy referred to as "bid what they ask for, not what they want," winning contracts by promising to do what the government requested and then counting on contract modifications (providing additional work) when what was requested did not solve the problem.[13]

Rules also created unintended consequences. An example was the Defense Department's specifications for everyday items, from ketchup to cookie mix. These emerged from the "buy low bid" practice based on distrust of government officials, who might show favoritism if allowed to exercise more discretion in choosing a bidder. To buy the low bid, the government needed to specify exactly what it was buying, so that it could choose among comparable offers. Whenever it was discovered that a low bidder had cut a corner, a new element was added to the specification to "tighten" it. Over time, some element emerged that commercial vendors could not meet. Unwilling to adapt products for government, a tiny part of their business, these vendors stopped bidding. Gradually, the only firms bidding became ones with no commercial market presence, who had come into existence exclusively to bid on these items and had high costs and poor responsiveness.

In a related vein, rules imposing cost reporting requirements on contractors caused many commercial companies to shun government business, because they either lacked accounting systems with which to comply, were unwilling to reveal sensitive information, or refused to accept the low profit margins this environment imposed. As of 1992 five of the ten largest semiconductor firms refused to accept defense contracts requiring provision of such data.[14] This limited bidding to firms working only on government business, firms that often were more expensive and less innovative than those in the commercial sector.[15]

More generally, rule proliferation (along with hierarchical approval requirements) dramatically slowed the procurement process. It frequently took two or three years to award a contract of any significance. Indeed, the benefits of each rule singly might have outweighed its costs, but the agglomeration of rules created so much delay that the system of rules had greater costs than benefits.[16]

However, in my view, the most important problem with rules was not what they contained but what they left out. Nothing in the rules prohibited people from looking for better ways to do business in areas the rules did not address. Most rules involved processes people needed to follow (for example, "Allow everyone to bid" or "Allow at least thirty days for bidders to respond to a solicitation"). No rule admonished, "Get a good deal for the government," if for no other reason than that such a "rule" would provide insufficient guidance and hence would not fill the role rules are supposed to fill. Furthermore, when rules regulate most parts of a person's job, it is natural to conclude that the job consists only in following the rules. So a rule-based system sent a signal to focus on process rather than results. Put another way, a rule-based system, by delineating minimally acceptable behavior, easily slides into delineation of maximum performance.[17] In the pithy phrase of Henry Mintzberg, "An organization cannot put blinders on its personnel and then expect peripheral vision."[18] The milspec for cookies described in the previous chapter did not violate the rules. Nor did buying individually shrink-wrapped software rather than site licenses. (Indeed, government probably got the best price in the world for individually packaged software.) So no one noticed these practices made no business sense.

Hierarchy within procurement organizations, and the functional wall separating procurement and program people, had analogous effects. Beyond its function in promoting good decisions by tapping greater expertise at higher organizational levels, hierarchy also had an important control function. But this occurred at the expense of discouraging people on the front lines from thinking themselves about what course of action made the most sense. Because such decisions would go through many reviews, it generally made sense to hew closest to the most-trodden path or to let the people above do the thinking. The same was the case for specialization. Specialization could promote good decisions because it allowed greater procurement expertise to develop in specialized procurement organizations. But it also served as an important control mechanism: a buying function separated from the program office was able to serve a "check and balance" function in policing abuse by program officials. Again, however, the effect was to dramatically reduce buying offices' orientation toward the organization's mission. Ensconced in a stovepipe without mission responsibilities, procurement developed an ideology that paid little attention to accomplishment of mission goals. Nor did the ideology give any value to creating good working relationships between the government and suppliers, which is often regarded, in contracting between private sector firms and their own suppliers, as an important element in gaining value out of a business relationship.[19] Instead, it emphasized procurement's police role in controlling program people and contractors. Program people were seen as being "in bed" with favored contractors and seeking wastefully to "buy a Cadillac instead of a Chevrolet," to use an oft-repeated expression among traditional procurement employees. Contractors were seen as being out to cheat the government.

The problem of the traditional system was that the tail wagged the dog. Controlling abuse—making sure people did not do bad things—became the focus of attention. The system did little to encourage people to do good things, in particular to focus on meeting their agencies' mission needs. A contractor might never overcharge the government for its services, but the contract may have done a poor job describing the performance the government wanted from the contractor in the first place, or the contractor's performance doing what the government asked might have been only marginal. The procurement system became like a police department that never mistreated suspects but also never solved crimes; or like a professor who never sexually harassed a student but was a poor teacher and never did any research.

The Messages of Procurement Reform

In March 1993, early in his administration, President Bill Clinton instructed Vice President Al Gore to take charge of a National Performance Review to examine how government management could be improved.[20] The effort became known as "reinventing government." Later that year, the report, *From Red Tape to Results*, appeared.[21] (It became known as the Gore Report.) The report featured a chapter on procurement, and a supplementary volume made specific procurement reform recommendations.

The overarching message of reinventing government in general, and of procurement reform in particular, was that bureaucracy was the enemy of good government. "The problem is not lazy or incompetent people; it is red tape and regulation so suffocating that they stifle every ounce of creativity. . . . The federal government is filled with good people trapped in bad systems. . . . Faced with so many controls, many employees have simply given up. They do everything by the book—whether it makes sense or not."[22]

Within the overall antibureaucracy theme of reinventing government, there were somewhat different messages. The Gore Report itself reflected the views of program people, who generally saw buying offices as unresponsive and unhelpful. The most persistent criticism program people made was that buying was too complicated and took much too long. In particular, the procurement section in the report was addressed mostly to people buying everyday items (such as office supplies) for incidental use, who resented having to go through a buying office, complaining that this often meant they waited weeks or months before receiving what they needed. Thus the Gore Report saw reform mostly as getting procurement out of the way. It sought to streamline the system so people could get what they needed faster—reducing steps, reviews, and required waiting periods to receive bids, all of which slowed down buying. A key recommendation was to allow program offices to make small buys using government-issued credit cards, without having to route them through a buying office.

The buys I had studied in *Procurement and Public Management* were large purchases of information technology systems, so my own experience involved mission-critical purchasing.[23] Similarly, weapons buys were mission critical for the Defense Department. Program managers using the system for mission-critical buys also complained that procurement was too slow. However, both for me and for Defense procurement reformers, this was far from the only problem the system created. We wanted to build a system that delivered better value from contracting—a "better value agenda." We sought reduced bureaucracy, and less emphasis on controls, because we felt the traditional system reduced focus on supporting agency missions and attaining good business results and inhibited the innovation we believed would produce better results. We focused less on getting around procurement than on getting a better system. Our approach was thus ideological, in the sense it was tied to a view about how procurement should be changed to promote the public good.

The central example of problems with a bureaucratic procurement system discussed in my earlier book was the failure to use past performance in making new contract awards, a subset of the problem of buying from the low bidder. Generally, I argued that government officials should be released from the shackles of rules (I emphasized hierarchy less) and instead be encouraged to use their brains to develop better, innovative ways to do business. For example, people should focus on developing intelligent buying strategies—buying commercial food distribution capabilities rather than milspec cookies, buying site licenses rather than shrink-wrapped software. To help develop intelligent buying strategies, government people should gather more information about how successful firms bought similar products or services for themselves. (How did American Express buy information technology? How did WalMart buy logistics capabilities?) People should focus on asking contractors for the right thing in the first place—placing performance requirements in contracts rather than telling the contractor what activities to perform (which might well not produce the underlying results the government sought and which failed to take advantage of contractor expertise about what activities would best produce results the government sought). People should think more about putting powerful incentives into contracts.

Another important part of the better-value agenda was to reduce stovepipes between procurement and program by establishing teams of program and procurement people to work together on a buy. The goal was for procurement people to develop a commitment to helping their agency accomplish its mission—to see themselves as a service function, not as police. Finally, I argued that the system needed to move from an adversarial relationship between government and industry toward a more partnership-style one, as was occurring in customer-supplier relations in business.

Defense Department reformers also had a better-value agenda, but it emphasized different themes, mainly better access for the military to commercial technology. The basic criticism Defense reformers made was that reliance on milspecs, along with onerous controls over contractors (especially submission of cost data and compliance with government accounting rules), created barriers to entry for predominantly commercial firms that might otherwise sell technology to the military—a high-tech version of milspec chocolate chip cookies. Reformers argued that this left the military too dependent on traditional defense contractors, many of whom were not at the cutting edge of technologies the military wanted, particularly information technology and biotechnology. They therefore sought to reduce reliance on milspecs and imposition of government oversight requirements (such as cost reporting) on contractors. This put them into conflict with the distrust of contractors important to the ideology of the traditional system, since they were recommending reduction in control activities.

Like the Gore Report, I was concerned about buying faster as well, but only secondarily, and mostly for reasons related to a better-value agenda. One result of the enormous time it took to evaluate lengthy proposals was that program managers seldom assigned good people to the exercise, since it was likely to keep them away from their jobs for months on end. This meant that judgments about bids were not being made by high-quality employees. The time it took to get on contract also meant that threats to cancel a poorly performing contractor's work were empty (since it would take so long to redo the competition), further reducing government's ability to get good performance. More broadly, I believed it was incongruous to tell those responsible for delivering programs that their missions were crucial and we wanted them to feel urgency about producing results—but that they would need to wait years to receive what they needed to accomplish those missions. A slow-as-molasses procurement system sent a message of mediocrity—that slow and poor performance could be deemed "good enough for government work."

One technique for speeding up buying would be to establish more program-procurement teams, since an important reason buying was slow in the traditional system was that program and procurement offices lobbed documents back and forth over stovepipe boundaries: program offices developed bid documents on their own, procurement critiqued them and sent them back, and so forth. In a team environment, documents could be developed jointly, which would save time. Teams were good in the context of the better-value agenda as well, since they promoted greater mission orientation on the part of procurement people. Finally, streamlining more generally would allow resources to be redirected to managing contracts better after they were signed.

Why Organizational Change Is So Hard

At the beginning of a new administration, then, a message went out that the new political leadership wanted procurement to be made less bureaucratic. Few, probably, would have bet the call would result in much change.

Most people have an intuitive sense that it is hard to change organizations. In many classics of organization theory, ranging from Robert Merton's essay, "Bureaucratic Structure and Personality," through Michel Crozier's *The Bureaucratic Phenomenon* and Karl Weick's *The Social Psychology of Organizing,* the difficulty of organizational change is a central theme.[24] Indeed, a major school of organization theory, originated by Michael Hannan and John Freeman under the name "population ecology," has as its core the premise that few organizations can adapt to shifts in their environment; new ways of structuring organizations develop not, they argue, because existing organizations have changed but rather because natural selection has occurred, whereby organizations whose existing structures happen to fit the new environment prosper, while those whose structure is no longer appropriate die.[25]

To bring about change on the front lines of an organization in response to an effort initiated at the top requires successful implementation of plans announced by top leaders. The large literature on the general difficulty of implementing new programs reflects the cautionary, almost ominous tone adopted in the classic establishing the genre, Jeffrey Pressman and Aaron Wildavsky's *Implementation:* "The view from the top is exhilarating. Divorced from the problems of implementation, federal bureau heads, leaders of international agencies and prime ministers in poor countries think great thoughts together. But they have trouble imagining the sequence of events that will bring their paths to fruition. Other men, they believe, will tread the path once they have so brightly lit the way."[26]

In explaining why change is hard, there is a tendency to resort to the general statement that "people resist change." Surely, however, this is incomplete. If management were to announce that it was tacking $5,000 onto everybody's salary, would employees be likely to resist? Yet that is a change. We need to ponder more deeply why organizations, and especially the people inside them, might find it difficult to embrace change. In doing so, we need to distinguish various sources of the problem, especially the following:

—factors that encourage people to resist changing their existing behavior in any context (that is, whether or not they are in an organization)

—ways that organizations, in general, act on the individuals within them that make those individuals likely to resist changing the way they do their jobs

—ways that bureaucratic organizations, in particular, promote resistance to change

—ways that government organizations, in particular, promote resistance to change.

Why Individuals May Resist Change

Individuals, in their everyday lives inside or outside organizations, may resist change for a number of reasons. First, change may make people worse off; it scarcely takes feats of analytical acrobatics to explain why people resist changes that make them worse off. Change requires, at a minimum, learning something new, which may itself be a cost. We tend to be better at performing actions we have performed many times. Continuing existing behaviors thus economizes on effort. ("Civilization advances by extending the number of operations we can perform without thinking of them," Alfred North Whitehead once wrote).[27] Furthermore, we value the self-perception of competence engendered by the ability to perform oft-repeated behaviors.

Second, behavioral consistency is often seen as a virtue. Consistency, it has been said, "is the heart of logic, rationality, stability, and honesty."[28] Public figures who change their positions ("flip-flop") on an issue are subject to criticism. In one psychological experiment in which subjects were shown attitude surveys purportedly filled out by another person, those who had given different responses at two different times were rated as more insincere and unreliable (though also more open minded and flexible) than those whose answers were constant.[29] The perceived virtue of consistency privileges existing behaviors.

Third, mere exposure to something tends to increase people's liking for it. Albert Harrison illustrates this "mere exposure effect" through the changed attitude of Parisians toward the Eiffel Tower. Now a beloved treasure, the landmark was initially seen as hideous and evoked a storm of protest. However, "because of its tremendous height, the tower was ubiquitous and inescapable and hence was likely to be seen day after day. . . . It became a familiar part of the landscape."[30] A 1989 review article counted more than two hundred experiments on this phenomenon.[31]

Mere exposure creates commitment to a previously undertaken course of action. In one experiment by Charles Kiesler, subjects played three rounds of a card game.[32] Four strategies for playing the game were presented. Subjects were then randomly assigned one of the strategies for either one, two, or all three rounds of the game. After playing, some subjects were given a communication arguing against the strategy they had played. They were then asked which strategy they would play the next time. The more times subjects had played the criticized strategy previously, the more likely they were to state they would choose it again.

Fourth, behaviors can become embedded. Switching from driving a car to the office, for example, to taking the train requires more than learning schedules and how to buy tickets. It also may require buying clothes for dealing with inclement weather and finding an alternate way to eat breakfast once the coffee mug below the dashboard is no longer available. Existing behaviors thus can become enveloped in a larger set of activities. They can also take on symbolic significance: drivers and mass transit riders may have different self-images. When during the 1960s the New York City police department tried to get police officers to move from a three- to a four-shift system to increase patrols during high-crime hours, officers resisted, partly because the change disrupted other aspects of their lives (breaking up patrol partner groups as well as upsetting carpooling arrangements) and partly because the three-shift system was originally established as a labor protection and had become a symbol of the balance of power between labor and management.[33]

Finally, people tend to misperceive the distance between their own performance and what they would view as good performance. Shelley

Taylor notes considerable evidence that people have "positive illusions" about their own abilities: in one survey, for example, 90 percent of respondents rated themselves as "better than average" drivers.[34] Evaluations people offer of themselves are typically more favorable than judgments others make about them. Positive illusions make it harder to change because they hinder our ability to notice a gap between current and desirable performance.

How Organizations in General Promote Resistance to Change

Organizations have an impact on the attitudes and behaviors, particularly work-related ones, of their members. Some features of organizations in general—abstracted from the specifics of any individual organization—tend to discourage individuals inside them from changing existing job-related attitudes and behaviors.

The first of these is the inherent tension between organizing and innovating. What it takes to organize activities makes it harder to reconfigure them. Getting people organized is not easy. People are ornery, with their own preferences for how they wish to spend their time. Organization involves thrusting a stake in the ground in defiance of entropy. We take for granted what is an astounding achievement, the ability to get large numbers of people moving in similar directions, making collective action possible. To accomplish this feat, organizations develop structures, training, a culture, and incentives to enable them to do their current job well. A Federal Trade Commission organized around hungry young attorneys seeking to win lawsuits will win more cases than one consisting of academic economists.[35]

But this has consequences for the ability of an organization to change. As Weick puts it, "Adaptation precludes adaptability." Adaptive organizations (such as those that are good at winning lawsuits) will have difficulty being adaptable (switching to rule making based on policy analysis).[36] "Core capabilities," as Dorothy Leonard-Barton puts it, can become "core rigidities."[37]

Moreover, organizations recruit for and reward current practice. Traditionally, organizing people often required either physical coercion or taking advantage of economic desperation that made people willing to buckle under to the commands of those above them. These days, most organizations in rich countries use carrots more than sticks, subtlety more than steamrollers. They try to recruit people predisposed—based on personality or previous professional education—to want to do what the organization needs them to do. Thus police departments recruit Clint Eastwoods, not Alan Aldas, and research universities recruit graduates of research-oriented doctoral programs. Organizations also develop systems to reward people for behaving in ways the organization wishes. These recruitment and reward systems create workforces oriented to behaving according to current practice.

Second, organizations create member commitment to current practice, seeking to inculcate a sense of commitment to—emotional identification with—its practices and values.[38] Research shows that employee commitment is related to higher performance. Commitment inoculates people against setbacks, providing "support for persistence in the face of apparent failure."[39] Persistence can be positive, as in "the dedicated struggles of missionaries and doctors battling disease and starvation in the jungles of South America or Africa."[40] But when the setbacks are practices that continue to fail and should be changed—as when an army fighting guerillas persists in ineffective combat methods—this inoculation is a problem.

Third, change may be difficult because it affects power relationships. One study, tracking what happened following introduction of automated testing equipment in hospital laboratories, has found that few hospitals made organizational changes rendered appropriate by the new technology.[41] Thus, for example, in all the labs studied, the new equipment could be used only by specially trained technicians, although the new technology was simple enough that it could have been handled by assistants with less training. Such a change, however, would have upset established authority arrangements. Resistance to change originating in a worry that changes will upset power relationships is an organizationally created example of how existing practice becomes embedded in something larger.[42]

Finally, knowledge structures created by organizations make it hard for people to notice signals that change is needed. In organizations, people are frequently exposed to situations that are similar to one another, to which the organization develops a standard response. Repeated exposure to patterns of stimulus and response generate what psychologists call "knowledge structures" (sometimes called "mental models" or "schemas") surrounding these situations. These are constructs for "placing stimuli into some kind of framework," providing "a summary of the components, attributes, and relationships that typically occur in specific exemplars."[43] A knowledge structure creates a composite picture of what a situation is "about," which can be used to guide the interpretation of individual situations.

When people use knowledge structures, they let the generic structure, rather than actual data from the specific instance, do a good deal of the mind's interpretative work.[44] The knowledge structure suggests what is important and what is unimportant among signals coming in from the environment. This provides enormous benefits by helping people make sense of the cacophony assaulting them. As John Van Maanan puts it, "The raw empirical world is essentially absurd."[45] Someone unable to distinguish the important from the unimportant features of a situation "would hear background noise as loudly as a voice or music . . . and would be driven crazy by the coughs and chair squeaks at symphony concerts."[46]

However, the very advantages knowledge structures create by bringing order to our understanding of the world can create problems as well. (No bane, no gain.) To gain the benefits of knowledge structures, people "unconsciously attempt to match incoming information cues with the previously developed set of schemas."[47] Consequently, our interpretation of the world around us thus becomes "guided by expectations or preconceptions."[48] This engenders what is sometimes called "perceptual confirmation"—people perceive new situations in ways consistent with preexisting knowledge structures, reinterpreting or even ignoring information that does not conform to the established structure. As a result of perceptual confirmation, people see what they want to see or what they expect to see.[49] Using knowledge structures, people act according to the maxim "I'll see it when I believe it"—one of the greatest bons mots in organizational behavior research.[50] In one experiment, male students were given pictures of women with whom they were told they would be having a telephone conversation, though in fact the students had conversations with completely different females.[51] Females who were attractive in the pictures (but whom the students did not actually see) were rated as more lively, personable, and intelligent than females appearing in the pictures as less attractive.[52]

Use of knowledge structures derived from current practice inhibits organization members from seeing a need for change because they become less likely to notice discrepant signals suggesting that current practice is not working. A knowledge structure "direct[s] attention toward restricted aspects of an object that . . . seemingly justify routine application of the procedure."[53] If you have a hammer, everything may come to be interpreted as a nail.

How Bureaucratic Organizations in Particular Promote Resistance to Change

The elements of bureaucracy—rules, hierarchy, and specialization—are examples of organizational practices that inhibit change. Rules may be seen as knowledge structures imposed consciously on people rather than arising spontaneously through organizational experience. As Weick notes, "A standard operating procedure is a frame of reference that constrains exploration."[54] Specialization, by limiting people's experiences, limits the scope of their knowledge structures. Rules and hierarchy play into and affect existing power relationships.

Changes to reduce bureaucracy in bureaucratic organizations are challenging for different reasons. The literature generally finds that rules and hierarchy are negatively related to innovativeness. In a pioneering study by Jerald Hage and Michael Aiken on organizational innovativeness, one of the highest correlations was a negative relationship between innovation and the presence of bureaucracy.[55] Fariborz Damanpour's meta-analysis finds that hierarchy was negatively related to generation of innovative ideas, and rules were negatively related to innovativeness, for organizations producing services (but not in manufacturing) and for nonprofit and government organizations.[56]

Bureaucratic organization limits the competence of employees and thus their capacity to behave differently. In a bureaucracy, rules are developed by thinkers, often in staff positions (such as, classically, Frederick Taylor's acolytes using stopwatches to measure the best way to perform a task). Decisions not covered by the rules are sent up the hierarchy for decision at higher levels. In this arrangement, the employee's role is intentionally limited; Henry Ford once stated, "All that we ask of the men is that they do the work which is set before them."[57] In such an environment, employees become increasingly incompetent to do anything but follow rules or buck decisions up the hierarchy, making it harder for them to develop the skills needed to change, in particular, to learn to take greater responsibility for decisions, as a change to a less bureaucratic organizational form would require. Hierarchy makes it more difficult for new ideas employees might develop to get accepted, creating a disincentive for generating such ideas in the first place.

Bureaucracy is also hard to change because rules provide defense in the face of criticism. As Michel Crozier notes in his classic, *The Bureaucratic Phenomenon*, rules provide important benefits for organization members by providing "protection against too harsh treatment in case of error."[58] If disaster occurs, rules provide an excuse. Think of the dilemma of a government contracting official, notes James Q. Wilson:

"A decision you made is challenged because someone thinks that you gave a contract to an unqualified firm or purchased something of poor quality. What is your response—that in your judgment it was a good buy from a reliable firm? Such a remark is tantamount to inviting yourself to explain to a hostile congressional committee why you think your judgment is any good. A much safer response is 'I followed the rules.'"[59] Since making an organization less bureaucratic removes one defense against criticism, employees can be expected to resist such change.

How Government Organizations Promote Resistance to Change

Behavior in government organizations is harder to change than in other organizations—and bureaucratic organization in government is particularly resistant to change. Business firms face an environment more unforgiving than do most government agencies, and those wishing to prosper in a competitive marketplace have a strong incentive to seek to improve performance and pay attention to inadequate performance, both of which may require organizational changes.[60]

The structure of government makes it easier for employees who do not wish to change to resist change efforts that leaders initiate. Any reader of the comic strip "Dilbert" knows that in all large organizations people at the bottom who are unhappy about the prospect of change adopt delaying tactics to slow down implementation in the hope that leader attention will wander to something else and that "this too shall pass." As Rosabeth Kanter notes, "Foot-dragging . . . is the one 'weapon' even the most powerless people possess: simply withholding effort."[61] An evocative quote by an aide to Franklin D. Roosevelt captures the ability to resist unwanted direction: "Half of a President's suggestions, which theoretically carry the weight of orders, can be safely forgotten by a Cabinet member. And if the President asks about a suggestion a second time, he can be told that it is being investigated. If he asks a third time, a wise Cabinet officer will give him a least part of what he suggests. But only occasionally, except about the most important matters, do Presidents ever get around to asking three times."[62]

Such resistance is easier in government because top leadership turns over more quickly. To quote Donald Warwick's nice turn of phrase, "Possessed of a well-developed actuarial sense, [career civil servants] know that it will not be long before this particular madness is over."[63] Moreover, dismissing or reassigning recalcitrant employees is considerably more difficult in government than in most business firms; and resistant employees may seek support for resistance among allies in Congress, organized groups, or even the media.

Furthermore, government organizations are more likely to have (at working levels) more people with long tenure, and such people may be more likely to resist change. In corporate America it has become far less common since the 1980s for people to join a firm at the entry level and stay through an entire career.[64] Government has been less subject to pressures producing this change, and, compared with large firms, it continues to a greater extent to embrace the older model of lifetime careers. If career employees are more resistant to change than shorter-term ones (because many of the forces discussed here act more strongly on them), government organizations become more resistant to change because they have a larger proportion of such employees.

Third, in government, the environment punishes error more than it rewards excellence, encouraging bureaucracy because it makes it easier to avoid error and to have an excuse when error occurs. The dominance of uncovering error over promoting excellence applies to government agencies in general, not just to procurement. As Derek Rayner, whom Margaret Thatcher hired during the 1980s to improve government management in Britain, has noted (showing this is not just an American phenomenon), "Failure is always noted and success is forgotten."[65] Government organizations thus have relatively few incentives to soar to excellence but many to avoid disaster. This contrasts with business firms, where isolated errors are not usually a huge problem and success is richly rewarded.

Change is risky, and so the orientation to avoiding disaster discourages any sort of change. "The dirty little secret is that innovation requires failure. The corollary is that unless an organization tolerates . . . failure, it is unlikely to get much innovation."[66] Additionally, if a crucial goal is to minimize disaster, bureaucracy has many advantages. A concern with avoiding disaster encourages hierarchy, allowing more people at higher levels to consider actions before they occur and to check up on subordinate behavior; this argues for hierarchy if the upside of success is relatively less than the downside of failure.[67] People may therefore resist reducing bureaucracy for fear that the change will put them at greater risk for disaster.

As noted earlier, rules provide people with a shield from criticism. If avoiding criticism is especially important in government, this feature of rules will be particularly valuable. In particular, if disaster does occur, a bureaucratic infrastructure allows people to take refuge in showing that "everything possible" has been done to avoid it.

Fourth, the goals of government organizations are more likely to be vague and multiple, and this encourages bureaucratic organization. When the goals of government organizations are vague, people "have few direct, measurable indicators of how well they are doing." In such an environment, rules are a savior. They "have the advantage of being means-oriented, if not ends-oriented, guides to success. The official may not be sure of what he has produced or how well he has produced it, but he can be sure that he did it in the right way."[68]

Multiple goals also encourage hierarchy. The greater the number of goals, "the more discretionary authority . . . is pushed upwards to the top. . . . It is easier to allow front-line operators to exercise discretion when only one clear goal is to be attained. The greater the number and complexity of . . . goals, the riskier it is to give authority to operators."[69] Furthermore, political disagreement over the goals an agency should pursue creates a tendency to focus on enforcing adherence to rules more than on the substance of what the organization accomplishes, since "everyone can agree" that people should obey the rules.

Finally, rules and hierarchy have particular legitimacy in government as tools of democracy and "equal treatment." There are two substantive arguments growing out of political theory on behalf of bureaucracy. The first is that in a democratic society the basic foundation for decisions should be either constitutional requirements or laws the legislature passes; only elected officials should make public decisions. The president, and by extension the executive branch, in which agencies reside, is required by the Constitution to "take care that the laws be faithfully executed." As Herman Finer bluntly states in a classic contribution, the role of nonelected officials is "subservience."[70] These considerations establish the virtues of rules and significantly limit the right of non-elected officials to exercise discretion.[71] A similar argument is made for hierarchy. As the first Hoover Commission report on government organization stated in 1949, the public cannot hold political officials accountable without hierarchy. "Responsibility and accountability are impossible without authority—the power to direct."[72]

The second argument for rules involves how government treats citizens: rule-based organization is necessary to ensure equal treatment of citizens. By treating people the same, rules treat people fairly. For Weber, an advantage of rules is that "the abstract regularity of the execution of authority" they provide establishes a government of laws, not men.[73]

I believe these arguments are substantively flawed.[74] However, they have significant resonance. The arguments in support of bureaucracy thus decrease the willingness to change bureaucratic forms of organization.

Change and the Traditional Procurement System

It is striking that, in James Q. Wilson's classic account of government organizations, *Bureaucracy,* the specific examples dominating a chapter called "Problems" in a part called "Change" involve dysfunctions of the procurement system and reasons why the mess will never be fixed. The chapter begins with the saga of New York City's effort to contract for rebuilding the ice-skating rink in Central Park during the 1980s. After six years of effort and expenditure of $13 million, the rink had still not been rebuilt. Then Donald Trump offered to take charge, committing to having contractors he selected complete the job within six months at a price no greater than $3 million. The job came in one month ahead of schedule and $750,000 under budget.[75]

Why could Trump run the procurement so much more quickly and effectively? The basic reason was that government procurement was more rule-bound than Trump's and thereby reduced the ability to get the job done.

> The Parks and Recreation Department was required by law to give every contractor an equal chance to do the job. This meant it had to put every part of the job out to bid and to accept the lowest without much regard to the reputation or prior performance of the lowest bidder. Moreover, state law . . . forbade the city from even discussing the project in advance with a general contractor who might later bid on it—that would have been collusion. Trump, by contrast, was free to locate the rink builder with the best reputation and give him the job. . . . [Furthermore], to reduce the chance of corruption or sweetheart deals the law required Parks and Recreation to furnish complete, detailed plans to every contractor bidding on the job; any changes after that would require renegotiating the contract. No such law constrained Trump; he was free to give incomplete plans to his chosen contractor, hold him accountable for building a satisfactory rink, but allow him to work out the details as he went along.[76]

Moving beyond the rink, Wilson notes that Defense Department acquisition officials do their jobs in an environment overloaded with rules. "What dominates the task of the contract officer are the rules. . . . Contract officers are there to enforce constraints" on program managers and defense contractors.[77] Wilson concludes that the demand that government treat people fairly and the pressure to design the contracting system to stop abuse doom efforts at change.

Amazingly as well, a book cowritten by one of the developers of business process reengineering in the private sector cites government procurement as a prime example of the challenges of organizational change: "When government agencies try to streamline their work," they write, "they often run into a hail of criticism prompted by the government's commitment to maintaining the fairest and most open processes—which, as in the case of procurement, are rarely the most cost-effective."[78]

Potential changes in power relationships are an additional reason procurement people can be expected to resist reducing bureaucracy. In the traditional system, the power of procurement people was tied to the rules. Procurement people possessed mastery of the complex rule structure with which end users were required to comply: that knowledge constituted much of this job description.

Change Strategies in a World of Resistance to Change

There is an enormous literature on achieving organizational change. The large social science literature on factors explaining organizational innovativeness is, unfortunately, only occasionally relevant to the prescriptive question of what might be done to promote successful change.[79] Much of the prescriptive social science literature about change actually dates from the 1940s and 1950s, produced by the renowned social psychologist Kurt Lewin and his students. Some attention has been paid to strategies for public sector change in the public management literature, particularly that on program innovation.[80] Most of this literature is heavily focused on leader actions and pays little attention to change processes on organizational front lines.[81]

The most important prescriptive literature on change is work by management "gurus" with a practitioner-oriented bent. To move from social science to the guru literature involves a significant change in focus and something of a jolt. Standards of evidence undergo a dramatic shift; multiple regressions give way to multiple assertions. Prescription often takes the form of lists ("The Top Ten Mistakes in Reengineering," "The Eight-Stage Change Process").

The most common prescriptions assume that people resist change and need the application of "a force sufficient to 'break the habit'" to divert them from continuing current behavior. Success therefore requires either "unfreezing" existing attitudes—to use the phrase popularized by the legendary social psychologist Kurt Lewin—or getting resisters out of the way.[82] Hence the emphasis in existing theories on tactics either of inducing attitude change (convincing people that their existing attitudes are mistaken and that they should embrace a new approach) or of "shock and awe" (overwhelming the reluctant with the necessity of change, despite their inclinations to preserve the status quo, or ramping up rewards and penalties tied to behavior change).

Research Approach and Design of This Study

Of the obstacles to organizational change presented earlier in this chapter, most come down to resistance from individuals at the working levels of an organization (although individual-level resistance may be explained by the ways membership in the organization has influenced individual attitudes of the people in them). Put simply, change is seen as hard because people do not want to change. Thus the fundamental research approach of this study is to take the individual front-line employee as the unit of analysis.[83] This approach is also consistent with the focus in implementation research on gaps between the policies leaders announce and what ends up happening on the ground. I proceed from the premise that unless large numbers of individuals on the front lines end up altering attitudes and behavior, change can be proclaimed, but it will not be performed. The research approach also presumes the inverse: organizational change has been successful, on the ground, when large numbers of individuals show reasonably high proreform attitudes and levels of reform-oriented behavior change. In other words, I seek to explain system-level success by explaining individual-level development of attitude and behavioral support for reform.

The data for this research come from two surveys of contracting employees at nineteen buying offices. Five offices were in the U.S. Army, four in the U.S. Air Force, two in the Defense Logistics Agency (which buys commercial items such as food and pharmaceuticals as well as weapon spare parts), and the rest in five different civilian cabinet departments, including four that were units of a single department.

Together, these surveys constitute one of the most comprehensive survey data sets of federal employees ever assembled.[84]

One, the Frontline Survey, was a printed questionnaire for all frontline employees (nonsupervisors and first-level supervisors), administered on the job on my behalf by the office ($N = 1,593$). Two central questions in this survey asked respondents to self-report their attitudes toward procurement reform and the extent to which they had changed on-the-job behavior as a result of reform. There were also about four hundred other questions, in most of which respondents were given a statement and asked how strongly they agreed or disagreed with it.[85] In addition, the survey included other questions (about education and number of years of work experience or job level within the organization as well as questions exploring general personality traits). Finally, each respondent record included information on which agency or department (such as the Army) and which of the nineteen local buying offices in the survey (such as one of the five Army buying commands) the respondent worked for. In this book, Frontline Survey data are generally analyzed using ordinary least-squares multiple regression, with the individual respondent as the unit of analysis. Multiple regression is a statistical technique allowing estimates of what factors influence some result one seeks to explain.[86]

The other survey, the In-Person Interviews, were face-to-face interviews a research assistant and I conducted ($N = 272$), using a standard questionnaire, with mostly open-ended questions to which respondents gave narrative replies (rather than simply indicating they agreed or disagreed). Responses were coded into categories for analysis. Senior local management as well as frontline employees were interviewed, including local office heads and their deputies. All were career civil servants, except for a few military officers.

This book draws conclusions both about why it was possible to achieve successful change in the procurement system and also what can be learned from this of general relevance for change processes in large organizations, particularly in government. Thus I need to worry about both the accuracy of explanations for the results of the case of procurement reform and the generalizability of findings to other situations.[87] Although I am concerned mostly about accuracy, I at least speculate about generalizability, lest the question be asked, "So what?" The central methodological challenge for establishing accuracy and generalizability is that the empirical material for this study consists only of one case, procurement reform. I discuss this issue in appendix B.

Finally, a word is in order about my research approach in the context of academic research on public administration and public management. The reliance here on quantitative analysis reflects a trend in public administration and public management research; my view is that though quantitative approaches should not be allowed to take over research in these areas, quantitative analysis has, in the past, played too modest a role.

In terms of research approach, this study adds to intellectual traditions appearing in existing literature on organizational change in a number of ways. One is the use of writing on social movements and political revolution. Social movements (ranging from civil rights organizations to new religions) and revolutions are efforts at change, in a societal rather than an organizational context. One feature of these literatures is that they do not start with the assumption that people resist change. Instead, in this literature there is clearly a group that very much wants change, but it faces political and other challenges. Obviously, there are differences between change efforts in societies and within organizations, but the similarities and analogies are intriguing. Yet this literature goes largely undiscussed in work on organizational change. I note parallels between my results and these literatures.

Second, I make more extensive use than is common of literatures in two areas closely related to the study of organizational change: the study of organizational innovation and the study of diffusion of innovation among individuals in social groups. It is surprising how little these literatures figure in work labeled as being about organizational change. In the case of writing on organizational innovation, this may be because innovation studies tend to be focused on the introduction of practices that are both discrete and new, while organizational change literature tends to focus on changes that involve broader behavioral patterns and are not necessarily particularly new (except to the organization not previously practicing them). Innovation literature also emphasizes sources of variation in the innovativeness of different organizations, such as by arguing that organizations with certain kinds of employees—professionals, for example—are more likely to innovate than otherwise-similar organizations.[88] This does not closely fit the people-resist-change uniformity in literature on organizational change. The same is the case for writing on diffusion of innovation in social groups, which emphasizes differences among individuals in a group, such as "early" and "late" adopters.[89]

In explaining organizational change, this study also relies heavily on general theories from organizational behavior scholarship by social psychologists and sociologists, mostly working in business schools or disciplinary departments. These literatures have been applied surprisingly seldom to research on organizational change. More generally, they are virtually absent in public administration or public management. (Since these literatures will be relatively unfamiliar to most readers whose field is public administration and management, I spend more time discussing them than I would if greater familiarity could be assumed.) There are far more researchers studying organizational behavior in business schools or disciplinary departments than there are scholars whose field is public administration or public management. Research in organizational behavior is also methodologically closer to the scholarly social science mainstream than much research in public administration and management. For both these reasons, the isolation of public administration and management research from the broader field of organizational behavior research has been unfortunate. One aim of this book, therefore, is to contribute to mainstreaming public administration and public management research.

PART ONE

Initiating Change

CHAPTER 3

Discontent on the Front Lines

At the beginning of the new Clinton administration, senior leaders announced an effort to change the government's procurement system. However, given the obstacles to organizational change presented earlier, it would not have been surprising if reformers had, in effect, given a party to which nobody came. On the front lines of the system, reform might have been ignored or "slow rolled," passively resisted by foot-dragging. Procurement reform could well have ended up dead on arrival.

That, however, did not happen. Change was successfully initiated; it gained a foothold on the front lines. Furthermore, this occurred without the use of tactics recommended in the prescriptive literature on organizational change. This part of the study seeks to develop a new account of change initiation to explain how reform was successfully launched.

The basic story has two elements: First, there were people on the front lines, the "change vanguard," who were dissatisfied with the traditional system and desired change before any effort at change was initiated. Second, the actions of top leaders created an exogenous shock to the political environment at buying offices, providing an opportunity for those who already supported change to act on behalf of their beliefs and to become stronger politically. These two elements together constituted a path to successful frontline change initiation that may be called "activating the discontented."

Much literature on organizational change, with its refrain of "people resist change," is curiously apolitical. This account, by contrast, starts with the suggestion that change has supporters as well as opponents. It also presumes that to some significant extent decisions about how people in the organization behave are made collectively and that in the event of disagreement, there is a process through which such decisions get made.[1] The mixture of disagreement and collective decisionmaking means that organizational change should be seen as a political process.[2]

Initiating Change: Conventional Prescriptions

As noted in the previous chapter, the assumption that people resist change informs the most common prescriptions for the initiation of change, which propose either inducing attitude change by "unfreezing" resistance or using shock-and-awe tactics to propel people onto the path of behavior change, though their old attitudes may remain the same. Of three common prescriptions, one ("persuasive discussion") involves inducing attitude change by unfreezing existing attitudes. Two others (the "burning platform" and leader pressure) involve shock and awe.

The persuasive-discussion theory grows out of Kurt Lewin's experiments during World War II on how individual change is achieved—specifically, unfreezing attitudes to get people to eat unorthodox cuts of meat, such as beef hearts, because of wartime shortages. Lewin compared two groups of housewives: one was exposed to lectures by a nutrition expert, the other participated in discussions led by the expert. The discussion group showed dramatically greater behavioral change. Lewin argues that two factors explain the difference. One was the greater personal involvement discussion produced. The other was that the discussion gave "the leader a better indication of where the audience [stood] and what particular obstacles [had] to be overcome."[3]

The first application of Lewinian principles to organization change was an experiment involving an effort to introduce productivity-enhancing production methods in a factory.[4] The authors tried two different methods to gain acceptance for the changes. In one, the need for change (to meet competitive conditions) was presented in a dramatic way; the group was asked to discuss the plan and approve it in principle, and workers were involved, making suggestions for specific ways to implement the change. In the other, the changes were presented to the workers with an explanation of why competitive conditions made them necessary. Groups exposed to the second approach resisted the changes; the productivity of groups exposed to the first increased.

The other two common theories of change initiation—"burning platform" and leader pressure—are well nigh universal in the "guru" literature on change. The burning-platform theory argues that because change is hard, people must be made to understand that failure to change is even harder. As often put in presentations of management consultants, getting people to move requires—in a reference to what it takes to rouse drilling workers on oil rigs from complacency—a "burning platform." Until the platform is actually burning, people will keep doing what they have always done. This theory is most commonly presented in a business context, wherein the burning platform is the threat that if change does not occur, the company will decline or even go bankrupt.

The key role of leaders in the burning-platform theory is "establishing a sense of urgency"—a realization that the organization's prosperity and even survival are at stake.[5] John Kotter notes that change efforts "start more easily with a natural financial crisis." Absent this, Kotter recommends that leaders "create a crisis by allowing a financial loss," "allowing errors to blow up instead of being corrected at the last minute," or insisting that "people talk regularly to unsatisfied customers, unhappy suppliers, and disgruntled shareholders."[6]

The leader-pressure theory emphasizes the personal commitment of top management. Kotter notes that resistance to change cannot be overcome without top leaders' relentlessly pressuring the reluctant troops below. "It is an unalterable axiom," Michael Hammer and Steven Stanton write, "that [change] only succeeds when driven from the topmost levels of an organization."[7]

None of these theories explains the successful initiation of procurement reform. Change leaders did communicate with the front lines but did not really involve the "troops below" in a discussion that attempted to "unfreeze" existing attitudes. Those few organizations that faced some sort of crisis around the time procurement reform was starting were not more likely to initiate reform more successfully. Leaders played a crucial role in change initiation, but it involved neither creating a sense of urgency nor pressuring the reluctant.

Organizational Change as a Political Process

On reflection, the suggestion that people in general resist change contradicts much experience of our everyday lives. We seldom encounter situations in which people have the same reactions to societal or personal questions, be it opinions on abortion or attitudes toward taking the time to keep physically fit. Why shouldn't the same be so about issues of organizational life? Furthermore, any social arrangement is likely to create discontent as well as satisfaction. Those discontented with established arrangements form a natural constituency for change. Politics, in the sense of disagreement about what an organization collectively ought to do, should therefore be expected.

The first key to the successful initiation of procurement reform was that frontline discontent with the traditional system existed before reform got launched. Some had actually been hoping for something resembling procurement reform. They were procurement reformers before reform began. When reform was announced, this group, whom I call the "change vanguard," was joined by a second group, people who had not previously been advocates of change but became favorably disposed to giving reform a try soon after it got started. I call this group "early recruits." Together, the two groups constituted a "reform coalition." Even together, they were a minority; but they formed a sufficiently large group, and were sufficiently well positioned in their organizations, to get the change effort launched.

Evidence that there was significant discontent with the traditional system comes from a question in the In-Person Interviews asking people to recall the period when reform was getting started. The question asked, "If somebody had asked you about five years ago, 'Is the procurement system broken?' what would you have answered?" Forty-three percent of nonsupervisory respondents answered yes, 36 percent no, and 21 percent volunteered a response coded as "not 'broken' but had real problems."[8] These percentages (and those for other recall questions discussed in this chapter) almost certainly exaggerate the discontent actually present at the time.[9] Furthermore, discontent did not necessarily translated into membership in the reform coalition, since there might have been countervailing forces leading a person on balance to support the traditional system. Still, the high percentage who believed the system was "broken" or "had problems" before reform began is noteworthy.

Based on their responses to the Frontline Survey, employees were classified in terms of their initial reactions to reform, as members in one of four groups: the change vanguard, early recruits, fence-sitters, and skeptics or critics. Responses to two questions were used to establish this categorization. The first asked respondents to agree or disagree (on a five-point scale) with the statement, "When I first tried out some of the new ideas of acquisition reform, I was doing it mostly because my bosses told me to, not because I was convinced they made sense." The second asked, "Which of the following statements most closely describes your own personal overall attitude toward acquisition reform?" and presented ten alternatives (see box 3-1), with a request that the respondent check the most accurate characterization.[10] Based on this categorization, 18 percent of the sample—a substantial group, though a clear minority—were in the change vanguard, and 25 percent were early recruits. Seventeen percent were fence-sitters, and 41 percent were skeptics or critics. In only 12 percent of buying offices were half or more of nonsupervisory respondents in the reform coalition. According to these findings, however, the traditional system, as of when reform started, was already controversial.

Sources of Discontent

Around the time change began, many people in local offices believed the system had problems.[11] How was this possible? Does that mean the argument about resistance to change was wrong? No. Factors promoting resistance to change provide what may be called the comforts of bureaucracy. But paying attention only to comforts gives an incomplete picture. Conditions in bureaucratized government organizations create a constituency for change as well as for the status quo.

What were the sources of discontent? Four factors are explored here. Together, these may be seen as the bureaucrat's complaint.

The first is the desire for autonomy. In a work context, *autonomy* refers to people's ability to decide for themselves how, and perhaps also when or at what pace, their work should be performed. This has been called "self-control and self-management" or the extent to which workers are "left on [their] own to do [their] own work."[12] Bureaucracy— under which rules and superiors determine how work is performed— reduces autonomy. In everyday parlance, the word used for autonomy is often *empowerment*.[13]

Second, the introduction of total quality management and the customer concept also contributed to workers' discontent with bureaucracy. Total quality management (TQM) was an American response to

---

BOX 3-1. **Responses to Procurement Reform View Question**

1. This is something I was hoping for for a long time. I was enthusiastic from the beginning and didn't need any persuading.

2. Before the acquisition reform movement got started, I didn't have any strong views one way or another. But I became convinced toward the beginning of the push for acquisition reform that this was the right way to go.

3. Originally, I was skeptical about whether this was the right way to go. But I changed my mind pretty early on and would now call myself a supporter of acquisition reform.

4. For a long time, I was skeptical about whether this was the right way to go. But seeing how many other people were going along with this, I eventually changed my mind and would now call myself a supporter of acquisition reform.

5. For a long time, I was skeptical about whether this was the right way to go. But when I tried some of the new ideas out, it eventually changed my mind so that I would now call myself a supporter of acquisition reform.

6. I'm a good soldier. If this is something my bosses are for, I'm for it, irrespective of my personal opinion.

7. I have mixed feelings about acquisition reform. There are some things I like and some I don't.

8. I'm still not really convinced that this is a good way to go, and my worries are strengthened by the opinions of other people around this organization.

9. I'm still not really convinced that this is a good way to go, based on negative experiences with the acquisition reform ideas I've tried out.

10. I am critical of the acquisition reform direction that is being promoted these days.

Japan's economic success in the 1980s, based on Japanese firms' ability to produce high-quality products and satisfy customers.[14] After entering corporate America, the TQM concept spread to government. "Customer" was the TQM mantra. Total quality management involved an organization's identifying its "customer" and changing its business processes to serve customers better. For buying offices, program offices were the customer. Total quality management represented a challenge to another element of bureaucracy, specialization and its consequent stovepipes.

A third factor was the job burdens and stress caused by bureaucracy. Rules and hierarchy may force people to do more work than they otherwise would. Rules tell them they need to go through numerous hoops before finishing an assignment.[15] Sign-offs make them prepare justifications for what they want to do. Each new procedure and review adds to a procurement official's workload. In addition, new procedures, which slow the system down even more, make program people even angrier with procurement, adding to job stress.

Finally, the better-value contracting ideology challenged bureaucratic preoccupation with process over results. For reasons similar to those embraced by the leaders of procurement reform, some people criticized this preoccupation of the traditional system.

It should be noted that these last two factors—job burdens and support for a better-value contracting ideology—might create discontent through two separate paths. They might do so both directly and also indirectly, through creation of support for job autonomy. These two paths are not identical. A person concerned about job burdens might simply be dissatisfied with the system and want job burdens reduced by any means available, such as direct elimination of some number of rules or sign-offs. This would be a direct path between job burdens and discontent. However, in addition, high job burdens might also be one source creating the demand for job autonomy (the ability to decide for oneself whether one should follow some procedure or consult a superior), which is a specific solution to the job burden problem. This would constitute an indirect path between job burdens and discontent. Conversely, one might be dissatisfied with the system because it created job burdens without favoring job autonomy—one might, say, believe that job autonomy will simply increase burdens by forcing one to make more decisions oneself. Analogous arguments may be made about the direct and indirect impacts of support for a better-value contracting ideology. I test for both direct and indirect effects of these variables.

Desire for Job Autonomy

Two questions from the Frontline Survey suggest that hostility to bureaucracy based on a desire for autonomy was a major source of discontent with the traditional system. One question asked about job autonomy in general, presenting a "feeling thermometer" whereby respondents were asked to state how "warm" they felt, between 0 and 100 degrees (50 degrees being neutral), about the suggestion that there should be "more freedom for people doing the work to make their own decisions, with fewer reviews and approvals."[16] The other focused specifically on dislike of rules, asking respondents to agree or disagree with the statement, "I feel uneasy when I have to make a decision where there's no rule that tells me what to do." The mean response for dislike of hierarchy was 80.3 on a scale of 1 to 100 ($N = 1,340$). The mean response for dislike of rules was 3.55 on a scale of 1 to 5 ($N = 1,230$). Both answers showed strong support for job autonomy.[17]

People might value greater job autonomy for a number of reasons. First, many derive satisfaction from using their minds to exercise judgment, make choices, or display self-reliance.[18] This may reflect what philosophers call a "motivated" desire, growing from one's belief that some particular end (in this case, the opportunity to choose) is valuable.[19] It might also grow from an unmotivated desire that simply assails us; a person might well up with frustration when ordered around, as a small child might throw a temper tantrum when asked to walk in one direction rather than another.

Second, one may seek autonomy to reduce job burdens. As noted above, rules and hierarchy can create extra work, as well as job-related stress in interactions with other parts of one's organization.

Third, one may seek autonomy to get better organizational results. As noted in chapter 2, procurement reform leaders supported greater autonomy to give frontline procurement employees an opportunity to use discretion to improve the value procurement delivered.[20]

It is plausible that the desire for autonomy in order to exercise judgment might increase with increasing education, job level, and affluence. Employees making decisions for themselves must use their minds more than those who simply follow the rules or send decisions up the chain of command. The better educated people become, the better able they are to use their minds and thereby to make decisions. In addition, education lowers the cost of making decisions and thus increases the likelihood people will value the opportunity to do so. Education also generally instills the value of thinking for oneself.

Moreover, to develop a motivated desire for autonomy is to value an abstract idea. In an influential essay, Philip Converse has argued (in the context of how people think about politics) that as education and political information decrease, the ability to think in terms of abstract belief systems rapidly declines.[21] Higher education helps people conceive of an abstraction such as autonomy as having value because education helps people develop the capacity for abstract thought generally. Similarly, James Walsh suggests that those at higher organization levels develop more complex knowledge structures, involving a greater ability to abstract, because they get exposed to a wider range of stimuli and deal with complex situations requiring the use of their minds.[22] The higher a person rises in government (particularly into a supervisory position), the more experience he or she gets in dealing with policy issues, which also are abstract. For this reason, job level, like higher education, has the capacity to promote the desire for job autonomy.

The view that affluence might lead a person to value choice is associated with the writings of Ronald Inglehart, who has argued that as societies have become more affluent, "postmaterialist" values have become more important than satisfaction of economic wants.[23] This view is based on the theory of an innate "hierarchy of needs," beginning with physiological (hunger and thirst) and safety needs.[24] Once these have been satisfied—as occurs with affluence—the hierarchy proceeds upward to a need for "self-actualization" (self-fulfillment and personal growth), coming from the opportunity to realize a life plan that has been chosen rather than one that is imposed.[25]

Additionally, a number of psychological traits might facilitate the desire or ability for work involving choice and thus directly or indirectly promote the desire for autonomy to exercise choice or judgment.[26] One is venturesomeness or risk tolerance. The more one likes trying new things, the more one might value a job with the opportunity to do so. A second is deference. Deferent people might be less apt to seek autonomy, since they would be more comfortable letting those in authority make decisions. Also, in the context of a long-standing system backed by those in authority, this may measure a tendency to accept the values of that system, which substantively devalued autonomy. A third is self-confidence. The more confident one feels about one's ability successfully to realize projects one has chosen, the more valuable the ability to exercise choice might be perceived to be.

These factors all have implications for the course and nature of a process of organizational change seeking to reduce bureaucracy. The more distinct reasons there are to value job autonomy, the higher will be the likely support for bureaucracy-reducing reform. Moreover, if increasing education or affluence increases the desire for autonomy, then as education and income levels rise, one can expect a secular trend toward growing dissatisfaction with bureaucracy over time, increasing the constituency for this kind of organizational change. However, if different people seek autonomy for different reasons, this also means that people will be seeking different things under the same rubric; someone seeking autonomy to reduce job burdens would not be expected to behave the same way, if rules and hierarchy were reduced, as one seeking autonomy to produce better organizational results.

To what extent did procurement employees seek autonomy for each of the reasons discussed, and to what extent was the desire for autonomy associated with higher education, job level, and affluence? To explore these questions empirically, two models were developed with a number of predictor variables that might explain respondents' desire for job autonomy and dislike of rules.[27] Specification of the models appears in appendix A.

Many variables to be tested here might affect the desire for autonomy both indirectly and directly. Therefore, rather than ordinary regression, a structural equation model was used, which allows testing for both indirect ("mediated") relationships and direct paths—though owing to the many links between the two, these models can be daunting to interpret.[28]

Results of the two regressions are presented in figures 3-1 and 3-2. Only variables with a statistically significant relationship explaining support for autonomy are shown. For each variable, a coefficient is presented that shows the variable's effect size.[29] With a few exceptions, variables that best explain the desire for job autonomy and a dislike of rules were the same.

The results indicate that gaining the opportunity to exercise judgment or choice was the most important reason for seeking job autonomy. The variable measuring the opportunity to exercise judgment had the largest effect of any variable (.11). Its effect size was twice as large for specifically disliking rules (.23) as for seeking job autonomy in general. Nor was there evidence that the desire for autonomy simply assailed people who felt an aversion to being controlled by others, rather than being a motivated choice.[30]

By contrast, the desire for burden reduction did not drive support for autonomy. In neither model was high job burden and stress positively related to the desire for autonomy. Indeed, for disliking rules, greater job burden and stress was associated with liking rules *more*, a result

FIGURE 3-1. Structural Equation Model Predicting Support for Job Autonomy

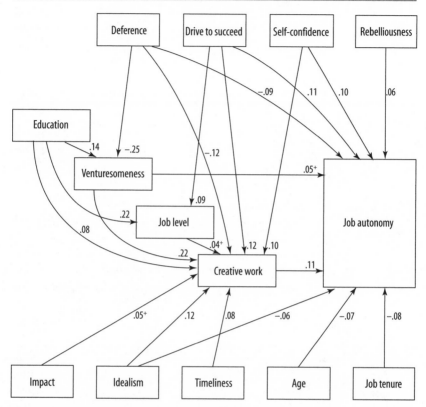

Note: CFI = .92; *N* = 1,341. Standardized coefficients. All coefficients are statistically significant at .05 or better, except those indicated by a +, which means they are significant to .1.

suggesting overworked respondents regarded rules as a welcome short-cut obviating a need to spend time thinking.

In addition, there was some evidence that the desire to produce better organizational results promoted the desire for autonomy indirectly by promoting desire to exercise judgment or choose.[31] The link between the desire for better organizational performance and support for autonomy was tested in a number of ways. The results show that a number of bet-ter-value variables tested—the perceived impact of the respondent's job on organizational performance, idealism, timeliness, and the drive to succeed—did help explain the desire to exercise judgment or choose, which, in turn, was linked to desire for autonomy. However, this con-

FIGURE 3-2. Structural Equation Model Predicting Dislike of Rules

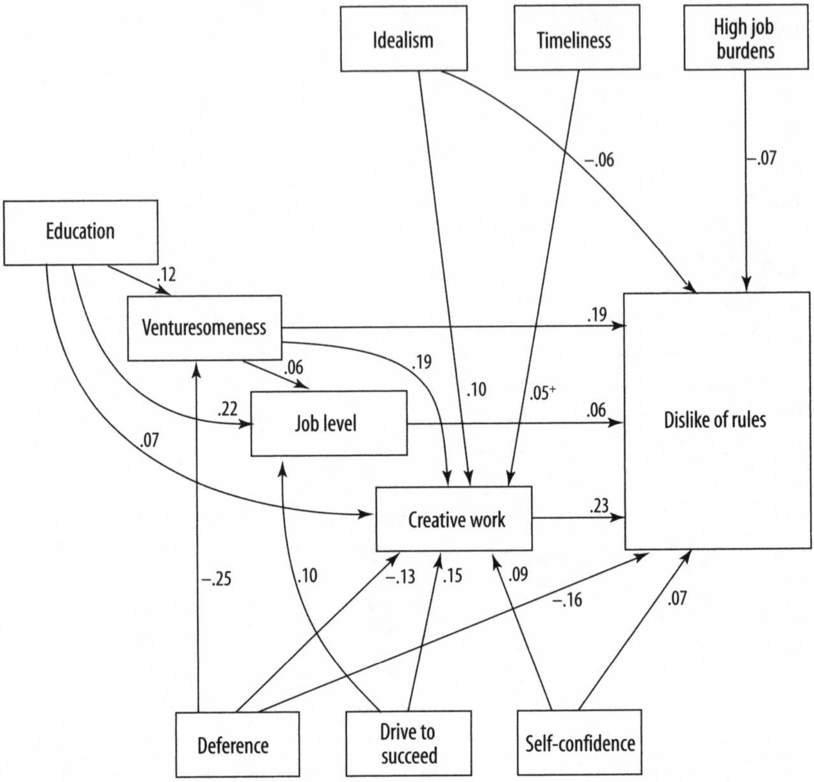

Note: CFI = .92; N = 1,341. Standardized coefficients. All coefficients are statistically significant at .05 or better, except those indicated by a +, which means they are significant to .1.

nection was generally smaller for those variables that were most closely connected with the reformers' agenda.[32]

Psychological traits were powerful predictors of desire for autonomy. All three variables—risk tolerance, self-confidence, and lack of deference—were significant predictors, with above-average effect sizes, particularly for dislike of rules.[33] All of these variables also indirectly explained support for autonomy by creating, with large effect sizes, a desire to choose or exercise judgment. Venturesomeness or risk tolerance had the largest effect size (.22) of any variable.

Education helped explain a desire for autonomy predominantly through its impact on other variables. In both models, greater education influenced three variables that predicted support for autonomy: desire for creative work, risk tolerance, and job level. Education also had a modest direct impact predicting desire for job autonomy, reflecting some impact of the ability to think abstractly on desire for autonomy, but it was insignificant for dislike of rules. This is one of the first empirical demonstrations of a relation between education and desire for job autonomy. Thus it can be argued that as education levels rise, desire for job autonomy will rise as well, producing increased dissatisfaction with bureaucracy over time.[34]

Affluence (expressed as a function of age) may help explain desire for autonomy. Controlling for education and job longevity, lower age significantly predicted a desire for autonomy, although the effect was modest.[35] Controlling for education, age, and job level, lower job tenure predicted lower desire for autonomy.[36] However, in these models age did not significantly predict a desire for creative work. This raises questions about Inglehart's postmaterialism hypothesis, which would predict an impact of affluence on desire for autonomy mediated by desire for creative work. Thus although age was related to desire for autonomy, something other than affluence might have been driving the relation. One explanation would be a secular change in society's cultural climate, placing greater value on choice. Such a climate change might be driven by growing affluence and education, but its potential impact on an individual would not be dependent on individual affluence or education, since the effect comes from social, not individual, factors. This in itself would explain a desire for autonomy, independent of any personally felt desire for work involving original thinking.[37]

The Customer Concept

By coincidence, shortly after I had observed the traditional system, total quality management arrived in the federal government.[38] The traditional procurement culture, operating through a stovepipe, was separated from and hostile toward program people. In interviews for my 1990 book, procurement people generally referred to program people as "they." So when I entered government in 1993, I was startled to hear procurement people calling program people "the customer." This enormous change grew out of TQM.[39] "Before TQM," one senior local official stated in the In-Person Interviews, "contracting people thought *they* were the customer. They didn't see themselves as helping *others* to be successful." A local office head recalled that his previous boss had once blurted out at a TQM meeting, "I have had it! I do not have customers.

My job is to protect the taxpayer interest and to prevent the government from being ripped off."

How was such a major cultural change possible? The very word *customer* may have helped. The virtue of this word is its ready cognitive availability; it is the opposite of a consultant's neologism. Everyone is a customer in everyday life. Everyone has an idea of what it means to be treated well, or badly, as a customer. The idea of treating customers well in the world outside government is uncontroversial. Thus the word itself supported the legitimacy of the demand.

The In-Person Interviews presented a good feel for the change that occurred:

> Years ago we weren't necessarily concerned about the customer. Our goal was to get a contract package that was right. It didn't matter how long it took. It didn't matter whether customer concerns were taken into account. I remember when I was a [contract] specialist my supervisor arguing with the customer all the time. We had little teaming and partnering, lots of tossing things over fences. I would consider us an organization that had built a fence around ourselves.

> We began to change about ten years ago. The customer started to show on our radar screen. We started to break down the walls. I think that TQM, although people considered it a fad, made the concern for customer focus begin to rear its head. We realized that we're only here because of our customers. [My boss] and I used to sit around late at night and talk concepts. The vision was customer service.

> TQM in contacting led to a significant change in mind-set. There had been a great deal of emphasis on what was labeled as professionalism, but actually it was *control*. The climate was one of "we're the experts; you, customers, have to play by the rules as we describe them and interpret them." There was a conflict between contracting and customers. With TQM, there was a cultural change—better partnering with program people.

> Personally, it was a hard change, because, like 90 percent of people in procurement, my objective was to be a contract negotiator. And the image of a negotiator was somebody who was tough. Part of the image was to be tough on everybody, both the contractor and

the end user. If you had a satisfied end user, you must have compromised. You'd almost be proud if you made everybody unhappy. You might even brag about it. All of a sudden you were being asked to be a soft person, to be sympathetic and to listen. You were moving from bully to sissy.

One step along the way was when I got into a higher grade and started doing [information-technology] procurements. I became close with some of the computer specialists and found myself evolving over time to an attitude of trying to help them achieve their mission.

Then, when I started my current job, my boss was a strong supporter of TQM. She kept on saying, "Who are your customers? Who are your customers?" She kept on asking. I remember one time we spent three hours discussing it. It forced me to think about some of this stuff, and it finally hit me. You keep on hearing this stuff in speeches, conferences, reading material. Hearing the term "customer" over and over again made you focus on what you're buying. Finally you say, "Maybe this isn't so foreign after all."

At a number of buying offices, total quality management produced the first-ever systematic evaluation of the office's "business processes." (In fact, the term itself was new.) One office adopted its first mission statement, placed on the outside wall by the local office head's door. The office also established groups to map processes used for various kinds of buys. "When we were done, we put process charts up on the wall with a supply of stickies," one local office head recalled. "We gave people the message, 'If you have an idea about where we could make the process better, take a sticky and put it there." Another local office head "talked to customers and said, 'What can we do better?' They said we needed to tell them what to do when they were preparing a requisition so we didn't have to bounce it back to them. So in 1992 we put out a requisitioner's guide to procurement. And we began to send acknowledgements to them telling them we had received their forms. It was pretty basic, but the program folks loved it."

Total quality management represented a challenge to stovepipes, one of the pillars of bureaucracy. In so doing, it confronted people with a new conception of their job: the role of procurement was not to act as police but to serve program customers. This was a conception that could make an impact on an employee's ideological view of the system. It was also likely to make people more sensitive to the most insistent criticism made by program people, that the system was too slow. Additionally, the impact of TQM might be more personal, making complaints about poor service to program offices more stressful because more salient. For any of these reasons, anyone who liked TQM might have been dissatisfied with the traditional system.

Growing Job Burdens and Stress from Bureaucracy

A perception of bureaucracy-driven job burdens might have created a desire for autonomy, though no empirical support for that relationship was found in the models predicting support for job autonomy. However, discontent with job burdens and stress from bureaucracy might cause dissatisfaction with the traditional system directly, not mediated through support for greater job autonomy.

During the 1980s two things happened to procurement that tightened the vise of bureaucracy. The first was spare parts "horror stories" during the Reagan-era defense buildup, alleging—incorrectly, as it turns out—that the Defense Department paid outrageous prices for everyday items such as hammers and toilet seats.[40] The second was the "Ill Wind" corruption scandal involving bribes of government officials to obtain inside information about proposals submitted by rival bidders during contract competitions. This double whammy produced two pieces of legislation, the Competition in Contracting Act of 1984 and the Procurement Integrity Act of 1989. The Competition in Contracting Act increased bureaucratic requirements for choosing contractors. The Procurement Integrity Act made it a criminal offense for contracting officials to provide contractors with sensitive information, and the result was a significant clampdown on any contacts at all between government and contractors. In the Defense Department, more reviews were introduced, and more cost data sought from contractors to justify prices being charged. Contracting people continued to play a police role vis-à-vis program people and contractors, but the question, who will guard the guards? increasingly arose. More and more, controls that contracting officials had applied to others started getting applied to them as well. As one respondent stated in the In-Person Interviews, "The hammer and toilet seat led to a point where people were afraid to do anything for fear of being criticized. It made effective folks go head down and pencil up." The anger of program people at an ever slower and more complex system rose, increasing job stress. (In the words of one interviewed respondent, "Some people were ready to kill me, with what we went through to buy computers.")

This environment created a cry for "relief" from bureaucracy. Indeed, once reform began, requests by frontline people for elimination of various rules increasingly began with "We request relief from. . . ."

Better Value for Government from Contracting as an Ideology

Problems with the traditional system that interfered with getting good value from contractors might have produced a desire for autonomy and might also have been a source of dissatisfaction directly. A number of grievances involving the traditional system's failure to provide the best value for the government were expressed in the In-Person Interviews, mostly involving criticisms of the buy-low-bid mentality.

> We'd been doing business this other way for a long period of time. However, it's quite different from how you'd do business in your personal life. Best value is something you do in your personal life. You'd look at past performance. You'd check out *Consumer Reports*. And in our personal lives, different things are important to different people. When buying a car, the sound system is important to my son, leather seats to my wife. We needed to do the same thing for the war fighter.

> The emphasis on adhering to the rules mattered more than whether we had a good-quality job being done by the contractor.

> It was frustrating to explain to the customer why we had to keep dealing with lousy contractors.

> There was a strong preference to develop an exact specification and then take the low bid. Procurement was geared to low bid. There was no way to interject common sense. The regs didn't prohibit best value, but it was instilled that you can't do it that way.

Other respondents expressed dissatisfaction more broadly with how the system did a poor job creating value:

> We were not doing a good job of using taxpayer dollars wisely. We followed form over substance—we were more concerned about

making sure we put page numbers on contracts than with getting the right clauses in our business deal with the contractor.

I was trained the old way. The process was the end-all and be-all. My job was to enforce the rules and follow the process to the letter. The [*Federal Acquisition Regulation*] was the Bible, the literal Word. We went by the book.

Back in 1986 a new commanding general comes in and sees we're getting one protest a week. He called the deputy director and me down and said, "Set up a system where industry can talk with us informally so they don't protest as much." So we set up an ombudsman to hear informal complaints, and that became my job, along with chief of compliance.

What changed me was serving as ombudsman, seeing the stupidity and waste in the procurement process, realizing we couldn't do things the old-fashioned way. We were buying a [certain kind of field telephone] which had been in the field for forty years. But we were still requiring environmental stress testing for it. I asked why, and I was told, "Somebody in headquarters said everything has to be field tested. You have to follow the rule." I said I was waiving it. There was a mounting bracket we used for trucks that was also used in the space shuttle under much harsher conditions than ours. Testing it cost more than the total cost of the brackets themselves. Our engineer said, "We checked that testing block last time we bought it," and wanted to do it again. I said, "If it's good enough for the last guy, it's safe for me." So we waived it. Hewlett-Packard shipped computers to their commercial customers within twenty-four hours. But we were requiring special protective packaging for shipping it that added five weeks to the delivery schedule. And the packaging added 25 percent to the price. It made absolutely no sense, since the product had a 100 percent warranty anyway. These kinds of things were routine.

First, you sat in a room by yourself and developed a milspec; you didn't care what the customer needed. You felt forced to deal with the processes you had without working with other folks to develop a solution. And during the early stages of the process, there were limited opportunities for communication with vendors. It was very tightly controlled, with a strong sense that you had to bend over backwards not to say anything differently to one vendor than another. The safest interpretation was to do everything in writing and [send a carbon copy to] everyone.

Second, proposals were a boxful of documents. It took months of technical evaluation. The technical proposals from the [bidders] were being written by people who weren't going to do the work.

Finally, the selection process bordered on being exclusively formulaic. The Competition in Contracting Act forced the program people to accept [a bidder] other than the one they wanted, because the evaluation criteria before you see proposals didn't capture what you see in the proposals. There was such an emphasis on points, scores, numbers that it became very hard to make adjustments.

The desire to serve society by better fulfilling agency mission is a source of support for change in government organizations, whereas in firms, desire to serve others is less important for job choice.[41] Thus just as there are special reasons for resistance to change in government, so too is a desire for better mission attainment a special reason for discontent with the status quo in government.

Overall Patterns from the In-Person Interviews

In the In-Person Interviews, respondents who stated they thought the traditional system was broken were asked a follow-up question, "Why would you have said that?" The frequency distribution of their replies, coded into categories, was then calculated. The patterns are clear (see table 3-1). Dissatisfaction with lack of autonomy—expressed in general terms describing the system as "too bureaucratic" or having "too many rules" (reported by 45 percent of respondents) or with the more specific criticism of excessive hierarchical reviews (25 percent)—was by far the most important source of discontent. Relatively frequent mentions of the system's being too slow (19 percent), as well as of poor relations with program people (11 percent), show the influence of TQM. Thirteen percent of respondents expressed dissatisfaction with personal job burdens (coded as "'too much paperwork' or cumbersome"). Only a modest number expressed dissatisfaction involving problems the traditional system created for achieving better value. (These were responses criticizing excessive reliance on low-bid source selection and on following rules rather than seeking a good deal for the government—15 percent—as

TABLE 3-1. Reasons Procurement System Was Viewed as Broken
or as Having Problems

Reason	Percent[a]
Relating to job autonomy	
Bureaucratic, "too many rules"	45
Too many higher-level reviews	25
Relating to personal job burdens	
To much paperwork, cumbersome	13
Relating to TQM and personal job burdens	
Too slow	19
Poor relations with program	11
General ideology	
Not oriented to best-value contracting, following rules instead of getting good deal	15
Risk averse, did not support innovation	10

Source: In-Person Interviews.
a. $N = 96$. Column totals add up to more than 100 percent because respondents could give multiple answers.

well as the criticism that the existing system failed to support innovation—10 percent.) No respondent expressed dissatisfaction with problems buying commercial items, an important theme for Defense Department reformers. Nor did any proffer the criticism reformers made that
some burdens placed on industry, as well as restrictions on partnership
with industry, hurt the government's ability to achieve better value.

From Discontent to Membership in the Reform Coalition

Dissatisfaction with some elements of the traditional system was relatively high. Not everybody, of course, was dissatisfied. Furthermore, not
every dissatisfied person joined the change vanguard before reform was
launched or became an early adopter of reform once it had been
launched. The next chapter examines what led people to join—or not—
the reform coalition.

CHAPTER 4

Joining the Reform Coalition

Not everyone discontented with the traditional system joined the reform coalition. The factors encouraging resistance to change discussed in chapter 2 reduced the level of discontent below what it would otherwise have been. But these factors may also have held people back from becoming part of the reform coalition, even if they felt dissatisfaction with the status quo. Conversely, factors in addition to the level of discontent may have encouraged some to become initial supporters of reform.

What drove people to join the reform coalition, and what differentiated the change vanguard from early recruits? In the "activating the discontented" theory of change initiation, successful initiation requires a change vanguard that is waiting for an opportunity to spring into action upon receiving encouragement from above. Had there been no change vanguard, successful change initiation could not have occurred, and there would have been no reform effort for early recruits to have joined. Thus it is important to learn what made people procurement reformers before procurement reform. Moreover, there are differences between people in the change vanguard and early recruits that were important for the course of procurement reform after it was launched.

Factors Influencing Joining the Reform Coalition

The two most obvious factors—already discussed—influencing whether somebody joined the reform coalition were the degree and kinds of discontent with the traditional system (for example, the desire for autonomy, burden reduction, providing better customer service, or a system oriented toward producing better value) and the degree of resistance to change. In addition to the sources of discontent and to factors promoting (or discouraging) attachment to an organizational status quo, two other considerations—not yet discussed—might promote (or discourage) joining the reform coalition: personality or demographic factors leading people to become early adopters of changes in general, and the influence of leaders and co-workers.

Early Adopters: A Perspective from Diffusion of Innovation Research

Research on the diffusion of innovation has investigated how innovation, typically a new technology, product, or practice, spreads among individual users. Early research investigated farmers' adoption of new seeds, doctors' adoption of new antibiotics, and families' adoption of family planning in poor countries.[1] This research has, puzzlingly, received little attention in literature on organizational change.

One of the virtues of research on the diffusion of innovation, from the perspective of the argument of this book, is that it takes differences of opinion seriously. Rather than simply assuming that people resist change, diffusion-of-innovation research sees people as ranging from enthusiasts to critics with regard to innovations.[2] Indeed, according to this literature some people actually *enjoy* change in general, independent of discontent with concrete features of the status quo, or they may have characteristics making it easier for them to translate discontent into early support for a change. Such people are among the "early adopters" of innovations—a category somewhat, though imperfectly, corresponding to what I call the change vanguard.[3] At the extreme, some might become early supporters of change even absent dissatisfaction with the status quo, just because they like trying new things.

Why might some enjoy change? Some people enjoy trying new things just because they are new; they value new experience for its own sake. "Venturesomeness is almost an obsession" for the earliest adopters.[4] Venturesome people are those who like to explore a strange city by themselves, even if it means getting lost. (The flip side of this is that if there is a penalty for failure—and there usually is, at least to some extent—those more averse to taking a risk in trying a behavior with a benefit if it succeeds but a penalty if it fails will be hesitant to try new behavior until they have watched others do it and seen it work.)

Second, some people are "cosmopolitans" who derive satisfaction from responding to ideas from the wider world outside their local community. This may occur either because the outside world is attractive to them or because they feel alienated from their local environment (what Georg Simmel has called "strangers" in the local social system).[5] Since diffusion literature sees innovations as typically entering a local system from outside (family planning in a rural village in a developing country, for example), those who enjoy responding to outside influences are likely to become early adopters of externally initiated changes.[6]

In addition, other demographic or personality traits make it easier for people to translate discontent with the procurement status quo into reform coalition membership. Put another way, these traits make it more likely that a person will join the reform coalition at a given level of discontent. Some people, for example, are good at thinking abstractly. The status quo is tangible, while the new activity or behavior is abstract. Before procurement reform started, the ideas it embodied were theories about how the system should work. They had not been tried. "Innovators must be able to adopt a new idea largely on the basis of rather abstract stimuli. . . . Later adopters can observe the innovation in the here-and-now of a peer's operation. They need less ability to deal with abstractions."[7] The literature on diffusion of innovation typically sees education level as a good measure of a person's ability to grasp abstract ideas.[8] In the context of an organization, job level might be a more powerful measure of the significance of the ability to abstract, since it would reflect a person's ability to deal with abstractions involving the organization in particular, rather than the generalized abstraction ability that education provides.

However, these measures are contaminated in the context of support for an organizational change, particularly in government procurement organizations, because education and job level reflect other things besides ability to abstract. As is noted in somewhat greater detail in a different context later in this chapter, it is commonly believed that those at higher job levels will oppose change because their rise to higher levels may show an ability to have succeeded by the rules of the traditional system. They may also feel grateful to the traditional system for having provided them with promotion and educational opportunities. (Many procurement employees during the period under study received college or professional degrees while on the job, paid for by the government; one might expect that gratefulness might be particularly strong for individuals educated in this way.) These influences may well confound the positive impact of education and job levels on early adoption coming from increased ability to abstract.

"An individual is more likely to adopt an innovation if he or she is efficacious and believes that he or she is in control."[9] Particularly in an organizational context, people who do not believe their actions can "make a difference" in changing broader conditions in the organization are less likely to be early adopters of a change, given their tendency to believe their efforts will not succeed in actually changing the organization. Also, idealists might be more willing to take up long-shot (even lost) causes because it is the right thing to do and to worry less about practical consequences of pursuing quixotic quests. And rebellious people might experience satisfaction from acting against mainstream opinion.[10]

Influence of Leaders and Co-workers

Leaders (both systemwide procurement leaders and local office heads or first-line supervisors) might exert influence on individual decisions to join the reform coalition. Such influence might be of several sorts. The leader-pressure theory of change initiation suggests that leaders can get change initiated through relentless application of pressure on people lower in the organization. It is implausible to believe that top system leaders, who were far away from people on the front lines of buying offices, could have exerted the kinds of pressure these theories envision. It is also unlikely that local office heads or first-line supervisors would have put real pressure (as opposed to gentle encouragement) on individual employees to participate in reform activities; such pressure would be unusual as a general matter in a government organization, especially with regard to something, such as participating in a change program, not critical to its mission. In any event, I have defined the reform coalition as consisting of those who were either in the change vanguard or early recruits for reform, excluding people who were unpersuaded but nonetheless went along because of pressure from their bosses. (To be counted in the reform coalition, a respondent needed to have disagreed with the statement that when they first tried reform, they were "doing it mostly because my bosses told me to.")

However, leaders and co-workers might have influenced decisions to join the reform coalition in other ways. One is through persuasion, particularly trying to reach the uncommitted after the reform effort was launched. Leaders might provide a vision of an alternative system, a role emphasized in theories of managerial leadership that address a leader role in creating a vision for an organization and in those that emphasize "symbolic action" in the repertoire of managerial behaviors.[11] In a typically pithy phrase, Karl Weick has suggested that "the appropriate role for the manager may be evangelist rather than accountant."[12] Upon launching the reform effort, systemwide leaders could play a different role—providing reassurance or cover. For those on the front lines who support system change but are afraid that moving away from a focus on control would bring on political wrath, the belief that systemwide leaders could protect them would allow them to support changes they might otherwise be afraid to embrace.

Leader and co-worker influence might also involve social influence or support rather than persuasion. Leaders and co-workers who are themselves in the change vanguard might make it easier for a discontented person to join by providing social support for what at the time would have been a lonely stance. The flip side is that at the beginning of the change process, only a minority support reform. To the extent that a workgroup exerts social influence on individual group members, they will, on balance, dampen rather than promote reform coalition membership. Thus the lower the support for change in a person's workgroup, the less likely it is that the person will join the reform coalition.

Testing for Explanations of Reform Coalition Membership

Different reasons a person might join the reform coalition, either by joining the change vanguard or by becoming an early recruit, were tested using two ordinary least-squares regression equations. In one model, the dependent variable was whether a respondent was in the change vanguard or an early recruit. This model compares the two groups in the reform coalition to see what encouraged a person to oppose the traditional system before changing the system had been raised as an issue. In the second model, the dependent variable was whether the respondent was an early recruit or a skeptic or fence-sitter. This compares early recruits with those who did not join up when change was first launched. Specification of the models appears in appendix A.[13] Table 4-1 presents results, with standardized and nonstandardized coefficients; lower values imply earlier support for change.[14]

The battle for hearts and minds was in significant measure waged between a desire for autonomy impelling people to join the reform coali-

TABLE 4-1. Predictors of Early Support for Change

Predictor	Change vanguard versus early recruits		Early recruits versus initial skeptics and critics	
	Standardized coefficient	Nonstandardized coefficient	Standardized coefficient	Nonstandardized coefficient
Job autonomy				
Dislike rules	−0.14**	−0.15		
Job autonomy	−0.16***	−0.01	−0.13****	−0.008
Burden reduction				
Job burdens			−0.09**	−0.10
Customer service				
Timeliness			−0.07*	−0.08
Satisfy program customer			−0.07*	−0.07
Support for better-value agenda				
Idealism	0.17	0.18		
Idealism × job level	−0.37+	−0.10		
Trust	0.19	0.30		
Trust × job level	−1.03***	−0.22		
Early adopter, "diffusion of innovation"				
Education	0.06	0.08	0.05	0.06
Job level	1.06***	1.13	0.11	0.12
Education × job level			−0.26+	−0.06
Venturesomeness	−0.17***	−0.25	−0.11***	−0.16
Rebelliousness	−0.11*	−0.11	0.08*	0.71
Individual self-efficacy	−0.07	−0.08	−0.21****	−0.25
Support for traditional system and resistance to change				
Deference			0.12***	0.19
Drive to succeed	0.13**	0.19		
General resistance to change			0.16****	0.18
Worried about inspector general			0.09*	0.84
Social influence/leaders				
Most-respected co-worker attitude	−0.50****	−0.66		
Workgroup percentage in change vanguard	−0.15+	−1.07	−0.11*	−0.81
Supervisor attitude	0.14**	0.17		
Systemwide leader influence			−0.09**	−0.09
Crisis				
Work for Defense Logistics Agency	−0.09*	0.31		
Work for Defense Department			0.08****	0.30
Control variable				
Distortion	−0.02	−0.001	−0.14****	−0.008
Adj. R^2	0.49		0.26	
N	438		914	

Source: Frontline Survey.
a. Empty cells indicate that the coefficient for the variable was not statistically significant at the .1 level.
+ ≤ .10   * ≤ .05   ** ≤ .01   *** ≤ .001   **** ≤ .0001

tion and forces of resistance to change keeping them aloof. The other source of discontent driving people into the change vanguard was an ideological criticism of the traditional system, including support for the better-value agenda, while the additional source of discontent driving people to becoming early recruits was desire for burden reduction. Some early-adopter variables also played a role in moving people into the reform coalition, though effect sizes were generally smaller. Most early-adopter variables distinguished not only change vanguard members from early recruits but also early recruits from skeptics and fence-sitters, so being an early adopter helps explain not just the earliest support for change but also decisions of the next adopter group. Generally, enough of the results support ideas from diffusion-of-innovation literature to suggest that this literature can usefully be imported into studying organizational change. Finally, supportive co-workers were important in explaining reform coalition membership, although local leaders did not influence frontline employees to join the reform coalition.

Why Did Some People Join the Change Vanguard?

Four sources of discontent with the traditional system were discussed in chapter 3. For the desire for autonomy, members of the change vanguard were like early recruits, only more so. Both autonomy and opposition to rules were significant, each controlling for the other and each with a large effect size. Together, they were powerful predictors of change vanguard membership. The other two sources of discontent—with high job burdens and poor service to program customers—did not distinguish change vanguard members from early recruits.

However, virtually the only factor uniquely distinguishing change vanguard members (particularly at higher job levels) from everyone else in the sample—both early recruits and initial skeptics and fence-sitters—was *ideological* discontent with the traditional system. The better-value agenda that systemwide leaders advocated when procurement reform began seems to have played a role in explaining reform support only for the change vanguard. Such considerations were, in fact, central to their break with the traditional system.

Both trust and idealism were strongly associated with change vanguard membership, the more so the higher a person's job level.[15] For those at the highest job level (first-line supervisor), trust actually had the largest effect size in the model; for supervisors, idealism had a quite large effect size as well.[16]

TABLE 4-2. Mean Values for Agreeing That Reform Is Burden Reduction among Categories of Early Supporters[a]

Group	Mean value
Early recruits	
1	3.09
2	3.46
Change vanguard	
3	3.63
4	4.23
$N = 189$	

Source: Frontline Survey.
a. Based on responses on a five-point scale, from "strongly agree" (1) to "strongly disagree" (5).

Trust and idealism are both personality traits. These results indicate that at higher job levels, where people developed a greater ability to think abstractly about procurement issues, these personality traits got translated into an ideological critique of the traditional system for being based too much on mistrust and for not doing enough to create a better (procurement) world. This in turn propelled people into the change vanguard, in that it constituted a view of how the procurement system should be organized to promote the public good, as opposed to a view based on how some change in the system might address personal concerns. The focus on control growing out of the distrust underlying the traditional system took attention away from substantive goals of the system, such as obtaining better value from contracting. Obtaining better value would also seem to be a goal that would be embraced by somebody seeking a better procurement world. It is thus plausible to believe that part, or perhaps even the central element, of this ideological critique involved the failure of the traditional system to focus on providing better value.[17]

There is additional evidence, though it is not fully unambiguous, that a desire to focus the system on better value was important to change vanguard members, especially at higher job levels. A question in the Frontline Survey asked respondents to agree or disagree with the statement, "When acquisition reform first was getting started, I thought it was mostly about reducing the burdens on government contracting officials." As can be seen in table 4-2, the strongest change vanguard members (group 4) overwhelmingly disagreed. By contrast, for the weakest early recruits (group 1), almost half saw reform as mostly about burden reduction. In all, 31 percent of early recruits perceived reform as about burden reduction, while only 15 percent of change vanguard members did. It is plausible to believe that getting better value was at least one of the other things people thought reform was about.[18]

The strongest evidence that discontent with the traditional system for its failure to promote better value through contracting was important in driving people at higher levels, who thought ideologically to a greater extent, into the change vanguard comes from the question in the In-Person Interviews about why people were dissatisfied with the traditional system. Among respondents most closely corresponding to change vanguard members, a substantial 38 percent of supervisors (though only 7 percent of nonsupervisors) volunteered a response coded as "not oriented to best value contracting" as a reason they regarded the traditional system as "broken" ($N = 35$, p value = .04 for two-tailed test).[19] Furthermore, though the numbers are very small,[20] every local office head in the change vanguard for whom information was available criticized the traditional system for lack of attention to best value.[21]

Virtually none of the resistance-to-change variables distinguished change vanguard members from early recruits, though they sharply separated early recruits from skeptics and fence-sitters. Thus change vanguard members were no less (or more) likely to be influenced by a generalized resistance to change than were early recruits. All reform coalition members were less swayed by generalized resistance to change, while those initially opposing reform were strongly influenced by such resistance. One exception was that change vanguard members were actually *less* likely than early recruits to report being driven to succeed at their jobs—and the effect size for this was quite large. Supporting change when doing so was not "politically correct" was apparently seen as not career enhancing, which promoted resistance to change before reform got under way (with endorsement of the system's leadership). This result is especially interesting because as reform proceeded, the desire to succeed became associated with support for reform, not opposition to it.[22]

Some, but not all, early-adopter variables helped predict change vanguard membership. Venturesomeness or risk tolerance was associated with being in the change vanguard, with one of the largest effect sizes in the model.[23] People who liked change for the sake of change were more likely to join the change vanguard.

The results presented earlier indicate that the ability to abstract made it easier to translate generalized idealism and trust into joining the change vanguard. That is a bit different from the argument in the litera-ture on diffusion of innovation that the ability to abstract encourages early adoption by making it easier to conceive of an alternative to cur-rent practice that does not currently exist. The evidence from this model, combined with that from the one explaining being an early recruit, is also suggestively positive but must be interpreted speculatively. Run sim-ply as a main effect, job level was unrelated to change vanguard mem-bership ($p = .92$),[24] while more education, although with marginal signif-icance ($p = .10$) and small effect size, was actually associated with a lower likelihood of membership in the change vanguard. One interpreta-tion of these results is that both promotion and gratefulness effects would normally have produced a negative association between these fac-tors and change vanguard membership, so the nonassociation suggests that something was counteracting the effects that would otherwise have occurred—the positive impact of the ability to abstract, both directly and interacting with idealism to produce ideological discontent with the status quo.[25] Confidence in this explanation is increased since, as noted below, when reform was launched and the gratefulness effect thus elimi-nated, both education and job level became associated with becoming an early recruit rather than a skeptic or fence-sitter.

None of the cosmopolitanism variables—exposure to outside media covering procurement ($p = .18$), professional association membership ($p = .32$), or keeping up with systemwide leader statements ($p = .42$)—was associated with change vanguard membership. Diffusion-of-innova-tion literature may be wrong in assuming that the outside world is always a source of new ideas and that therefore those who like exposing themselves to the outside world get exposed to new ideas. Before 1993, systemwide leaders in the executive branch and Congress were not gen-erally promoting change, certainly not loudly; nor was the professional association of the procurement community. If the outside world is not a source of new ideas, cosmopolitanism will not produce exposure to new ideas. Furthermore, sociability was not significantly related to change vanguard membership (or to being an early recruit). Those in the change vanguard were thus neither social deviants nor "strangers" in their local systems.

Individual-level self-efficacy did not predict change vanguard mem-bership ($p = .23$). Collective self-efficacy—the view that a person can make a difference in creating social change—was just short of statisti-cally significant ($p = .12$), with modest effect size. Rebelliousness was a significant predictor of change vanguard membership, with a moderately large effect size; people who derived satisfaction from going against conventional opinion, like people who enjoyed change, were more likely than others to join the change vanguard.[26]

One social influence variable—measuring whether one's most-respected co-worker was in the change vanguard—turned out to have a larger effect size than the combined (additive) effect of the desire for job autonomy and dislike of rules. Indeed, except for the impact of high interpersonal trust among people at the highest job level, the attitude of one's most-respected co-worker had the largest effect size in the model. The percentage of workgroup members in the change vanguard also predicted individual change vanguard membership, again with a large effect size. These results are consistent with the description one member of the change vanguard gave in the In-Person Interviews: "There were cells or pockets of people who wanted to change the system."

These effect sizes seem large as measures of social influence alone—it seems implausible that this should have exerted such strong influence, especially since, as discussed later in this chapter, attitudes of respected co-workers did not differentiate early recruits from skeptics and fence-sitters. Instead, what may have been going on was not so much social influence as social support. Those discontented with the traditional system in an environment that discouraged expression of such views may have developed ties to like-minded colleagues, which might have allowed them to sustain a conception of themselves as people seeking change. Social support thus enabled people to join the change vanguard.

Support for change coming from local leadership did not move people into the change vanguard. Having a local office head in the change vanguard was not associated with joining the change vanguard ($p = .80$).[27] Amazingly, there was a quite strong relationship, in terms of both statistical significance and effect size, between having a proreform immediate supervisor and a *decreased* likelihood of being in the change vanguard.[28] As discussed later in this chapter, supervisor attitude was also unrelated one way or another to being an early recruit versus a skeptic or fence-sitter. The lack of influence—or even negative influence—of one's supervisor's procurement reform attitude on a respondent's own attitude recurred as the change process proceeded (see chapter 8). Speculatively, the strong negative results here might reflect a variant of the negative impact of extrinsic reward on intrinsic motivation (discussed in a somewhat different context in chapter 9): for those who might otherwise have been intrinsically attracted to an alternative to the status quo, the support of an authority figure for challenging that status quo might have reduced the attractiveness of such a challenge.

Why Did People Become Early Recruits?

Early recruits were less strong than change vanguard members in their desire for job autonomy, but stronger than skeptics and fence-sitters. Two sources of discontent specifically drove people to become early recruits (that is, distinguished them from skeptics but did not distinguish change vanguard members from them). These were the desire for burden reduction and discontent with poor customer service.[29] Neither trust ($p = .62$) nor idealism ($p = .84$) was a significant predictor of being an early recruit.[30] Generalized resistance to change strongly distinguished skeptics and fence-sitters from early recruits.

Respondents experiencing high levels of job stress or job burden were more likely to become early recruits, though the effect size was fairly low. Another sign of the importance of burden reduction to early recruits was that dislike of rules, which had distinguished change vanguard members from early recruits, did not distinguish early recruits from skeptics or fence-sitters ($p = .27$). As noted in the context of models explaining support for job autonomy, those feeling overworked may actually like rules because they reduce their work burden, and this would be expected to counteract, and perhaps (as here) even neutralize, the connection between the desire for job autonomy and reform coalition membership. Both customer-service variables also explained becoming an early recruit, though with the smallest effect sizes of any of the significant variables in the model.

Most variables measuring resistance to change, in contrast to the change vanguard model, were significant and had large effect sizes, in particular those measuring fear of change and deference. That greater deference inhibited becoming an early recruit is especially interesting, since—like the drive to succeed—it came to promote reform support as the change effort continued. Fear of external criticism from control organs was also significant, though its effect size was modest. One resistance-to-change variable that did not help explain being a skeptic or fence-sitter, however, was length of service in government procurement, although surely at least part of the explanation is that coefficients were biased downward by the departure of older reform skeptics after 1992.[31]

Most of the same early-adopter variables that were significant in explaining change vanguard membership also helped explain being an early recruit. Both job level and education, representing abstraction ability, were significant for explaining becoming an early recruit. There was also a significant interaction effect between the two, such that their effect was multiplicative (that is, the higher one's education level, the greater the impact of higher job level). At the highest job level, the effect size of education was actually the largest in the model.[32] These straightforward results, in contrast to the more complex ones for the change vanguard, can be explained by the implications of the launch of reform by systemwide leaders and endorsement by many local office heads. This would have eliminated the impact of the gratefulness effect before reform was launched and made it easier for the effect of abstraction ability to come to the fore.[33] Collective self-efficacy—one's belief that one could make a difference in a collective effort—had the largest effect size in the model (except for education at the highest job level), so a view about whether one could make a difference by joining a change effort was crucial for people deciding whether to sign on once reform had been launched. Venturesomeness was significant but had a more modest effect on being an early recruit than on joining the change vanguard. As in the change vanguard model, sociability was not significant ($p = .17$), suggesting that early recruits were not deviants or "strangers."

Keeping up with top leaders, a cosmopolitanism variable, not significant in explaining change vanguard membership, was significant here, with moderate effect size. The reason, consistent with the explanation of its lack of importance in the change vanguard model, is that top leadership began to push reform. Listening to top leaders now encouraged reform support. The extent to which this influence was based on providing a vision and providing reassurance or cover cannot be determined from the data.[34]

As in the change vanguard model, the higher the proportion of members of the change vanguard in one's workgroup, the more likely a person was to become an early recruit, and the effect size of this variable was quite large. This is likely to reflect both change vanguard proselytizing and a weaker antichange workgroup majority that lowered antireform conformity pressures. Surprisingly, having a most-respected co-worker who supported reform was unrelated to being an early recruit ($p = .47$). This was puzzling, both given the large effect size for this variable in explaining change vanguard membership and because one would assume that if change vanguard members were collectively influencing respondents, then that influence would, if anything, be stronger for the dyadic relationship between an individual and his or her most-respected co-worker. Speculatively, one can imagine that the persuasive impact of some was counterbalanced by resentment against others who were seen as exploiting a trusted status to promote a long-held enthusiasm, particularly if they "came on too strong," as evangelists often do in the enthusiasm surrounding a new effort.[35] As for the change vanguard, the impact of local leadership was absent: neither proreform office heads not proreform supervisors influenced becoming an early recruit.

The Burning-Platform Theory

If downsizing or subjecting an organization to market pressures for the first time can be seen as a sign of organizational crisis, the results provided little support for the proposition that crisis helped trigger early support for change. The dummy variable for working for the Defense Logistics Agency, which had lost its appropriated budget just before procurement reform began, did not explain becoming an early recruit, which is when it might have had an impact.[36] The dummy variable for working in the Defense Department was significant in the early-recruit model, though with a fairly modest effect size, but in the opposite direction from that predicted by the burning-platform hypothesis: Defense Department respondents were *less* likely to be early recruits.

One way to explain this is that crisis *reduces* support for change.[37] Assuming that this is not in fact the result of a negative impact of crisis on change support, a plausible explanation is that Defense Department employees tend to be more cynical than those in civilian agencies with regard to short-term initiatives—such as, but not limited to, procurement reform—senior leadership announces.[38] This would be so, first, because senior procurement leadership in the Defense Department is more likely to consist of, or include, military officers serving short (typically three-year) stints, a situation with no counterpart in civilian agencies, where senior procurement leadership consists of career civil servants. Second, because of the importance of military procurement to the department, political appointees in the Defense Department are more likely to become involved in procurement issues. Together, this means that the influence of senior leadership over procurement is more likely in the Defense Department to come from short-term leaders, typically criticized by career civil servants (whether Defense Department or civilian) for excessive use of short-term "initiatives" used to "make a mark" and for lack of follow-through. Having been subjected to many such initiatives, Defense Department employees would be expected initially to be more likely to react with cynicism (viewing reform efforts as a "flavor of the month").[39]

Different Agendas and the Size of the Reform Coalition

To some significant extent, then, procurement reform was "about" different things for different members of the reform coalition—job autonomy as a route to better job satisfaction, the hope for burden reduction, and the belief the traditional system failed to get best value for the government. The presence in change movements of people with different conceptions of what they seek from the change is not untypical. In the early declarations of grievances (*cahiers*) appearing on the eve of the French Revolution, huge differences can be seen in what different people in the same movement were demanding. "From its outset . . . the Revolution was running fast in opposite directions. Its leaders wanted freedom, deregulation and mobility of labor; commercialization; rational economic activity. . . . [But a] striking number of *cahiers* both within towns themselves and especially from rural regions dependent on cottage weaving and spinning attacked mechanization and the amalgamation of industrial process into factories."[40] Similarly, as a college student observing protest movements in the 1960s, I wrote about how a "confrontation coalition" got established among students with different, even contradictory, agendas—student revolutionaries seeking a rigidly controlled communist society, alienated students hoping to live unconventional lifestyles, and moderate students seeking changes to policies on Vietnam and race.[41]

In both examples, people with different change agendas joined the same movement. This increased the number of those breaking with the status quo and hence improved the change efforts' chances for success. Indeed, one could go further and note that the more a change effort is able to unite such disparate sources of protest, the greater its chances of being successfully initiated.

Formal Leaders, Opinion Leaders, and Reform Coalition Membership

Table 4-3 divides respondents into categories of initial reaction to reform by job level—frontline, first-line supervisors, division chiefs, and local office heads.[42] What is striking is how initial support, and espe-

TABLE 4-3. Initial Support for Procurement Reform, by Job Level[a]
Percent

Group	Frontline[b]	First-line supervisors[b]	Division chiefs[c]	Local office heads[d]
Change vanguard	16	35	38	37
Early recruits	24	30	14	32
Fence-sitters	17	10	48[e]	32[e]
Skeptics and critics	43	25		
N	791	98	21	19

Sources: Frontline Survey, In-Person Interviews, and telephone interviews.
a. Column totals may not add up to 100 percent because of rounding.
b. Based on responses to initial attitude and view of procurement reform questions. See text.
c. Based on responses to view of procurement reform question only. See text, including caution on interpretation.
d. Based on author's characterization, using responses to view of procurement reform and other interviews. See text.
e. "Fence-sitters" and "skeptics and critics" combined. The data do not allow a distinction between the two groups.

cially change vanguard membership, increased as formal leadership level rose. The big jump occurred from nonsupervisors to first-line supervisors—being in the change vanguard increased from 16 percent to 35 percent, and in the reform coalition from 40 percent to 65 percent. The highest level of initial support was from local office heads (69 percent).

This finding may be seen as surprising. It is a commonly held view in the literature that leaders are the most resistant to change.[43] The literature suggests this is owing to a selection effect—that these people have succeeded in rising under the rules of the traditional system, or perhaps were selected for their positions partly based on their sympathy for values and approaches the traditional system embodies.[44] One may also imagine a gratefulness effect, owing generally to gratefulness at having been promoted within the traditional system and, in the specific context of government procurement organizations and some other government organizations as well, gratefulness at having been provided an education.

Yet on balance, the opposite was the case. This does not mean the selection and gratefulness effects were absent. Rather, they were outweighed by other factors. Desire for autonomy and support for a better-value ideology were stronger among formal leaders. Higher education level and greater venturesomeness among supervisors were early-adopter variables making it easier for them to envision alternatives to the traditional system and to enjoy change.[45] Finally, one may note that the more senior—and, in the government, hence more secure—position of supervisors may provide them a freedom to engage on behalf of their beliefs that lower-level employees may not feel; supervisors who feel they are unlikely to advance further may also feel greater independence than lower-level employees still hoping for promotions. Government organizations may be different from many private ones in this regard, and the transferability of conclusions about supervisors drawn from private sector experience may therefore be decreased.

Opinion leaders, who may or may not also be formal leaders, are those who exert influence over the attitudes and behaviors of those around them. Because of their influence over others, the literature on diffusion of innovation sees the views of opinion leaders as crucial to the success of a change effort.[46] However, in discussing adoption patterns of opinion leaders in diffusion-of-innovation research, Everett Rogers argues that the earliest adopters are typically *not* opinion leaders. More oriented to the outside, they may well be considered "deviant," with "low credibility" in the local social system.[47]

In the case of procurement reform, however, opinion leaders seem to have been disproportionately likely to be change vanguard members. Asked to characterize the reform attitude of the person they most respected as a procurement professional, two-thirds of respondents characterized that person as "an early enthusiast and evangelist for acquisition reform" (24 percent) or "an early enthusiast, but kept his/her opinions mostly to him/herself" (17 percent), although from the response categories available for the question it is hard to know whether these numbers come closer to describing change vanguard membership or being an early recruit (the best bet is somewhere in between).[48] Opinion leadership was measured a second way. Respondents were asked whether they got "more," "about the same," or "fewer" requests from colleagues for "information and advice about professional matters" than co-workers, other than supervisors, in their office. Table 4-4 presents mean responses from nonsupervisors and supervisors who were change vanguard members, early recruits, fence-sitters, and skeptics.[49] Those in the change vanguard reported having received the most advice requests; early recruits received more than skeptics.

To explore why opinion leaders were overrepresented in the change vanguard, a regression model was developed to predict whether a respondent got more requests for advice than others. The hypothesis was that the relationship between informal leadership and being in the change vanguard was similar to that for formal leadership, that is, that various characteristics predicting change vanguard membership were

TABLE 4-4. Mean Values for Requests for Advice Variable by Initial Support for Procurement Reform[a]

Group	Nonsupervisors	Supervisors
Change vanguard	1.42	1.29
Early recruits	1.58	1.38
Fence-sitters	1.64	1.66
Skeptics	1.71	1.55
N	758	84

Source: Frontline Survey.
a. Based on responses on a three-point scale, from "most advice" (1) to "least advice" (3). See text.

also associated with being a greater source of advice. So, for example, one hypothesis was that employees who desired job autonomy, or liked jobs requiring creative thinking, would be likely to be good sources of advice because, enjoying using their minds, they were likely to be more competent and inclined to provide advice (that is, they were likely to have thought through, or be intrigued with the idea of thinking through, tough or unusual situations about which people are most likely to seek advice). Similarly, it was hypothesized that people less inclined to defer to higher-ups, more confident of their ability to see plans through, and more venturesome would be more inclined to offer, and perhaps to be seen by co-workers as good sources of, advice. Finally, it seemed likely that the higher a person's job level, the more likely others would be to seek that person's advice.[50]

Results of the regression are presented in table 4-5.[51] Job level was highly significant, with the largest effect size. Dislike of rules and preference for creative work were also highly significant, with a combined effect size somewhat larger than job level. Additionally, respondents seeing themselves as less deferent to authority were more likely to be advice sources. Interestingly, the simple desire for job autonomy, controlling for dislike of rules and preference for creative work, was not significant: stripped of those two elements, what was left may have just been someone wanting to be left alone.[52]

How did members of the change vanguard avoid being seen as "deviants"? Important for answering this question is an old distinction in the literature on supervision and leadership between "task" leadership (directed toward the content of the work) and "interpersonal" leadership (directed toward maintenance of group cohesion).[53] The latter kind of leadership requires being sociable and relating to group values;

TABLE 4-5. Predictors of Being a Source of Advice

Variable	Standardized coefficient	Nonstandardized coefficient
Job autonomy	0.02	0.0005
Creative work	0.11***	0.08
Dislike of rules	0.12***	0.06
Job level	0.20****	0.12
Education	−0.04	−0.02
Deference	−0.06*	−0.05
Venturesomeness	−0.006	−0.004
Sociability	0.008	0.008
Control variables		
Age (log)	0.02	0.066
Job tenure (log)	−0.03	−0.05
Reform attitude	0.04	0.001
Adj. R^2 = 0.10		
N = 1,370		

Source: Frontline Survey.

$^+ \leq .10$ $* \leq .05$ $** \leq .01$ $*** \leq .001$ $**** \leq .0001$

the former requires competence. Although parts of Rogers' discussion of opinion leaders suggests, appropriately, that they provide information and advice, his discussions of opinion leaders' being well liked and personally admired suggests he conflates these two kinds of leadership, and his argument for why the earliest adopters are not typically opinion leaders is an argument for why they are not particularly personally popular. Both the question in the survey about receiving advice requests and the one about the reform attitude of one's most-respected co-worker emphasized the task-related, rather than interpersonal, side of leadership, since they talked about the person most respected for "his or her skills as a procurement professional" and advice "about professional matters." What the results show is that, for that kind of opinion leadership, people go to those they think are competent to offer and inclined to give advice. (The data show that people from whom advice was requested did not see themselves as more sociable than those receiving fewer advice requests.)

The strong overrepresentation of both formal and opinion leaders in the change vanguard boded well for reformers' ability to be successful in local politics when reform got initiated. This occurred only to a limited extent through leaders' ability to act as opinion leaders, bringing along early recruits, swelling their ranks, and increasing chances of success

owing to increased numbers: the higher the percentage of change vanguard members in a respondent's workgroup, the more likely the respondent was to become an early recruit, but neither local office heads, supervisors, nor most-respected co-workers influenced others to join reform as
it was getting started. However, formal leaders surely had an effect on
successful initiation through a different route, namely, disproportionate
local political influence, as people with formal authority to direct office
activity.[54] The same was most likely so for opinion leaders, who would
generally be more active in the political processes in their offices.

Frontline Discontent and the Procurement Reformers' Agenda

In this and the previous chapter I have looked at discontents with the
traditional system from the perspective of frontline employees. So I have
spoken of the desire for job autonomy—something *individuals* wanted.
This is in contrast to the perspective of chapter 2, where I address criticisms of the traditional system from the perspective of reformers in the
White House and the Pentagon. There, I spoke of reducing bureaucracy—a change in *organizational* design. As administrator of the Office
of Federal Procurement Policy, I almost always used the word *discretion*
rather than *empowerment* to describe what I sought to accomplish,
mostly because *discretion* evoked for me a principle of organizational
design rather than something centering on an individual's personal work
situation. Here I try to compare, and mesh, the two perspectives, to
explore what the "it" is that gained a foothold on the front lines when
reform was initiated—that is, what effort various people thought they
were joining when they first began to participate in the change effort.

As noted in chapter 2, the agenda of the reformers at the top of the
system was ideological. They criticized the traditional system for being
insufficiently focused on delivering to government better value from
contracting. They wanted to refocus the energy of the system on getting
better value. They believed that reducing bureaucracy would, among
other things, encourage innovative ways of doing business that would
provide better value.

By contrast, many of the discontents driving the front lines to support
change were personal. The range of discontents—and hence the range of
what people initially sought from reform—was large. Furthest from the
views of the reform leaders were those who felt overworked and wanted
"relief." Such individuals might not even want more autonomy, only

fewer "hoops" to go through. People thinking this way were not a majority of the discontented, but neither were they an insignificant group. About a third of early recruits, when they heard about procurement reform, saw it as mainly about reducing their own personal job burdens. They heard the word *streamlining,* originally identified mostly with concerns of end users about burdens the traditional system created for the end user, and saw reform as a way to reduce their own burdens as procurement people.

Discontent connected to the reformers' better-value agenda was lower. Statements of discontent with the failure of the system to provide best value appeared only occasionally in the In-Person Interviews, and those interviews showed no evidence of interest in the reformers' desire to obtain more commercial items for the Defense Department or better cooperation with industry. Mean values for recall questions measuring discontent with service to program customers and with contractor quality seemed to show only modest discontent—the means, respectively, were 2.44 (N = 394) and 2.50 (N = 401), where 1 was most content and 5 least content, though the numbers on discontent with poorly performing contractors may be misleading.[55] On the other hand, many wanted job autonomy to gain an opportunity for work involving original thinking; the mean sample value for liking a job involving creative work was 3.88, where 1 represented lowest interest and 5 highest (N = 1,012).[56] The data in chapter 3 explaining the desire for autonomy suggest that wishing to achieve better organizational results was one factor driving that desire.

For many, the various discontents got clumped under a demand to "streamline" to remove rules and clearances. The demand incorporated a broad range of concerns, from liberating those seeking a chance for creative work from the tyranny enchaining them, at one end, to eliminating requirements and supervision and reducing job burdens, at the other—and in the middle, eliminating time-consuming steps and allowing people to provide more timely service.[57]

The Reformers' Agenda: Contrasts between the Change Vanguard and Early Recruits

In the evidence presented earlier, the change vanguard, especially those at higher job levels, was the one group showing evidence of ideological discontent with the traditional system, including support for a focus on obtaining better value from contracting. Idealism and abstraction ability nurtured ideological dissatisfaction with the status quo, just as the desire for autonomy or resentment at job burdens were sources of discontent. A greater number of grievances meant greater discontent. (Put schematically, somebody worried about autonomy, burdens, and failure of the traditional system to deliver good value would be more discontented with the status quo than somebody with only two of those grievances.) In turn, the greater the discontent—controlling for other factors producing change vanguard membership—the more likely one was to become an early opponent of the traditional system.

In understanding differences between the nature of discontent with the traditional system among the change vanguard and early recruits, it is useful to look at evidence from social and revolutionary movements.[58] Lenin makes a distinction between "two groups with different sorts of political capacities and ambitions: a revolutionary class whose discontent provides the energy and whose members supply the manpower, and an intellectual local vanguard providing ideology and leadership."[59] There is a difference between demands the two groups raise. Michael Walzer argues that during the exodus of the Israelites from Egypt, the mass of slaves were "moved by the vision of 'a land of milk and honey,'" while Moses was "moved by the vision of 'a nation of priests and a holy people.'"[60] To use Lenin's language, "The idea of radical transformation is carried into the revolutionary class by the men and women of the local vanguard."[61] Revolutionary leaders also come from a different social and educational background from that of their followers. Moses was not a slave but an educated child of Pharaoh's court. It has also frequently been noted that party activists typically have a more articulated ideology than rank-and-file party voters—Democratic activists are more liberal than Democratic voters, Republican activists are more conservative than their voters. In addition, analogous to initial supporters of procurement reform, party activists are better educated than the population as a whole.[62]

This analogy should not be taken too far.[63] But some elements apply. Revolutionary leaders often have an idealistic desire for a better society and, because of their education, a greater ability to think abstractly. In initiating procurement reform, as in revolutionary movements, this combination differentiated first organizers and early followers.[64]

The analogy to revolutionary movements is also a reminder of the impacts of creating a coalition of people seeking different things from a change movement. Although the coalition makes it easier for change to get started by increasing the size of the group seeking change, these different agendas create potential problems for a change movement, particularly for leaders, who are likely to find that many of their followers seek something quite different from the movement than they themselves do. These problems have often become visible as revolutionary movements came to power and would become an issue for procurement reform leaders as well.

CHAPTER 5

Changes at the Top and the Unleashing of Reform

At the time procurement reform was announced, there was support on the front lines for the traditional system but also discontent. Yet there was little sign of any brewing frontline movement for change. Proclamation of reform by leaders at the top, an action undertaken independently of the development of discontent on the front lines, constituted a sort of exogenous shock to the politics of buying offices. This shock provided the change vanguard with the opportunity to initiate reform, something they had wanted to do even before reform was announced. Through their actions, top leaders, in effect, intervened in the politics of local buying offices. Their actions authorized, energized, and strengthened the hand of the change vanguard. People who, absent a signal from above, mostly would just have nursed their grievances and gone about their jobs in the old way, rose up and launched change. In this way, leaders at the top unleashed a change process at the bottom.

Top Leaders and the Initiation of Reform: A Personal Account

Before coming to Washington, I was aware of literature on the difficulties of achieving organizational change.[1] Also, for my research for *Procurement and Public Management*, I had interviewed some procurement employees and seen how committed they seemed to the traditional system. I assumed career people would react unfavorably to a nonprocurement outsider, especially an academic, trying to suggest how to improve the system they ran. At the Office of Federal Procurement Policy (OFPP), I would have a staff of about twenty, none of whom actually bought anything. The challenge of locating leverage points over a large, decentralized system seemed daunting. Though I knew that the OFPP had considerable influence over the content of regulations, I was skeptical that regulation changes by themselves would bring about frontline behavior change. Deregulation might eliminate constraints but could not require people to use judgment, so behavior might just continue according to the old rules. Although I was eager for a job in the new administration, I hesitated to take this one when offered. There was a better-than-even chance, I guessed, that despite my best efforts, nothing would improve.

I spent a good deal of time between being told I would be selected (June 1993) and arriving in Washington (September 1993) thinking about a basic strategy. I decided to focus on buying offices more than Congress—a subversive idea since success in Washington is traditionally measured in terms of laws passed, not lower-visibility activities inside agencies. But I thought that achieving change within buying offices would be no more difficult than achieving it from Congress (where support for the traditional system was high). This approach at least had the virtue of being consistent with my personal interests as a management professor.

I believed I possessed one significant asset, my perch in the Executive Office of the President, with a physical location in the White House complex. This meant my words would be heard and that if I called a meeting on my turf, people would most likely show up. But I had a hard time seeing how I could connect this to my goal of achieving frontline change.

The plan I developed was based on getting actions started quickly. I was influenced by articles in the public management literature, written by Robert Behn and Olivia Golden, advocating "groping along" as a method for innovation.[2] Their idea was that managers should implement some part of a change quickly, rather than studying the idea to death until perfected, and make corrections along the way. I had also somewhere been inspired by the idea, perhaps from the guru literature on change I had read (I now do not remember), of the importance of "early wins." If an example of successful change could somehow be achieved quickly, it might be possible to use that to set other changes in motion.

My thought was that, to increase the chances that an early win might encourage further change, the early change had to be something with visibility, at least within the procurement community. The method I thought could be used to gain visibility was to pursue a single change simultaneously among many organizations, as a common project of senior agency procurement leaders, in some way, I hoped, through the auspices of the OFPP. Such a joint effort would also focus attention on the OFPP as an organizer of improvement efforts, which would, in turn, augment its standing to push other innovations.

I was not confident such an initiative would be possible. My thought was to convene agency procurement executives (the senior officials in charge of procurement in each cabinet department) for a one-day meeting to brainstorm ideas for a joint initiative and conclude the meeting by agreeing on one that they would commit to pursue jointly. My (Kurt Lewin–style) idea was that if those involved agreed to some change, they would be more likely to implement it. I was relatively confident that agency people would show up at a meeting, and I had a number of possible ideas I hoped gingerly to inject into consideration. High on the list was increased use of past performance in awarding contracts, the major theme of my 1990 book. But since I believed there was a significant chance that procurement executives would not believe that anything needed change, I concluded that agreement on some joint initiative, however modest, was more important than what its content might be.

The second element of my plan was that my rhetorical theme would be antibureaucracy, based on the view that this frame would give the issue its best chance. The positive rhetorical image I wanted to emphasize was "commercial practices"—the idea that the government's procurement methods should become more like those used by the most successful business enterprises. I saw this as a way to sell reform to other policymakers—and give myself breathing space against those, especially in Congress, who would be wary of my ideas, so I could have some time to focus on initiating change in buying offices.

One of my first phone calls was to Mark Abramson, the founder of a good-government organization called the Council for Excellence in Government. Abramson arranged for me to meet with him and two council members (working as a trade association executive and a lawyer for the professional services industry), both advocates of a less bureaucratic procurement system. One part of the conversation particularly stuck with me. I was aware, I told them, that most of the relevant people in

Congress were likely to consider my ideas dangerously radical, and to avoid getting stopped before getting started, my inclination was to "fly below the radar screen" to achieve small changes and, I hoped, build up momentum. That was one possible approach, they replied. But they wanted to suggest an alternative: rather than being cautious, I might boldly announce an alternative vision—as one of them put it, of "excellence instead of mediocrity." Yes, I might get my legs cut off. But nobody would be inspired to follow the cautious words of a cautious professor. My only chance for arousing ardent support, creating a willingness to defend me against criticism, was with a vision of procurement capable of inspiring (at least some) people. I was intrigued, though the idea seemed risky. I realized that being bold, rather than flying under the radar screen, was a fundamental choice I needed to make.

The position to which I had been appointed required Senate confirmation, which takes several months. Once the president had announced I would be nominated, I could begin to work as a "consultant" but could not yet assume my job. These months allowed me to sit in on meetings inside the government without responsibility for making decisions (or even being required to talk, though I was allowed to) and to get to know the people with whom I would be working. During this period, I learned a great deal that turned out to be crucial to the strategy I would follow. The cumulative message was that chances for reform were greater than I had thought.

One thing I learned was that "reinventing government" was for real. As it turned out, procurement had been mentioned frequently in town meetings, organized by Vice President Al Gore, at a number of agencies to publicize and get ideas for the effort. During the week in September when the Gore Report came out, the vice president appeared on the David Letterman show to make fun of a procurement specification for an ashtray requiring that the glass break into no more than a certain number of pieces when hit. (On national television, Gore put on safety glasses and smashed the tray with a hammer.) A few days later, Gore and President Clinton held an event on the White House lawn launching their reinventing government plan, featuring forklifts with internal regulations, including procurement regulations, as a backdrop. In late October a procurement reform event, with both the president and vice president in attendance, was organized to announce a procurement legislative proposal. I also learned that senior Defense Department officials were interested in reform; I had been ignorant of criticisms (analogous to but not the same as mine) defense reformers had made of the traditional system. All this would help both in getting the attention of senior career procurement people and in fending off Congress.

Given my plan, the most important and surprising thing I learned was the existence of reform-minded senior career procurement officials and frontline employees. For example, the three people working on procurement recommendations for the Gore Report were all career procurement people basically using reinvention as an opportunity to make recommendations for changes they had favored all along.

Second, after *Procurement and Public Management* came out, I had consulted briefly for the procurement operation at the U.S. Postal Service, a government corporation not subject to procurement laws, working to make their system less bureaucratic. On coming to Washington I arranged to meet with the person who had hired me. He mentioned that friends who were procurement executives in some of the civilian cabinet departments had formed a group called the Procurement Executives Association. They were reform minded, and he thought I should meet them. I called the head of the group, and we got together. I was amazed to discover that he thought the traditional system needed significant change. He seemed honored I had called. I hesitantly broached my idea of trying to get procurement executives together on a joint project. He was enthusiastic.

I also called another member of the Procurement Executives Association, at the Department of Health and Human Services. It occurred to me it would be worthwhile to spend time visiting buying offices to listen to employees—again, in a sort of Lewinian spirit—about what (if anything) they did not like about the system and to get reactions to some of my ideas. The department's procurement executive offered to let me visit some offices. The meetings, with groups of ten or fifteen sitting around a table, made a tremendous impression on me—indeed, this may have been the most important experience of my apprenticeship. To my astonishment, I discovered that the dominant view, among those speaking at any rate, was that the system had too many rules and too much red tape. I now cannot recall the specific criticisms they made. What struck me was that they were making criticisms at all.

A few images from that week stand out. One was how often frontline people used the word "customer" to describe program officials. (Entering the office of one supervisor, I noticed one of the few books on his bookshelf was on total quality management.) Something had changed since I had done my research in the late 1980s. Another image was visiting a buying office and talking with an employee at her workspace who was complaining how the rule that all purchases under $25,000 be made from small businesses, applying even to the purchase of a few computer disks, made it impossible for her to go across the street, where an inexpensive computer superstore was located, to get such items quickly for those needing them.

How had I missed such critics' existence? Partly, as the new word "customer" suggested, changes had occurred since I had interviewed people in 1988. In addition, it would have been easy for me to miss the existence of a change vanguard, given that even in 1993 fewer than one in five would have so classified themselves.[3]

The main effect of this period was to lead me to realize I had allies inside the system and that I should try to use the visibility of my White House perch to encourage them to act to change the system. The discussion at the Council for Excellence in Government in my mind, I decided to opt for the "bold vision" approach. Hoping it might now be possible for me actually to make suggestions to senior procurement officials about changes they might make, without a day of meetings, I adapted my original idea. Riding back to Washington one day with the senior procurement executive of Health and Human Services, I ventured the suggestion that perhaps a group of senior procurement executives might agree to double agencies' use of the government credit card (a "reinventing government" initiative) over a one-year period. While sitting there, I thought out loud that perhaps this might be called a "pledge," a strange-sounding word reminiscent of the "taking the pledge" refrain temperance advocates use to get people to forswear alcohol. He said he liked it.

Thus was born the first activity of procurement reform, the pledges. Over the next year, the OFPP organized five pledges. The idea was to get some agencies to agree to voluntarily undertake some specific effort, typically involving specific contracts to be awarded, to show that reform could get started. Behind the pledges was the notion of gaining early wins to attract support for change through participation and to build momentum. I frequently repeated the message that I wanted to start with actions, not a study group or report. I also emphasized that by banding together, and in alliance with the OFPP, individual agencies could provide themselves with "cover" for trying something new and risky. Another idea I had was that those working on contracts in the pledges would become "ambassadors for reform" in their offices.

Pledges would also establish the OFPP as an active participant not just in the formation of procurement policy but also in its practice. To the best of my memory, I did not conceptualize the role of pledges as sending a message to supporters of change on the front lines.

The first pledge expanded the use of the government credit card, but the first big pledge for which significant media publicity was sought involved past performance. I spent weeks on the phone working to persuade agencies beyond the seven in the Procurement Executives Association to sign up. If we could get at least eight agencies, we would, I decided, go ahead. I asked procurement executives in the association to help by talking with their colleagues in other agencies and contacted senior information-technology managers I had interviewed for my earlier book. My staff used contacts they had, particularly in the Defense Department. After we got to nine agencies, participation started snowballing, and soon we could say to holdouts, "Almost everyone but you is participating." In the end, twenty agencies agreed to make past performance a primary factor in selecting the winner for sixty specific contracts they identified. The pledge ceremony occurred in the ornate Indian Treaty Room in the White House complex. Seated around a large table, agency procurement executives signed the pledge and got their pictures taken with the heads of the Office of Management and Budget and of the reinventing government staff. The event was covered in the *Washington Post* and the trade press (an editorial in *Government Computer News* was titled "Taking the Pledge").

Meanwhile, on a separate track, the Defense Department was proceeding with its own action effort, to reduce milspecs. In early 1994 the secretary of defense issued a memo that henceforth milspecs could be used only with higher-level approval. (This reversed the previous policy that eliminating milspecs required approval.) As with my choice of past performance, Defense Department reformers chose a change reflecting an idea about how the system might better serve the public good—and that some on the front lines who relished original thinking might find challenging—but doing nothing to appeal to those seeking to reduce their job burdens.

Providing an Opportunity

Why, if there were "reformers before reform," didn't they seek to initiate change on their own, without awaiting a proclamation from the top?

In fact, to a limited extent this did occur, at least in offices whose local head was in the change vanguard. According to material from the In-Person Interviews, at two of the eleven offices whose leaders were reformers before reform, local office heads instituted limited efforts to reduce bureaucracy before procurement reform started. The flip side is that nine of the eleven had not done anything—and one of the two who moved did so cautiously.

Most in the change vanguard would not move without a signal from the top because they would have felt their chances for success were small. The most obvious reason was that they were far from a majority. In a hypothetical vote on changing the system before reform began, the change vanguard would have gathered only about one-fifth of "votes," though their total would have been higher among supervisors. Beyond that, in large, hierarchical government (and most large private) organizations, it is not considered legitimate for people at working levels to initiate major changes in how their organization does business without authorization from "headquarters." Most career government employees share the norm that they should not act contrary to policies established by senior political leadership. Even those who would have welcomed reform would thus have been unlikely to initiate a local effort to change office policies away from those of the traditional system unless they believed senior leadership wished this to occur.

Finally, without a signal from the top, there were significant limits to what the change vanguard would be able to accomplish locally, even in theory. Many laws or regulations promulgated at the top prohibited people on the front lines from doing much of what the change vanguard wanted. According to one interview respondent, a change advocate who sought to introduce some reforms in the office he headed before reform began, any local changes had to be accomplished within the bounds of existing regulations, for "at the time, of course, we had no hope of ever changing the regulations themselves." Thus absent a signal that laws or regulations might change, many would have been discouraged from taking up the fight in the first place out of a conviction that local victories they might obtain would be rather empty.

Top Leaders and Initiation of Reform: Evidence from the In-Person Interviews and Frontline Survey

Both the In-Person Interviews and the Frontline Survey provide evidence that the change vanguard perceived the vice president's announcement of reinventing government, and of procurement reform, as an opportunity to do things they had wanted to do all along. The interviews suggest that reinventing government had high, early visibility among the discontented. One of the question posed was, "Do you recall when you first became aware that the new administration was making a push for acquisition reform?"[4] Responses indicate that those discontented with the traditional system[5] heard about reinventing government quite early. Twenty-six percent ($N = 110$) mentioned Gore's task force, which begin in the spring of 1993; another 35 percent mentioned Gore's appearance on Letterman (many cited his breaking an ashtray), Gore's appearance on the White House lawn with stacks of regulations, or information received early on from the respondent's own superiors or fellow employees. Only 9 percent said they could not remember when they had first heard of the push, while another 10 percent mentioned events after the fall of 1993.

The In-Person Interviews asked how the respondent had initially reacted to "reinventing government." It is interesting to note how many spontaneously used the word "opportunity." The following quotations express a common theme:

This is the greatest opportunity we've had in my career. For years we've bitched, complained, and moaned—about all the reviews and rewriting of acquisition plans, where we were subjected to English lessons about split infinitives; about bid protests; about the people in headquarters; about contracting people being at the tail end of the whip. I said, "If we don't take advantage of this, shame on us!"

This is a fantastic opportunity—once in a lifetime—to make a significant change. Let's not blow it and have it be just an exercise with a lot of work and no results.

When the vice president was first starting to put together the [reinventing government effort], I was hoping he would call me on the phone. My reaction was, "*Finally* we have an opportunity to make some changes!" Having always been far away from the conservative side, I saw this as an opportunity.

Now we could evaluate past performance—I'd waited my whole career for this!

TABLE 5-1. Attitude toward "Reinventing Government," by Initial Support for Procurement Reform[a]

Percent

Attitude	Change vanguard	Early recruits	Skeptics and critics
Is enthusiastic about "reinventing government"			
Agree	55	22	14
Mixed	31	51	48
Disagree	14	27	38
N	135	163	253
Sees "reinventing government" as an opportunity			
Agree	56	35	18
Mixed	30	33	43
Disagree	14	32	39
N	133	143	243

Source: Frontline Survey

a. Based on responses on a five-point scale, from "strongly agree" (1) to "strongly disagree" (5).

Whether they mean it or not, I'm going to take advantage of it. They threw me the ball. Until somebody tackles me, I'm going to run. You've empowered me to move out. I'm gone. I like chaos. I know what I'm doing, know where I want to go. I can use chaos as an opportunity for change. Just go do it—forgiveness is easier to get than permission! You guys handed me a blank check, I was going to get the store.

Additionally, two questions in the Frontline Survey asked how respondents had initially reacted to the announcement of "reinventing government" (officially and in the questions called the National Performance Review). One asked whether they agreed with the statement, "My initial reaction to the National Performance Review was very enthusiastic." A second asked reactions to the statement, "The National Performance Review gave people like me the support we need to make changes we wanted to make all along." Respondents as a whole were somewhat skeptical (see table 5-1)—not surprisingly, given that career people are generally skeptical of initiatives announced by political leaders, whether because they have seen so many before, because they are convinced that political leaders' attention spans are too short to accomplish anything announced in the initiatives, or just out of a tension between career and political types.[6] What is most noteworthy are differences between the change vanguard and everybody else. Most people in the change vanguard (55 percent) stated their initial reaction had been enthusiastic—especially impressive given the grounds for skepticism noted above—compared with only 22 percent of early recruits and 14 percent of skeptics. These are some of the most dramatic differences in the survey results.[7] Answers to the second question explain the startling enthusiasm among the change vanguard: 56 percent agreed that "reinventing government" helped them bring about changes they had wanted all along. This explains their enthusiasm, despite other reasons for cynicism or skepticism.

How Did Intervention from the Top Help the Change Vanguard?

How did the announcement of procurement reform provide the change vanguard with an opportunity? There is little evidence about the political processes at local buying offices following announcement of reform, so arguments must be deductive and speculative.[8] It is likely that the announcement provided an opportunity by authorizing, energizing, and strengthening the hand of the change vanguard, making it more likely they would be successful in getting reform started.

First, the announcement of the reform initiative gave an authoritative voice to the idea of reform. For reasons discussed earlier, career people are unlikely to act in defiance of the wishes of top leaders. Evidence from the change vanguard model suggests that members of the change vanguard mostly kept their opinions to themselves. Thus an important way top leaders provided those in the change vanguard an opportunity was to authorize them to act. Top leaders authorized the change vanguard to "come out."[9] In addition, top leader support for reform made it more difficult for critics openly to attack the change vanguard's efforts, because now the *critics* were in the same position the change vanguard had been in before reform: they lacked authorization to criticize.

Authorization from the top also eased people's minds about consequences of possible failure. This applied not just to the change vanguard but also to those deciding whether to become early recruits. If top leaders were urging that changes be tried, negative consequences of failure were lower than if changes had been undertaken at a person's own initiative.[10]

Second, the announcement energized those sympathetic to or supportive of reform. An announcement gets people talking, so local supporters discovered they had more compatriots than they might have known existed, decreasing their sense of isolation. Support from the top made supporters feel good about being associated with the views of senior leaders. It created the hope that system-level obstacles to change would be eliminated. It increased optimism about the possibility of change.[11]

Furthermore, the announcement encouraged the change vanguard to allocate time to working on procurement reform rather than other matters. Any person has a myriad of ways to allocate time, among any number of "causes" in all of which he or she believes. Announcements from top leadership directed attention to the particular "cause" of procurement reform, increasing the likelihood it would be chosen as a way the change vanguard might spend its time.

The announcement also strengthened the hand of reform. The intervention of top leaders provided the change vanguard with assets—new supporters and a new argument they could make—thereby increasing the probability they would be victorious in local political processes.

The most important way top leaders strengthened the hand of the change vanguard was in providing them with additional supporters, the early recruits, to add to the mere one in five (or fewer) they initially had. To some extent, evidence from the early-recruit model suggests that top leaders mobilized some into the ranks of early recruits directly. Probably more important, top leadership contributed to mobilizing early recruits indirectly, simply by putting reform "in play." Before, there had been people in buying offices who were not self-conscious change advocates but were more likely than others to have a high desire for autonomy, experience greater worries about job burdens, and place greater value on pleasing program customers. These people thus already held some values that, if more salient to them, would increase the likelihood they would support change. Before a change movement was initiated, these values were not uppermost in their minds, partly because the traditional system hardly encouraged their expression. If something could get them to focus on values they already held but that had not been prominent in their minds, these people could be made into reform sympathizers.[12] Once change was in play and people were asked to take a stand, many reacted positively because of who they already were. Thus were early recruits born.

The announcement of reform also strengthened the hand of the change vanguard by encouraging opponents in local leadership positions to leave. In the two years following the beginning of reform, three office heads in the nineteen local offices, all fence-sitters or skeptics when reform began, retired and were replaced by new people, all of whom were enthusiastic reform supporters. None seems to have been forced out, but in most cases, it appears, retirement decisions were speeded by lack of comfort with the reform direction from Washington.

Finally, intervention from top leadership offered the change vanguard a powerful argument—some version of "We are being told to do this; we have no choice" or "Our leaders want us to change" or "There's lots of pressure on us to change." What is interesting is that people who support change anyway—even in the absence of any "outside pressure"— point to the existence of such pressure. Thus "outside pressure" functions in significant measure as a tool used by those who agree with the direction the outside pressure is pushing to strengthen their hands. The suggestion that the local advocate is acting simply as a bearer of demands from the outside is appealing. It reduces interpersonal contention between supporters and opponents over whether the new policies are a good idea. The change advocate can, in effect, say, "This isn't about what you or I think is the right way to go. This is the direction coming to us."[13]

The Initiation of Reform: Analogies to Natural Selection in the Theory of Evolution

The role top leaders play in providing opportunity for already existing supporters on the front lines is analogous to the role a change in the natural environment plays in initiating natural selection in the theory of evolution. In evolution, there is natural variation in genetic material among creatures in the system (analogous to the organizational front lines here). An exogenous change occurs in the environment—say, it gets colder. This creates selection pressures favoring creatures who are already constituted to be more resistant to cold. Such selection pressures produce species change. Translated to the context of procurement, "natural variation" meant that there were on the front lines both supporters of the traditional system and supporters of change. The existing environment was the traditional procurement system. It selected for one kind of creature—supporters of that system—but not so strongly that alternate genetic material was eliminated. Then new leadership—the environmental change—helped those who already supported changes sought by the leaders (analogous to creatures already constituted to be more resistant to the cold). Selection pressures produced change. Without the selection pressures—the leadership change—those on the front lines seeking change would have just remained the unfavored minority. No leadership change, no successful change initiation. But because of the selection pressures the new leadership produced, those who had been last now became first.

Absent underlying natural variation, an exogenous shock will not produce species change. Had there been no creatures able to adapt to the cold, no change would have taken place, and the species would have died out. Absent the presence of change supporters before new leadership signals, those signals would not have produced organizational change—no change vanguard, no successful change.[14]

As it was, the intervention from the top in procurement reform succeeded. The reform coalition became strong enough in enough places that, to return to the metaphor from the beginning of chapter 3, when reformers gave a party, people came. Reform did not yet enjoy majority support, but it had survived birth.

CHAPTER 6

Initiating Change: Implications for Theory and Practice

The initiation of frontline change in this account is a story of politics. Procurement reform was not initiated by way of any of the three theories of change initiation—persuasive discussion, leader pressure, or the burning platform—present in the existing literature. As in the persuasive-discussion theory, support of people at working levels was an important factor in allowing change to get started. But contra the Lewinian tradition, change initiation required no unfreezing of existing attitudes. Contra the guru literature, there is little evidence that leaders dragged frontline people kicking and screaming to change or that they either created or exploited a crisis to persuade people that change, however unpleasant, was necessary. Instead, before the change effort began, there existed a change vanguard hoping for something like procurement reform. However, the change vanguard was a relatively small minority, peripheral to a system generally dominated by other behaviors.

Discontent at the working levels probably could have continued indefinitely had no change occurred at the top. In 1993 a strong signal from the top leadership proclaimed reform. The change vanguard took the message as a signal to launch changes they had already favored before the signal had come. Others, the early recruits, joined. Change gained a foothold.

Initiation of frontline change thus could not have been accomplished by either the change vanguard locally or by top leaders in Washington alone. Both were necessary, and neither was sufficient. The change vanguard was not strong enough politically to get reform started. Top leaders did not buy anything themselves; for them to have attempted reform without local support would have been like pushing on a string. Top leaders played an important role in initiating change by providing an opportunity for the change vanguard, but this role was different from the one envisioned in the literature.

What I call the theory of activating the discontented can be stated in general terms as follows: A system has two levels, call them "the top" and "the bottom." Some at the bottom would like to see changes in how the system works. However, those desiring change lack power to achieve it. An exogenous shock (exogenous from the perspective of the bottom), favorable to changes the bottom wants, occurs at the top. This creates a moment when those who sought change before the shock have a chance, a "window of opportunity," to become more powerful. The actions of change advocates at the top thus get coupled with change advocates at the bottom. It is this coupling that unleashes successful change initiation. Those at the bottom seeking change could not have initiated the change by themselves. But had they not been around, the tide at the top (to switch metaphors) would have ebbed away, leaving no trace.

Nothing resembling this idea of activating the discontented as a path to frontline change initiation has received much attention in the voluminous literature on organizational change. Other theories suppose that reluctant people are induced to change through some version of persuasion or shock-and-awe tactics. I am not suggesting that existing theories of change initiation are incorrect, that is, that they do not constitute possible paths to successful change initiation. My claim is more limited. What I have done is to construct a theory, with the hope that it becomes available as a possible path to successful initiation of organizational change—to open our minds, as theories should, to a generalization about how the world works. Others will need to test this theory against existing ones to see how often successful, or failed, change initiation is associated with different possible paths to organizational change.

I am aware of a few works with a similar perspective. The one closest to the approach presented here is Rosabeth Moss Kanter's *The Change Masters*. Although it is not a central theme of her book, Kanter's analysis bears many similarities to my activating-the-discontented path. She discusses what she calls the "prehistory" of successful change, which features advocates operating below the radar screen. Kanter argues both that a constituency for change in bureaucratic organizations exists and that the problem this constituency faces is political. Within bureaucratic organizations there are "'dissident' subcultures" and "bureaucratic insurgents." Such organizations may suffer not "from a lack of potential innovators so much as from failure to make the power available to those embryonic entrepreneurs that they can use to innovate."[1]

Furthermore, there is evidence that at least some change practitioners practice what the literature fails to preach. For example, Derek Rayner, who successfully led a number of management improvement change efforts in the British government during the 1980s, from a senior political position as efficiency adviser, believes that there were many civil servants who sought the changes he sought, and that his job was "the discovery and enfranchisement of that suppressed talent."[2]

Accuracy and Generalizability of the Theory of Activating the Discontented

Presenting a new account of some phenomenon is intellectually gratifying, but it also raises a red flag—analogous to the joke about the economist seeing a $100 bill on the ground only to have a colleague say, "That couldn't be a $100 bill or somebody would have picked it up," or to the put-down, "If you're so smart, why aren't you rich?" Given the voluminous literature on organizational change, a new theory must be scrutinized for accuracy and generalizability. A methodologically oriented discussion of these issues appears in appendix B.

However, one issue about generalizability should be noted here. Existing theories assume more or less universal "resistance to change" and propose what must be done to "overcome" it. Where such widespread resistance exists, activating the discontented has nothing to add to, and does not contradict, existing theories. It is not generalizable to such situations. So an important question about the generalizability of activating the discontented as a path to change initiation is how often the presence of nontrivial frontline dissatisfaction before initiation of a change effort occurs in government organizations outside the case presented here. If such discontent is rare, further testing will show that this theory applies to few situations.

Given the discussion of the sources of a desire for job autonomy presented earlier, there is no reason to believe that discontent with bureaucracy exists only in procurement organizations. Discontent is likely to be present wherever rules, hierarchy, and specialization are central features of organization design. If anything, the role of rules as a source of power for procurement employees would suggest that less discontent might be expected there than elsewhere. Indeed, one reason to argue that a constituency for reducing bureaucracy exists elsewhere in government is that at the beginning of procurement reform most would have regarded procurement as less likely than most government activities to change in response to the reinventing government initiative. Furthermore, evidence that a desire for autonomy grows with education and affluence means that the trend will most likely be in the direction of greater demand for reducing bureaucracy.

What about situations in which the change involves something other than reducing bureaucracy, as many change efforts do? Here I can only speculate. I suspect there is a larger constituency for change involving reducing bureaucracy than in many other areas. However, organization-specific sources of frontline dissatisfaction with the status quo may exist in many situations. If an organization is not performing as well as it should, some—given the role that "making a difference" in the area of the agency's mission plays in the choices of many to pursue public employment—are likely to be unhappy with that.

Implications of the Activating-the-Discontented Path for the Theory and Practice of Organizational Change

In contrast to the typical view, this argument is a hopeful one. The activating-the-discontented path suggests that there may be more opportunities for successful initiation of debureaucratizing organizational change, and conceivably other kinds of organizational change as well, than existing views imply. Thanks to the presence of frontline dissatisfaction, leaders have a less daunting task than existing theories suggest. Both existing theories and the activating-the-discontented path see leader behavior determining success or failure in change initiation.[3] But given the different starting points, the two theories proceed in different directions about the nature of the leader behavior required and the role it plays. Here, leaders need not persuade, pressure, or scare people. They need only provide the opportunity for already-existing supporters to move. At the same time, the theory suggests that, where there is some nontrivial level of frontline discontent, if change does not get successfully initiated, the fault lies with the top, not the bottom.

Why might leaders fail to unleash change when there exists potential at the bottom? I would speculate that the most important reason leaders do not more often provide an opportunity to supporters is that they never try. To be sure, political appointees, upon arriving in government, usually launch initiatives as part of "making their mark." But most have been attracted to government more by the opportunity to influence policy than to manage organizational production. So these initiatives typically involve new policies or programs added to existing ones, rather than efforts to change the existing organization.

Second, leaders may attempt change but not seek frontline allies. The view that employees resist change is widely held. Top leaders holding this view may seek to get change started behind employees' backs, so it gets established before the front lines can stop it. At a minimum, leaders with this view will not regard getting a change message to the front lines as a high priority. That they see themselves as unlikely to have frontline allies can thus become a self-fulfilling prophecy: their belief about people on the front lines generates behavior that makes the belief come true. For this reason, making the activating-the-discontented path available to leaders is perhaps the most important practical contribution of the theory. If it gets leaders to believe that providing an opportunity to frontline allies is a way to initiate change, acceptance of the theory may itself increase the chances of successful change initiation.

Third, even if leaders try to get a message out to the front lines, they might fail to communicate it frequently or loudly enough. Procurement reform leaders succeeded here, but through luck more than intention. My own early actions and those of others in reinventing government increased the amplitude of the signal sent to the change vanguard. Often, however, this occurred serendipitously. One crucial asset I possessed was my perch in the White House, giving my words and actions visibility. Initially, however, I saw this as helping vis-à-vis other senior-level players—I felt, for example, that agency procurement leaders would attend a meeting I scheduled—not as a tool for reaching the front lines. I saw the pledges as serving a large number of purposes, but these did not consciously include their role in amplifying the signal being sent to people in buying offices. However, I did consciously decide to speak in a visionary way—which, because it was so different, was more likely to be reported and thus heard on the front lines—after meeting procurement executives and frontline employees.

Finally, though activating the discontented does not require that the message leaders persuade otherwise recalcitrant people, it does need to resonate with the preexisting values of its targets. The discontented must see a connection between changes that leaders advocate and the discontent they themselves feel. If top leaders send a message to the front that is not resonant with frontline discontents, no opportunity will be perceived at the working levels, and change initiation will fail. To use the phrase David Snow and Robert Benford use in the context of social movements, there must exist "frame resonance" between leader messages and the values of those they seek to mobilize.[4] This is similar to the general advocacy tactic of getting people to focus on the most conducive "face of the issue" rather than seeking to persuade people to adopt new values: environmentalists seek to get people to focus on polluted streams, while opponents want them to focus on closed factories.[5]

Social change strategists are often conscious of this. Saul Alinsky, a longtime community organizer, has written that "a new idea must be at the least couched in the language of past ideas; often, it must be, at first, diluted with vestiges of the past." Organizers must avoid tactics that "go outside the experience of [their] people."[6] In a different context—conversion of pagans to Christianity in early medieval Europe—Richard Fletcher notes the that the church initially presented converts with only a small number of Christian behaviors, often those most similar to earlier pagan beliefs, and adapted Christian practices to familiar pagan ones.[7] The multiplication of angels bore resemblance to pagan polytheism. Early churches were frequently placed at pagan worship sites. Pope Gregory recommended allowing newly converted Christians, used to slaughtering cattle at ceremonies for pagan gods, to do something similar at Christian festivals. A ninth-century epic poem presenting the life of Jesus "is notable for its anonymous author's attempt to accommodate the gospel story to the tastes and expectations of a Germanic secular audience. He chose to write in the alliterative verse traditionally used for vernacular epic poetry. . . . The author . . . used stock phrases from secular epics to render the gospel narrative accessible to his audience. . . . [For example,] the apostles are the *gisidos*, 'companions, retainers' of Christ."[8]

When frame resonance is not naturally present between leaders and potential followers, a social movement organization "may have to extend the boundaries of its primary framework so as to encompass interests or points of view . . . incidental to its primary objectives but of considerable salience to potential adherents."[9] One example is peace movement literature that explains that popular community services cannot be funded because of the defense budget. Snow and his colleagues

quote a Hare Krishna leader on the group's strategy of trying to persuade people to read the cult's text by claiming a connection between it
and any interest displayed by the listener.

> The principle, basically, is just trying to relate the book to where a
> person is at. . . . Trying to be more sensitive to them, asking them
> what their job is and even going so far as X (a devotee known . . .
> as the king of book distribution), who would approach somebody
> and say: "What are you into, man?" Y: "I'm into guns." X: "Well,
> here, take this because in this book there are a lot of things about
> all kinds of ancient weapons from 5000 years ago."[10]

In initiating procurement reform, frame resonance occurred, but acci-
dentally. None of us driving the effort made a conscious effort to link
our message to the more personal sources of discontent on the front
lines. That my general message against bureaucracy happened to resonate with the most important source of discontent on the front lines
was a matter of luck, not strategy; I picked opposition to bureaucracy as
a theme because I thought it would present the most attractive face of
the issue to Congress and the media. Use of the term *streamlining* by
others in reinventing government, and the vice president's criticism of
procurement rules on the Letterman show and on the White House
lawn, grew out of criticisms expressed by program people, not from any
attempt to connect to procurement people. At the beginning, I seldom
used the word *empowerment,* the term that would have resonated most
strongly with potential supporters. I criticized rules but was unaware of
frontline discontent with hierarchical reviews, and this was something I
never mentioned, though it probably would have had greater resonance
(because it related both to a desire for autonomy and a desire for
reduced job burdens) than criticism of rules alone.

Some early reform leaders, including me, sent messages that were
either unrelated to widespread dissatisfaction on the front lines or actually harmed the ability to appeal to them. The Gore Report's rhetoric,
growing out of concerns of program people using the system, was hostile toward procurement employees, seeing them as part of the problem.
(Colleen Preston and I realized this, and never used such rhetoric, but it
was nonetheless part of the reinventing government message.) Choices
made both by Defense Department reformers and by me about our earliest targets, milspec reform and past performance, communicated

change, but the specifics involved our better-value agenda rather than issues with greater frontline resonance.

Seen from the perspective of frame resonance, systemwide leaders were lucky that our message happened to connect with frontline supporters. We were even more lucky that milspec reform, past performance, and criticism of the procurement workforce did not send a message so dissonant that resonance was lost. However, this may be good news for change leaders in other situations: if the overall message resonates, the change vanguard may be happy enough about the opportunity being provided to excuse discordant notes. After all, they are hoping for an opportunity to do something they want to do. They might strategically interpret an even moderately congruent message in a way more supportive of their own demands if doing so will help them win local political battles. Alternatively, to recall the research about failure to hear signals inconsistent with knowledge structures, perhaps they might not even hear the discordant part of the message.

The willingness of the change vanguard to put up with (or not hear) discordant notes is indicated by responses of local leaders in the change vanguard to a question posed in the In-Person Interviews, asking whether, when reinventing government started, they had heard a message that was hostile to procurement people, and, if so, how they had reacted to it:

> I heard the message more that the contracting officer served a role, but that role needed to be clarified. Lots of contracting officers were using it to control, and we needed to change to serve more as a businessperson, we needed to get more vested in the program.

> I did hear that message and thought it was correct. Contracting had a cavalier attitude. We were shortsighted in not learning more from industry. They took a little of an extreme stand. I knew that then they would back off once they had made their point.

> It was not necessarily critical, it was an honest assessment. This is just one more voice saying the current process is broken, it needs to change, and the people who implement the process need to change.

The "slack" the change vanguard was willing to give to top leaders made initiation of reform easier.

The Initiation of Procurement Reform and the Public Good

The ability of people on the front lines to initiate those features of change most consistent with existing grievances made the reform coalition bigger, thus increasing the chances for successful initiation of procurement reform. However, for top leaders with a broader agenda, and for the public, success in initiating change this way might reflect a Faustian bargain. Members of the reform coalition felt a wide range of grievances. Some corresponded with the reformers' ideological commitment to better value from contracting, but most were personal. The price paid by top leaders for change initiation based on existing grievances was that the changes initiated tracked discontents that were already felt rather than the larger agenda. Put another way, the change that got under way was only a subset of, or different in emphasis from, the change that leaders in Washington intended.[11] Relieving the sources of personal discontent would presumably be good for the individuals experiencing the problems. But one may ask whether a movement based significantly on personal discontent was likely to achieve public purposes. As reform began, it would not have been possible to give a definite answer to that question. This created a dilemma for reform leaders as change moved from initiation to solidification.

Activating the Discontented and the Size of the Reform Coalition

In the activating-the-discontented path, the behavior of the reform coalition is based on preexisting grievances. No demands are placed on them regarding the kinds of changes they need to endorse. People whose views of what reform was "about" differed from those of both top reform leaders and even some colleagues in the reform coalition were nonetheless able to participate in initiating change. This made change initiation easier by allowing the reform coalition to be as large as possible, increasing its chance of success.[12]

Others have noted, though in different contexts, a positive connection between limiting the scope of a change to its more resonant features and the ability of the change effort to succeed. "Fewer hurdles and resistances to change are encountered when a few, presumably easy, components of an innovation are implemented to a few, presumably supportive, stakeholders, than when all, easy and hard, components of a program are implemented in depth with all partisan stakeholders involved."[13] Studies of public school innovations have noted that frontline adaptation of the innovation to local circumstances was associated with innovation success.[14]

Activating the Discontented and the Reformers' Agenda

Reformers at the top criticized bureaucracy as part of a larger story about creating better government. Those on the front lines who were dissatisfied with the traditional system were generally discontented with bureaucracy as well, but this was mostly, though not exclusively, for a host of personal reasons.

The desire for job autonomy was essentially a personal one, sought largely (though not entirely) to gain greater job satisfaction. One might therefore argue that providing autonomy was unrelated to any larger public purpose. Indeed, the association might be negative. The large literature on principal-agent theory examines difficulties a principal (in a job context, the boss) faces in getting an agent employed by the principal (the employee) to do what the principal wishes. The starting assumption is that the agent seeks to work as little as possible—to "shirk," in the Victorian-sounding phrase used in the literature.[15] In this view, employees seek autonomy to be able to loaf. Principal-agent theory argues, instead, that a boss must be able to monitor employees and offer incentives to get them to act on behalf of the organization's goal; rules and hierarchy are possible ways, though not the only ones, to accomplish this end. Put into the language of public discourse, rules and hierarchy combat the tendency of government employees to be lazy.

The evidence presented earlier on sources of the desire for autonomy provides no evidence for shirking. Instead, the people studied sought autonomy mostly for an opportunity to use their brains.[16] While an employee seeking work that allows creative thinking might simply enjoy solving puzzles, with no public purpose, the data suggest that one reason people sought autonomy was to give themselves an opportunity to develop better ways to create value for their organizations. The desire for autonomy in order to use one's brain thus created the possibility that private desires might be used for public purposes.[17]

However, the increased or improved work effort that job autonomy might produce was not the same as reformers' better-value agenda. One might apply creative thinking to doing an existing job better, by being a better negotiator or a top-notch sleuth analyzing company-provided cost data, for example, rather than by innovating. Such behavior might improve the value government gained from contracting, but not through the reformers' goal of developing new ways to do business, and such improvements would not require organizational change. The reformers' agenda included policy innovations for achieving better value and sought to get people not only to use their brains in general but more specifically to come up with innovative ways to do business. There is not strong evidence that this part of the agenda had deep roots on the front lines.

Furthermore, a significant minority of members of the reform coalition initially thought that reform was mostly about reducing burdens—a view distant from why reform leaders were seeking to reduce bureaucracy but corresponding to the preexisting grievances among some on the front lines. Significant elements of streamlining were consistent with the reformers' agenda.[18] The streamlining efforts favored by leaders, however, fit into a larger strategy for obtaining better value. And important parts of their agenda did not streamline the system, however defined.

The activating-the-discontented path gives people on the front lines lots of influence over the content of the change that is initiated. This occurs not through the participation Lewin recommends but because frontline concerns get to play a central role in what gets launched. By contrast, since, according to Lewin, change initiated through other methods requires the unfreezing of attitudes, leaders play a more active role in establishing what the change is "about." Where change grows out of existing grievances, the top leader role is more passive. In the case of procurement reform, the content of change involved streamlining, and innovation in order to buy faster, much more than it would have had reform leaders in Washington determined the content of the change. Initiation of reform through activating the discontented thus contained both good and bad news for reformers at the top.

The Reformers' Dilemma

To use the language of social movements, the danger top leaders faced was co-optation, though not in the sense the phrase is often used, since leaders would lose their purity not to the ruling establishment but to their own supporters. The result, though, might be the same: success might occur at the price of sacrificing too many of the ideals in which top reform leaders believed. Indeed, in the empirical study in the literature on organizational change coming closest to the approach I have taken—Terry McNulty and Ewan Ferlie's account of business process reengineering in a British hospital—the authors present the change glass as half-empty.[19] One way to read their findings is that, in some units in the hospital (but not others), significant change occurred, owing to support from constituencies in those units. However, the authors' account emphasizes the limited nature of changes that occurred compared with top leaders' original intention of a radical transformation of clinical practice.

Thus as procurement reform proceeded, reformers faced two challenges. One was to solidify the change effort, which had gotten off the ground but still had only minority support. The second was to develop, or create, an inclination on the front lines to use autonomy to innovate. For most reform coalition members, this would require an expanded, even redirected, understanding of what they were supporting when supporting reform. Achieving this meant that reformers would need to open up a second front of a war that had started with only one. The dilemma was that any war on this second front might make winning the war on the first more difficult.

The reformers succeeded. A majority came to support reform, and many who initially had seen reform as involving only personal goals, including reducing job burdens, came to deepen their view of what changes they were willing to support, in a direction closer to the better-value agenda of the reform leaders' vision. This is the story of the next part of this study.

PART TWO

Consolidating Change

CHAPTER 7

How a Change Effort
Feeds on Itself: Theory

Initially, only a minority supported procurement reform. But by the time of the Frontline Survey, five years after the change effort had begun, a clear majority had a favorable attitude, and significant reform-oriented change in behavior had occurred. This part of the study examines how change got consolidated.

Just as there are conventional prescriptions for launching a change effort, so too there are corresponding ones for consolidating change, also based on the premise that people resist change. These prescriptions do a better job of explaining the expansion of support for procurement reform than did the conventional prescriptions for launching change. But they, too, are incomplete. This and the next chapter focus on a path to consolidating change that is absent from the literature—the idea that a change effort can "feed on itself." In this view, simply launching the change effort and continuing it over time generate forces building support for change. Thus launching and persisting in a change effort itself increases the likelihood the effort will succeed. What is amazing about this is that it occurs automatically, with no further intervention on the part of change leaders other than to launch and persist with the effort. It is also noteworthy that the list of potential positive feedback mechanisms that can promote consolidation of change is large and varied.

Discussions of how a change effort can feed on itself—a phenomenon social scientists call "positive feedback"—feature prominently in literatures on change phenomena in many contexts outside change in organizations, including literatures on the spread of fashions and fads, diffusion of innovations among individuals, social movements and revolutions, and even the spread of changes across different organizations. Furthermore, there exists a large body of social psychology research on the various mechanisms underlying positive feedback, though these mechanisms have seldom been related to feedback theory. These mechanisms have also been extensively discussed, in many contexts, in general research on organizational behavior.[1]

Yet positive feedback has been virtually ignored in both social science and the guru writing on change inside organizations. This is a serious shortcoming in the literature. Again, the mind-set that people resist change helps explain this lapse. Positive feedback theory sees many as open to change, ready to be influenced by positive feedback forces. Since most of the literature sees people as averse to change, scholars have not noticed how positive feedback might inform organizational change theory.

Consolidating Change: Conventional Prescriptions

Conventional prescriptions assume that people resist change and therefore efforts to consolidate change, like prescriptions for initiating change, involve either inducing attitude change or shock-and-awe tactics. Given resistance, change needs to overcome a sea of skepticism. The most promising way to induce attitude change is therefore to show that change works—it delivers organizational improvements or personal benefits (or both). In the guru literature, there is a strong emphasis in particular on the importance of "early wins" (quick examples of improvements from a change effort) for gaining support. The literature emphasizes the impact of early wins not on those generating them but on skeptical third parties who are watching: early wins "undermine cynics" and turn "neutrals into supporters, [and] reluctant supporters into active helpers."[2]

The guru literature also recommends shock-and-awe tactics to consolidate change. Financial incentives for employees and promotions, it is argued, should be tied to support for the change.[3] Opponents may need to be fired: "Confronting resisters and making it clear that termination is the consequence of their behavior is a very valid technique. . . . [Successful change managers agree that] if they had to do it over again . . .

TABLE 7-1. Attitude toward Procurement Reform, by Initial Attitude and Initial Experience
Percent

Attitude	Initial attitude	Initial experience
Negative	8	4
Somewhat negative	34	10
Neutral	19	26
Somewhat positive	27	37
Positive	13	23
N	1,166	1,131

Source: Frontline Survey.

they would have gotten rid of their naysayers more quickly."[4] These shock-and-awe tactics do not change minds, but they can change the behavior of those who stay, and they can get rid of people unwilling to change. Because, as noted in chapter 2, such tactics are more difficult to use in government than in the private sector, it is often argued that successful change is likely to be harder there.

Successful Experience and Consolidating Change Support

A central, commonsensical view in the guru literature on change consolidation is that successful experience is crucial to changing people's attitudes toward change, early wins being especially important. My discussion here and in the following chapter focuses on the role of feedback mechanisms in promoting support for change, not that of successful experience. Of course, successful consolidation of change is unlikely to be based on positive feedback alone, independent of the inherent features of people's experience. Positive feedback alone cannot continue to generate increased support in the face of ongoing negative actual experience. People will catch on. Furthermore, one impact of positive feedback is to give people more successful experience. If successful experience did not increase support, this path for the influence of positive feedback would not be available.

The data show successful experience strongly promoted support for procurement reform. Table 7-1 indicates that most people emerged from their first experience with a considerably more positive view of procurement reform than when they entered.[5] While 42 percent agreed they initially tried reform because their boss had told them to, only 14 percent reported that their actual first experience was negative. Sixty percent reported successful first experience. Mean successful first experience, on a five-point scale where 3 was neutral, was 3.65.

First experience strongly related to final support. Respondents with initially negative expectations of reform whose first experience was more positive than their expectation ended up with much higher average scores for reform support than initial skeptics with a poor first experience. Initial skeptics with a positive first experience had a mean reform support score of 71.0. This means that initial skeptics whose first experience trying procurement reform was positive ended up with an attitude toward reform that was, on average, somewhat above the mean value for the sample as a whole, quite an impressive finding.

What benefits did respondents experience in first trying reform? Responses to a question about this in the In-Person Interviews give us some indications.[6] The most common benefit cited was that the change made their jobs easier (29 percent) or got the system working faster (19 percent). Sixteen percent reported that the change had made their jobs both easier and faster, 21 percent that it improved mission attainment, and 15 percent that it improved job satisfaction.[7] For those, especially early recruits, who initially supported reform because of discontent over job burdens or slow service to program customers, it was good news for the effort that reform delivered what many sought from it.

Overall experience over five years of procurement reform was measured with five questions in the Frontline Survey asking respondents to agree or disagree with statements expressing various benefits (or costs) of reform: "Acquisition reform has empowered me"; "Acquisition reform has made my job easier"; "Acquisition reform makes it easier to choose contractors who provide best value to the government"; "Acquisition reform allows program people to get too close to contractors"; and "I've seen acquisition reform deliver positive results in contract actions in which I've personally been involved." Successful experience had a strong impact on reform support. Table 7-2 presents the results from a regression equation in which each variable, measuring a different aspect of an individual's experience independently, strongly explained support.[8] Together, experience variables accounted for a large 32 percent of variance in attitudes. (These results control for initial attitude and for the possibility the direction of causation went the other way, that is, the possibility that respondents decided they liked reform and then reported it had, for example, empowered them.)[9] The most impor-

TABLE 7-2. Successful Experience and Support for Procurement Reform

Variable	Standardized coefficient
Job easier	0.05*
Empowerment	0.15****
Get best value	0.10****
Worried about too close to contractors	0.09****
Success stories	0.16****
Control variables	
Distortion	0.33****
Initial attitude	0.11****
Adj. R^2 = .42	
N = 1,593	

Source: Frontline Survey.
$^+ \leq .10$ $^* \leq .05$ $^{**} \leq .01$ $^{***} \leq .001$ $^{****} \leq .0001$

tant source of support for changing the traditional system was a desire for autonomy. The results show that the specific experience most important for predicting support was whether respondents believed reform had empowered them.[10] Interestingly, the ideological questions (on getting best value and on worry about coziness with contractors) had a greater impact on support than experiencing burden reduction, a variable with a quite weak impact.

Mean values for all these variables, presented in table 7-3, also showed that people reported successful experiences on average.[11] However, the average level of successful experience was generally modest. Most favorably, respondents quite strongly agreed (mean value of 3.80, 68 percent agreeing) they had personally experienced success stories of some kind from reform. But on the two elements of reform most closely tied to discontents producing initial support, empowerment and job burden reduction, mean responses were only a bit better than neutral—3.20 for empowerment and 3.19 for burden-reduction, with only 43 percent agreeing (a mere 9 percent "strongly") that reform had empowered them and 41 percent that reform had made their jobs easier (8 percent "strongly").[12] Fifty-seven percent agreed with at least one of these statements, only 28 percent with both. Yet in the feeling-thermometer question reporting overall attitude toward reform, 70 percent of responses were positive.

This creates a puzzle, suggesting that reform support was higher than experience with it "warranted." The argument is that the various positive feedback mechanisms are important for explaining this gap.[13]

TABLE 7-3. Mean Values on Experience Variables

Variable	Mean value	"Agree strongly" (percent)	"Agree strongly or somewhat" (percent)
Empowerment	2.80	9	43
Burden reduction	2.81	8	41
Get best value	2.20	25	67
Not worried about too close to contractors	2.77	15	41
Success stories	2.20	25	68

Source: Frontline Survey.

a. Missing values have been excluded. A mean value lower than 3 represents a good experience. Values and percentages of the too-close-to-contractors response have been reverse coded (for example, 3.23 has become 2.77).

Positive Feedback

How did Communist East Germany move from quiescence to having millions of people on the streets in a few months? How do integrated neighborhoods change to segregated ones, or unsafe areas where few dare venture into urban stomping grounds? Why do certain pop artists become hot, while others, apparently similar, languish? How did support for procurement reform get consolidated? One of the hottest topics in both scholarly and informed nonacademic discussions about how changed ways of thinking or behaving spread in everyday life—and in the realms of society and politics—is that change can feed on itself. In common parlance, people speak of "snowball effects" or "momentum." The social science term *tipping point* has migrated into nonacademic discourse, as have (to a lesser degree) *contagion* and *path dependence*. In scholarly writing, the general term describing situations in which change feeds on itself is *positive feedback*. Crucial to note, positive feedback influences act independently of good experience.

Positive feedback is defined as a process whereby "a change in one direction sets in motion reinforcing pressures that produce further change in the same direction."[14] For example, if a government can influence television coverage, then a party coming into power can generate forces increasing the chances it stays in power. If people decide to live in a neighborhood based on its reputation, a neighborhood that begins to become less attractive can become increasingly so over time.

Positive feedback as a way to explain the spread of change has received the most attention in the context of "contagion" models.[15] In these models, adoption begins slowly. Then there is an inflection point ("critical mass" or "tipping point") at which time further spread of the phenomenon continues based on positive feedback mechanisms alone. At this point, change becomes self-sustaining; it will become consolidated unless something intervenes to stop or reverse it.

Positive feedback is often—as in contagion models—self-reinforcing. Self-reinforcement means that an increase in the phenomenon itself generates further increases, in turn generating further increases. Say, for example, people's opinions are influenced by opinions of their friends. If I am sensitive to the influence of my friends, I may adopt a certain attitude as soon as half of my friends hold it. My adoption increases the average support for the attitude in the friendship group, which may induce another member of the group, somewhat less sensitive to group opinion, to adopt the attitude. That further increase in the average attitude of the group, in turn, brings another person along, and so forth.

However, positive feedback need not be self-reinforcing. Say that the first time one tries a new behavior, but only the first time, one receives advice from an expert about performing the behavior. That advice provides positive feedback in terms of one's success with the new behavior, for it means that simply launching the behavior generates a force that increases the chance it will succeed. However, such positive feedback is a one-time event.

Contagion models also focus on one source of positive feedback, influences on individuals in a group from other group members. But positive feedback can also occur through mechanisms growing out of individual-level psychological phenomena or personality traits.

In the context of organizational change, positive feedback occurs when the very launching of a change, and the mere passage of time the effort continues, themselves generate forces that build support. Broadly speaking, positive feedback mechanisms may increase support for an organizational change in two different ways: indirectly, by promoting successful experience, which in turn produces more favorable attitudes toward the change; and directly, by promoting prochange attitudes.

The conventional prescription about the role of successful experience in attitude change assumes that one's experiences reflect only what may be called the "inherent" nature of an experience. To take an example from everyday life, if one invests money in a risky venture for the first time, and the investment generates a huge profit, the inherent nature of that experience was good, while if it produces a total loss, its inherent nature was bad. A successful experience is likely to generate a more positive attitude toward risky investments (and continuation of the new activity), while an unsuccessful one will generate a more negative attitude (and abandonment of the new activity). Positive feedback theory adds the idea that the very launch of a new effort, and its continuation over time, themselves generate forces promoting successful experience, independent of the inherent nature of the experience. Continuing the example given above, if a person has a prudent personality, simply making a risky investment will generate effort by that person to reduce the chance the investment will produce a bad experience—say, close monitoring of the investment, or setting a predetermined price at which to sell. Thus the effect of a prudent personality, a force unleashed in this situation merely by undertaking the risky investment, is to increase the chance of successful experience and hence the likelihood of developing a more positive attitude toward risky investments. In this example, a prudent personality is a mechanism generating positive feedback.

Second, positive feedback mechanisms may directly increase change support. A person may develop a more positive view of risky investments over time after becoming more accustomed to taking risks. If one begins over time to associate more with others who make risky investments (perhaps to share information or because one feels more comfortable with them), their influence may make one more positive over time toward risky investments.

Negative Feedback

Some mechanisms discussed in this chapter generate exclusively, or mostly, positive feedback. Others may generate negative feedback or, within a group, feedback that is positive for some and negative for others. For example, if a person feels a general sense of confidence in the ability to execute plans undertaken, this is a source of positive feedback for successful experience with a change effort. However, the mirror image can also occur: those who are lacking in confidence may be more likely to fail, creating negative feedback. For those in an antichange workgroup, group influence can reduce, not increase, support for a change.[16]

If a mechanism creates a mixture of negative and positive feedback, the mechanism will generate negative feedback on balance in the group unless the proportion of those for whom it functions positively is high enough. So, for example, self-confidence may not, on balance, generate positive feedback unless more people in the group are self-confident than not.

Positive Feedback and Successful Experience

The first way positive feedback may help consolidate a change is through increasing support for the change indirectly, by promoting successful experience with the change (independent of the inherent nature of the experience), which in turn produces more favorable attitudes. Feedback mechanisms that promote successful experience include "moving down the learning curve"; leader and co-worker behavioral facilitation; performance-promoting individual personality and demographic characteristics; the self-fulfilling prophecy; and perceptual confirmation.

Moving Down the Learning Curve

The learning curve is an empirical observation, first noticed in airplane production, that unit production costs decline as cumulative production increases over time.[17] The intuition is that practice makes perfect. Over time, workers get better at producing a product or service. Organizations, through trial and error, improve production processes. If people become better at producing a new behavior over time, they will have more successful experience with the change as time passes.

The learning curve begins generating positive feedback as soon as a change is initiated, and it is especially steep in the early stages of a change process. Although the learning curve becomes less steep over time, this mechanism generates no countervailing negative feedback.

Leader and Co-worker Behavioral Facilitation

Creating what an organization produces is often a group activity, where successful experience depends on others and not just oneself. So leaders and co-workers in favor of change can provide an individual in the organization what may be called behavioral facilitation in undertaking a change. This may occur both by providing direct assistance and by creating a conducive environment. Such behavioral facilitation increases the chances an individual will have good experience with the change.

Assistance involves provision of one-on-one cooperation, advice, or training about how to perform behaviors required by the change. It may also occur automatically when an individual watches and imitates the successful behavior of co-workers (what Albert Bandura calls "observational learning").[18] Alternatively, supportive supervisors can provide a favorable environment by organizing work to encourage good experience (such as by lightening up on other assignments for those having difficulty or pairing employees having difficulty with those having less). Prochange co-workers can create successful overall group experience, in which each member partakes simply by group membership; at the extreme, an individual might free ride on the efforts of others, gaining good experience without personal effort. Leaders can sponsor training to provide people with information and skills required to perform new activities more successfully. More generally, supportive supervisors and co-workers can provide what Amy Edmondson calls "psychological safety," so that individuals do not fear they will be rejected or embarrassed if they try something new and it does not work.[19]

Behavioral facilitation as a source of positive feedback begins with mere initiation of change. Unsympathetic leaders and co-workers are likely to content themselves with doing nothing to facilitate others' good experiences, rather than actively sabotaging them. If a minority tries to facilitate, and nobody tries to sabotage, this will provide positive feedback.[20] People who fail to get training (or who do not benefit from the training they receive) will not be helped, but neither will they be hurt.

Performance-Promoting Personality and Demographic Characteristics

Some personality and demographic traits make it easier for people to be successful at whatever they try. For example, some people simply have a strong drive to succeed at whatever they do. A higher education or job level may make it easier to perform tasks requiring cognitive or experiential skills. The greater likelihood that people with these characteristics will have successful experience applies to *any* new behavior they try—if a different change effort had been introduced, such individuals would have been more successful at that as well. The impact of these characteristics gets unleashed automatically with mere initiation of a change.

Some performance-promoting personality traits can create negative as well as positive feedback: people highly lacking in self-confidence may be less likely to be successful than one whose self-confidence level is only neutral. Increases in education and job level provide positive feedback only, compared with a baseline of no education and no job skills at all.

The Self-Fulfilling Prophecy

Robert Merton, who first transferred the phrase from common speech into social science, defines a *self-fulfilling prophecy* as an expectation evoking behavior that makes the original prediction come true.[21] How could this occur? Underlying the self-fulfilling prophecy is the observation that expectations can shape behavior. If I believe that another person is wary of me, I may behave in a cautious and suspicious way that makes the person wary of me. If my expectation to succeed evokes more diligent behavior on behalf of success, then the very existence of the expectation helps it to be realized. The self-fulfilling prophecy is a positive feedback mechanism because starting x generates forces producing more x. Those with positive expectations about their experience trying out a change will tend to have positive actual experience.

The best-known empirical study of the operation of self-fulfilling prophecies is *Pygmalion in the Classroom,* which examines learning in elementary schools.[22] Before the term started, teachers were presented with information that some students, but not others, were expected to show a learning spurt. In fact, selection of "spurters" was random. Several months later, it was found that students identified as spurters improved test scores significantly more than others. Examination of teacher-student interactions showed that expectations had changed teacher behavior. "Teachers who had been led to believe that their pupil was very bright were found to lean forward more during the interaction, to look their pupils in the eye more, to nod their heads up and down more, and to smile more than those who either had no prior expectancy about their pupils or who expected them to be somewhat slow."[23] Another well-known example is the placebo effect in medicine: patients given sugar pills have shown improvement compared with untreated patients, presumably in response to the body's release of disease-fighting substances based on expectations that the "medicine" will help.[24]

There is considerable research about the operation of the self-fulfilling prophecy in an area relevant to organizational change, the impact of expectations about future performance on actual performance. Psychological experiments show that the more people believe they will be successful at a task, the more effort they put into doing well—and thus the better they perform. In one study, one group was first given five easy anagrams to solve, while another was given five impossible ones.[25] After working on the anagrams, the groups were asked to estimate the probability they would successfully solve a second collection of anagrams. The second collection was identical for each group. At the end of stage 1, the first group had dramatically higher estimated probabilities of their ability to solve the next set of anagrams than the second group. The interesting finding was that they also performed better in actually solving the second collection of anagrams, though the two groups had been given identical ones. In another study, managers in two plants told employees that changes being introduced were expected to improve productivity, while in two other plants, employees were told that the changes were designed to improve relations with employees. Productivity improved in the first two plants but not in the second two.[26]

The self-fulfilling prophecy provides an alternative account to the one presented in conventional prescriptions about why early wins might help consolidate support. In the conventional prescription, early wins increase attitudinal support for change, both on the part of the individual experiencing the early win and among others observing early wins at the workgroup level. Here, early wins help generate later wins through operation of the self-fulfilling prophecy, and the better experience with the change so generated increases support for change.

The self-fulfilling prophecy can generate negative as well as positive feedback. For those expecting negative experience, operation of the self-fulfilling prophecy can help produce such experience. As long as the balance of expectations in a group is negative, operation of the self-fulfilling prophecy may on balance generate negative feedback in a group.

Perceptual Confirmation

Perceptual confirmation is a mechanism whereby a person's expectation of how some object will be evaluated itself affects how the object is evaluated, independent of experience with it. What this means is that the expectation of how much one will like something influences how much one does like it. (This is different from the self-fulfilling prophecy, whereby expectation generates action that actually does produce better experience, not merely a perception of it.) In an experiment involving perceptual confirmation relevant to experience in trying an organizational change, two groups of subjects were given an "unenriched" version of a job that involved processing student admission applications (coding data items from the applications), and two others were given an "enriched" version (also evaluating application quality). Within each pair, one group was given cues in advance suggesting that the task they would be undertaking was interesting, the other that it was boring. "Subjects who performed an unenriched task with cues that suggested the job was enriched expressed higher satisfaction than those who worked at an enriched task with unenriched cues."[27]

In the context of experience with an organizational change, operation of perceptual confirmation would involve the influence of one's going-in attitude on one's perception of how successful an experience was. Since an increase in perceived successful experience at time t generates an increase in change support at time $t + 1$, perceptual confirmation is able to translate a going-in attitude into a more supportive coming-out attitude.[28]

Perceptual confirmation is set in motion by mere initiation of a change. One would expect it to generate negative as well as positive feedback: while those with positive expectations would feel they had had more successful experience than the inherent quality of the experience produced, those with negative expectations would react the opposite way.

Producing Change Support Directly: As-Time-Goes-By Support

Positive feedback mechanisms can also help consolidate change by directly increasing support for change. One way this can be done is through mechanisms creating what I call "as-time-goes-by" support.

With the launch of a change effort and mere passage of time the effort continues, people are repeatedly exposed to and asked to try new ways to do business. Most end up participating in actions that embody the change. The more often people try an activity, the more they tend to like it. Psychologists have identified four mechanisms by which this operates: "mere exposure," commitment, cognitive dissonance, and "foot-in-the-door." These mechanisms act automatically and work independently of the inherent quality of experience with the activity. In honor of that renowned student of human behavior Humphrey Bogart, I christen these collectively as feedback mechanisms creating "'as-time-goes-by' support" for a change. Put another way, these mechanisms involve ways behavior influences attitudes, not the other way around. They generate positive feedback only, with no countervailing negative feedback. Many show their strongest effects toward the beginning of a change effort, contributing to increasing support during the crucial period before mechanisms that require greater support to begin generating net positive feedback kick in.

It is important to note a contrast between as-time-goes-by support and the early wins in the guru literature on change. The key in the guru literature is the word *wins*: the literature is clear that skeptics can be brought around only by demonstrated benefits. By contrast, as-time-goes-by support only requires initiation of change-oriented *activities*. These mechanisms generate support independent of results produced by the change-oriented activities.

"Mere Exposure" and Commitment

Two as-time-goes-by mechanisms are the "mere exposure" effect and the effect of commitment. There is no need to discuss these at length here, because both have been addressed earlier in this volume. Indeed, that is interesting in itself. The effects of mere exposure and commitment are discussed in chapter 2 as *obstacles* to change because both increase support for established practices, independent of their benefits. However, once a change effort has gone on long enough, and people have tried the new behaviors often enough, the mere-exposure and commitment films begin, so to speak, running backward. At some point in the history of a change, some of the same phenomena creating support for the status quo, and thus making change difficult to initiate, start working to expand support for change. Now, new behaviors that have been tried often enough begin to benefit from these mechanisms. The same factors making it hard to gain a foothold for change, independent of the benefits of the status quo, begin to promote support for new behaviors, independent of their benefits.

Cognitive Dissonance

Cognitive dissonance, one of the most studied phenomena in social psychology, is a concept introduced by Leon Festinger.[29] Underlying the theory is the observation that people frequently have many cognitions (bits of knowledge) about themselves and their environment. Often these are unrelated, but sometimes one cognition implies another. If I buy a Coke on a hot summer day over an equally priced, equally available lemonade, the implication is that I like Coke more than lemonade to quench a hot day's thirst. In this situation, the two cognitions "I bought a Coke" and "I like a Coke to quench a hot day's thirst" are consonant. By contrast, the two cognitions "I bought a Coke" and "I like a lemonade to quench a hot day's thirst" are dissonant (that is, clashing). Festinger's basic argument is that dissonance is psychologically uncomfortable, and people to try to reduce it by (nonconsciously) eliminating dissonant cognitions.[30] Most often, and most important in terms of the implications of dissonance theory, they do so by changing their attitude to fit their behavior.[31] They will decide they do not really like lemonade all that much, after all. Thus reduction of cognitive dissonance becomes one form by which behavior produces attitude.

Festinger and his students performed numerous lab experiments to demonstrate the operation of cognitive dissonance.[32] Many involved the attitudinal consequences of undertaking behavior that, given one's attitudes, one normally would not have undertaken.[33] Dissonance theory predicts that the more discrepant the behavior, the greater the dissonance and hence the greater the pressure for change toward an attitude consistent with the behavior. For example, in what are perhaps some of the most bizarre psychology experiments ever conducted, a majority of those assigned disgusting tasks (such as eating caterpillars), as part of an experiment in which they had agreed to participate, chose to go through with the tasks even after being informed they had a choice between the unpleasant task and a neutral one, but *only* when the subjects were given ten minutes alone between assignment of the task and presentation of the choice to avoid it. (Of subjects who were immediately told they had a choice, without intervening time to think about it, not one chose to eat caterpillars.)[34] How could anybody have agreed to eat caterpillars when given the opportunity to avoid doing so? The researchers' explanation involves cognitive dissonance. The initial assignment to eat the caterpillars after having agreed to participate in the experiment created severe dissonance between subjects' choice and their attitudes toward the choice. During the reflection period, subjects reduced cognitive dissonance by changing their attitudes toward the unpleasant task enough to make them willing to undertake it: some came to see themselves as braver than before, others as more deserving of suffering, while still others reduced their aversion to caterpillar eating.

Cognitive dissonance suggests that the more a person tries reform, the more he or she will like it, because the drive to reduce dissonance encourages people to change attitudes to make them more consonant with their behavior. Knowing they have already tried the new behaviors, they come to be more positive in their attitudes toward reform.[35] Cognitive dissonance would be expected to be especially important in influencing attitudes of initial skeptics and fence-sitters undertaking discrepant behaviors.

"Foot-in-the-Door"

Psychologists have studied two related mechanisms—both of which get their names from sales techniques—that encourage a willingness to engage in more significant behaviors after undertaking less dramatic ones. These are called "foot in the door" and "lowballing." "Foot-in-the-door" describes a technique door-to-door salespeople use, believing that if only they can succeed in getting inside a person's house, they will eventually succeed in getting that person to make a purchase. Lee Ross and Richard E. Nisbett define the foot-in-the-door technique as a phenomenon whereby "inducing people to take initial small, seemingly inconsequential steps [puts them] along a path that ultimately will lead them to take much larger and more consequential actions."[36] In car sales, *lowballing* refers to inducing a customer to make a decision to buy a car based on an unrealistically low price and then removing the low price (perhaps through a claim that the boss refused to authorize it), in hopes the customer will be willing to pay the higher price after having made the decision to buy the vehicle at the lower price. "The essence of the low-ball procedure . . . is for a requester to induce another to make a behavioral decision concerning a target action. It is assumed that the decision will persist even after circumstances have changed to make performance of the target action more costly."[37]

Foot-in-the-door was introduced into academic social psychology through a classic article using a natural-setting experiment in a neighborhood near Stanford University.[38] A person randomly knocked on doors and asked people to sign an innocuous petition or place a small sign in their car window supporting safe driving. Not surprisingly, virtually all agreed. Two weeks later, a different person went to the same houses and to an equal number of randomly selected houses that had not been approached with the original request. They asked people to place a large, crudely lettered "Drive Carefully" sign in their yard. Seventy percent of those who had earlier undertaken the innocuous action agreed, while only 17 percent who had not received the earlier visit did so.[39] Simon Schama presents a dramatic example of foot-in-the-door involving antiroyal riots during the French Revolution.[40] He notes Louis XVI himself had encouraged crowds to assemble at Versailles to observe hot-air balloonists, assemblages of a kind that had never occurred before. These gatherings initiated people into joining large, boisterous crowds on royal property, making riots during the subsequent revolution easier. A gruesome example of foot-in-the-door was the way the Nazis got doctors to perform innocuous experiments on concentration camp inmates and slowly graduated them to horrendous ones.[41]

One would expect foot-in-the-door, like cognitive dissonance, to operate less strongly on those with well-formed attitudes. In addition, one would expect it to be particularly important toward the beginning of a change effort.

Producing Change Support Directly: Organizational Impacts on Individual Attitudes

A second potential source of positive feedback that may directly promote support for change comes from the organization of which a person is a member. A person may be influenced to support a change by supporters within one's workgroup (over and above the indirect effects, through behavioral facilitation, that promote change support by helping create successful experience) or by organization leaders. Many of these mechanisms create negative as well as positive feedback.

Social Influence

Feedback from social influence involves situations in which individual attitude is affected by peer attitudes. Social influence can be a source of positive feedback (from prochange peers) but also of negative feedback (from antichange ones). There is a large literature on social influence, both developed on its own, mostly in social psychology and sociology, and also in the context of theories of diffusion of innovation and contagion.[42] Peers may influence individuals in three ways: through pressure to conform, the provision of information, and persuasion. Much of the older literature emphasizes conformity ("peer pressure") as the source of social influence. If social influence equals conformity pressure, then in the early stages of a change process, before mean group attitude[43] becomes positive, it would be on balance a source of negative feedback.

Might social influence also provide positive feedback during earlier phases of a change? There are several reasons it might. First, group members might perceive there to be a prochange majority in their group before one existed, because change supporters might be more vocal than opponents.[44] Second, desire to be fashionable may make some want to spot "trends" early. Trend spotters do not want to be doing something nobody else is doing—then it would not be a fashion. They also wish others to notice; like conformists, they care about others' reactions. (Fashion simultaneously satisfies "the demand for social adaptation" and "the need for differentiation, the tendency towards dissimilarity.")[45] The desire to spot trends then produces a form of social influence that, unlike conformity, acts early in a change process.

Third, other group members, rather than being a source of conformity pressure, may be a source of information. Individuals are often uncertain which of several actions they might undertake is best. Peers can provide information about whether an action produces good results, what Ronald Burt calls a "vicarious trial use."[46] In this view, a group member following others is like an investor buying stocks Warren Buffett has bought. In contrast to conformity, which generally operates only after majority support has developed, positive feedback from information provision can get started through mere initiation of change, when many seek information about whether a new behavior "works." The venturesome, generally inclined to try new things, can be expected to look for positive information more than negative and do not require a supportive majority before they conclude that enough information has been provided for them to proceed. Thus for the venturesome, though not for everyone, information-provision feedback from peers is likely to be positive from the beginning.

Information can also come from the workgroup's overall early experience with a change effort. Indeed, one of the arguments for the importance of early wins is that they have an effect on undecided third parties within the group who witness them. Majority support is not required for this to generate positive feedback, but good group experience is, so this may exert negative as well as positive feedback.

Fourth, one's group may provide arguments in support of a change that persuade a person the change makes sense.[47] Early in the change process, while opponents are a majority, persuasion might act on balance to produce negative feedback. However, it is possible that change advocates, enthused and evangelistic, will seek to persuade while skeptics stay quiet (the "silent majority" phenomenon). During the early stages of student protests in the 1960s, virtually no grassroots counterorganization by opponents occurred, though a majority of students were not radicals.[48] During the early years of activism surrounding the legalization of abortion, there was less mobilization by opponents than by supporters; opposition became more vocal only after abortion became legal.[49] If only change advocates seek to persuade, while opponents remain silent, persuasion might generate positive feedback from the time the change is launched.

Finally, some may wish to "go with a winner," feeling they stand to gain practical benefits, or at least enhanced self-worth, from attaching themselves to a movement that appears to be winning. As a French official stated during the war in Indochina, "Eighty percent [of the people] are less interested in ideology than in being on [the] winning side."[50]

Leader Influence

One would expect any influence from systemwide leaders to provide positive feedback from the beginning of a change, since systemwide leaders initiated the change in the first place. Local leaders (supervisors and local office heads) might be a source of negative as well as positive feedback (though in the case of procurement reform, the sample did not include any overtly antireform local office heads).

First, leaders might directly influence attitudes through several mechanisms. They might persuade people to support their vision. As discussed in chapter 4 in the context of the leader role influencing people to join the reform coalition, the view that leaders persuade by articulating a vision is consistent with a common view of the roles leaders play in organizations. Second, subordinates might follow the lead of proreform leaders because the subordinate tends to defer to authority. The operation of deference would be ironic in a situation, such as procurement reform, in which what the "bosses" were seeking was for subordinates to be more independent, not less. In such a situation, deference would produce a situation in which the obedient followed an order to become less obedient.[51] Third, leader persistence in pushing the same message might promote change support by counteracting perception that the change was merely a "flavor of the month." Fourth, sponsorship of training about the change might influence not just experiences but also attitudes. Such sponsorship might partly be a function of leader support for the change, but it might kick in with the mere passage of time, as local leaders conclude that if the change effort is continuing, they need to get people trained in how to do it. Fifth, there are practical benefits of going along with leaders. Supporting a change effort one's boss supports may give a person an advantage in gaining valuable resources (such as good job assignments and promotions) or avoiding bad treatment.

Finally, psychologists study "locus of control," the extent to which one sees oneself as controlling one's destiny or as jostled by outside forces.[52] Locus of control is not the same as self-confidence. One reason to believe one does not control one's destiny is poor self-confidence. But one may also believe this, despite high self-confidence, because one simply sees outside forces as strongly influencing one's fate, despite one's efforts.[53] People with an external locus of control would be expected to go along with an established reform effort more than those believing they had greater control.

Producing Change Support Directly: Replacement

A third potential source of positive feedback that may directly promote support for change comes from replacement of change-skeptical employees in the organization with change-sympathetic ones. Replacement does not change individual attitudes, but it changes the distribution of attitudes within an organization.

Replacement depends on mere initiation of change (some may leave as soon as it is clear there will be a significant change effort) and then on the passage of time as an effort continues. It is likely that replacement will create, on balance, positive feedback from the beginning, assuming any differential departure will be from antichange people and differential arrival from prochange ones. Replacement may also be self-reinforcing: the more critics leave, the higher the average support for change in the rest of a workgroup, thereby encouraging still other critics to leave.

One reason a person might leave an organization after a change process has begun is unease with the change. Thus on average, people leaving an organization might be more skeptical about a change than those who remain.[54] The outflow of skeptics provides a source of expanded change support.

In addition, it is possible that new people entering an organization might be more supportive of the change than those already there. This might occur through some mixture of conscious hiring decisions, self-selection by new hires (who chose to come into an organization undergoing a certain kind of change), or simply the greater sympathy on the part of newer people with no investment in the previous status quo or with personality or demographic characteristics making them more supportive of the change.[55] Promotion decisions might also produce new local leaders who are more in favor of reform than those they replaced.

Replacement might automatically promote support for change as a feedback mechanism. Replacement might also be a conscious strategy:

critics might be encouraged to leave, while supporters might be promoted. Replacement as a strategy is one shock-and-awe technique appearing in the guru literature on consolidating change.

Positive Feedback and Change Consolidation: Potentials and Challenges

Three of the mechanisms hypothesized here to create feedback effects on attitude toward and successful experience of reform are directly self-reinforcing. These are conformity-based social influence from one's workgroup, operation of the self-fulfilling prophecy, and perceptual confirmation. So, for example, if operation of the self-fulfilling prophecy at time t increases successful experience at time $t + 1$, that in turn increases the expectation-induced force of the self-fulfilling prophecy next time around, further increasing successful experience, and so forth.

In addition, the other feedback mechanisms are indirectly self-reinforcing. The reason is that all are hypothesized to increase individual reform support (either indirectly, by promoting successful experience, which in turn increases support, or directly). Any increase in successful experience increases operation of the self-fulfilling prophecy, and any increase in individual support increases group support—both of which are directly self-reinforcing. A similar point can be made with regard to perceptual confirmation, which is also self-reinforcing.

These self-reinforcing feedback mechanisms create the potential for self-sustaining increases in, and eventual consolidation of, change support. Once a self-reinforcing feedback mechanism starts generating, on balance, positive feedback promoting support for change, the mere passage of time will continue to increase change support automatically, unless the feedback mechanism stops functioning as the change process proceeds or something else—such as negative actual experience—intervenes to counteract the automatic increase in change support over time that self-reinforcement generates.

However, these same self-reinforcing mechanisms also threaten to extinguish change support early in a change process. The problem is that these mechanisms share two other characteristics. First, they generate negative as well as positive feedback. Second, at the beginning of a change process only a minority is likely to have values for these variables that generate positive feedback. Workgroups and individuals will, on balance, be negative toward change. Thus mean workgroup attitude and operation of perceptual confirmation may, on balance, generate negative, not positive, feedback. If negative feedback dominates in the early period of a change, this will reduce successful experience and support for change, setting in motion a self-reinforcing process diminishing and eventually extinguishing that support—again, unless actual experiences are positive enough to counteract the tendency toward extinction. The early period of a change effort is thus a hazardous time in terms of the impact of feedback effects.

What might prevent feedback from being negative on balance, despite lack of majority support at the beginning of a change process? One quick assumption would be that feedback would be negative on balance unless the group's mean value for the mechanism is above that associated with positive rather than negative feedback. (So if self-confidence can generate negative as well as positive feedback, the mean workgroup value for confidence level would need to be positive.) However, operation of a mechanism producing negative as well as positive feedback might be asymmetric: a value producing negative feedback might not operate as strongly as one producing positive feedback. So, for example, self-confidence might enhance the performance of self-confident people more than lack of self-confidence depresses it. In such a situation, the mean value for the mechanism would not need to be positive for it to generate positive feedback on balance. (Note, however, that the opposite could also be the case—lack of self-confidence might depress performance more than self-confidence promotes it.)[56]

Second, conformity-based social influence from an individual's workgroup can begin to have a net positive effect on change support early on, even if the workgroup on balance is antichange. The reason is that, in the activating-the-discontented model of change initiation, a group of change supporters appears as the change process begins, even given the conformity-based social influence of the antichange majority. A workgroup whose average change attitude is negative at the beginning of the change process produces a certain quantity of negative feedback. Even with that negative feedback, however, some number of change supporters appears. If some other source of positive feedback, operating at the beginning of the change process to generate positive feedback, increases average workgroup change support somewhat, then, even though the mean workgroup attitude is still negative, the net amount of negative feedback will diminish compared with what it was when the change process got launched, because average workgroup attitude has become *less* negative. With lower negative feedback, some additional group members will be willing to let other attitudes override negative group feedback, and the number of change supporters will increase. This process is self-reinforcing, acting to increase change support over time even while average workgroup attitude toward change is still negative, because it is becoming less so. What is necessary for this to work is that some feedback mechanisms, other than mean workgroup change support, are generating positive feedback on individual change attitude and, through that, generating less-negative workgroup attitudes.

Those potential sources of positive feedback are the mechanisms set in motion with launch of a change process and that generating only positive feedback—education, the learning curve, behavioral facilitation, or as-time-goes-by support. If these forces manage to generate positive feedback on balance—taking all feedback mechanisms into account, including those generating negative feedback—this will increase individual support for change, making mean workgroup attitude less negative and setting self-reinforcement in motion.

Third, even a person with a negative attitude toward change may have a positive first experience with it. Indeed, in the case of procurement reform, I have noted that respondents on balance reported positive first experiences trying reform. If the mean value for first experience is positive, earlier experience begins, starting with one's next experience, to generate positive feedback on successful experience through operation of the self-fulfilling prophecy early in the change process, even if one's overall attitude toward the change still remains negative (and perceptual confirmation is therefore still generating negative feedback).

Fourth, the mechanism most likely to generate negative feedback is operation of perceptual confirmation, since most individuals will remain skeptical of the change and that skepticism will generate on balance negative feedback through the operation of perceptual confirmation.[57] Thus a key question for whether a change effort will get nourished or suffocated early on is whether the other positive feedback effects on successful experience outweigh negative feedback from the operation of perceptual confirmation. This depends both on the balance of positive and negative attitudes toward the change and on the effect size of perceptual confirmation, as well as on the existence and size of countervailing positive feedback mechanisms set in motion simply by the launching of a change effort.

Ultimately, whether feedback mechanisms nourish or stifle change at the beginning of a change process is an empirical question, answers to which are likely to vary from one change effort to another. This analysis indicates what to look for empirically to find out whether during the early stages of a change effort feedback mechanisms in a given change situation will generate positive feedback, allowing change support to grow, or negative feedback, extinguishing support. This includes, for example, the size and existence of feedback mechanisms that can counter the expected negative influence of the operation of perceptual confirmation at the beginning of a change process and whether early experience is on balance successful.

The analysis also provides a theoretical account for why early experience is crucial. The early-wins prescription suggests quite generally that early wins promote change support. The argument here would be that early wins occur not just because of the inherent quality of the experience but also because of feedback; furthermore, early wins promote subsequent successful experience through operation of the self-fulfilling prophecy, and this successful experience in turn promotes support.

Finally, this analysis suggests that the fate of a change process may get established early on even more than advocates of the early-wins prescription realize. During people's first experiences, the change effort can get propelled on a self-sustaining path dominated by positive feedback, assuming nothing intervenes to stop it; or it can move on a path to extinction dominated by negative feedback whereby, if nothing intervenes, support will eventually get snuffed out. Thus the stakes for early experience with a change are high.

CHAPTER **8**

How a Change Effort Feeds on Itself: Evidence

Positive feedback promoted support for procurement reform, allowing it to increase beyond the level warranted by inherent features of experience with it. Indeed, one central finding in this chapter is quite dramatic: at the very beginning of procurement reform, the effort was launched on a path producing a self-sustaining increase in, and hence eventual consolidation of, reform support through positive feedback mechanisms alone, providing nothing acted to slow or reverse consolidation of support (such as, most obviously, poor actual experience). This finding is based on empirical impacts specific to the case of procurement reform. There are reasons to believe we might see the same result in some other change efforts, but this is an empirical question.

Leaders and Consolidating Support for Reform: A Personal Account

Systemwide procurement leadership played its role in encouraging positive feedback by pounding a drumbeat that the change effort was continuing, providing a backdrop that allowed positive feedback through the mere passage of time to occur. The years following 1993 can be seen as a series of adrenaline shots injected into the working levels of the system to demonstrate that change was "for real." I did not at the time conceptualize the purpose of my activities as being to communicate to the front lines that change was continuing in order to create an environment where positive feedback forces could help consolidate change support. But that was one of their effects.

As noted in chapter 5, I came to Washington less interested in legislation, which I doubted would by itself change much on the ground, than in working with buying offices to achieve changes directly. As it happened, it was impossible to avoid becoming highly involved in legislative issues. I had not understood before arriving that there was movement for procurement reform legislation, mostly involving Defense Department access to commercial items. I probably spent the largest block of my time during my first ten months working on what was to become the Federal Acquisition Streamlining Act (FASA) of 1994. A mixture of strong support, including from industry, for provisions to ease Defense Department access to commercial items and the "only Nixon can go to China" impact of a proreform Democratic administration on congressional Democrats, the heart of political support for the traditional system, made legislation possible. The frontline employee I had met during my "apprenticeship," who had told me about her problem buying computer disks (a problem that a provision in FASA eliminated), was invited to the bill-signing ceremony at the White House and was acknowledged in the president's remarks. Right afterward, the last of the five Office of Federal Procurement Policy pledges was signed.

The new law itself accomplished less than the rhetoric surrounding it suggested. It removed some rules and included language authorizing the use of past performance in selecting contractors.[1] It did not address (except with the past-performance language) the process used to award large contracts, where mission-critical relations between government and suppliers are crafted and in which I was most interested. And, of course, legislation could not command development of innovative business practices. What I did not understand at the time, though, was that it was not just political appointees who care about legislation. More than I imagined, FASA sent people on the front lines a thundering message—louder than any I could send through speeches or other activities—that change was under way. This statement went far beyond specific changes in the law. One soon began hearing about changes agencies were introducing "as a result of FASA" that did not involve anything in the law at all. Legislation suggested the changes were permanent, not just a whim that would disappear when top leadership turned its attention to something else or (as all political appointees sooner or later do) left. Finally, legislation sent the signal that, at least for the time being, the political environment would be benign: Congress would be focusing on improving the contribution of the system to mission accomplishment, rather than on abuse. Legislation thus encouraged the front lines to conclude that supporting reform was safe and that change was "for real."

With FASA done, I wanted to start devoting my attention to nurturing change in buying offices. In an interview, I announced that 1995 would be "the year of implementation." Testifying before Congress on the progress of reform, I decided, instead of discussing laws and regulations, as one typically would, to center my remarks around a half-dozen examples of local improvements frontline people had initiated. In each case, I mentioned the name of the team leader in charge of the change; I also sent letters about these individuals to each of their representatives in Congress, assuming they would follow up with their own recognition letters.

Not long after I assumed my intense legislative involvement was over, it began again, as an unprecedented effort got launched to pass a second major piece of procurement reform legislation the very year after FASA became law. At the beginning of 1995, Bob Murphy, the senior procurement policy person at the General Accounting Office, requested a meeting to present proposals for reducing bureaucracy in the awarding of larger contracts. Given the respect Congress accorded to the General Accounting Office, Murphy's views suggested that further legislation was possible. On a separate track, the new chair of the House Government Reform and Oversight Committee—Republicans had just taken control of the House in the 1994 Democratic electoral debacle, for the first time since 1954—began preparing legislation with a number of radical proposals for reducing rules in the system.

Although the details are not relevant here, the legislative battle on these new proposals was fierce, with strong opposition from defenders of the traditional system, particularly bid-protest lawyers and small businesses whose competitive advantage was their expertise about the old system. Out of these battles emerged the Federal Acquisition Reform Act of 1995, in some ways even more radical legislation than FASA. The law included many changes proposed by the General Accounting Office, eliminated an onerous bid-protest body, the General Services Board of Contract Appeals, that heard vendor complaints regarding computer procurements, encouraged innovative contract incentive arrangements, and further limited government oversight rules when commercial items were being purchased.

Meanwhile, in the middle of this battle, a revision to part 1 of the

Federal Acquisition Regulation was finalized, stating a set of "core guiding principles" for the system reflecting the better value from contracting agenda. The revision began by stating the central doctrine of this agenda: "The role of each member of the Acquisition Team is to exercise personal initiative and sound business judgment in providing the best value product or service to meet the customer's needs."[2] The principles also included a crucial antibureaucracy statement that "in exercising initiative, Government members of the Acquisition Team may assume if a specific strategy, practice, policy or procedure is in the best interests of the Government and is not addressed in the [regulations], nor prohibited by [statute or case] law, Executive order or other regulation, that the strategy, practice, policy or procedure is . . . permissible." The idea was to reverse the traditional presumption that anything the regulation does not specifically allow is prohibited.

The legislative battle was followed by an even more brutal one over a major rewrite of the part of the *Federal Acquisition Regulation* dealing with awarding contracts for major procurements. These changes did not just involve streamlining but also eliminated rules restricting government's ability to get a good deal, such as restrictions on what the government could negotiate about with potential suppliers.

The core guiding principles, the second piece of procurement reform legislation in two years, and the *Federal Acquisition Regulation* rewrite continued the adrenaline injections. In particular, elimination of the hated but previously unassailable General Services Board of Contract Appeals was a powerful signal to people who tended to go with a winner that reformers had political clout.

Despite continued legislative and regulatory work, I started spending more of my time directly interacting with people in buying offices. My thought was to approach frontline change like beating a large feather pillow into submission. One needed to hit and hit from every direction, hoping eventually to diminish its ability to spring back. (This metaphor, which I had in my mind but do not think I ever used publicly, suggested that I still thought of change, at least in part, as involving overcoming resistance.)

One initial thought was to transfer the pledges into local offices. I suggested to the Procurement Executives Association that an agency's procurement executive and I cosign a letter to each frontline employee, asking them to make a personal pledge to undertake during the upcoming year some specific action (of their choosing) to improve how procurement functioned in their offices. The procurement executives were not enthusiastic, so I dropped the idea. Another thought was to make myself available as often as once every two weeks to visit a buying office, where I would give a talk and conduct a "town meeting" at which contracting professionals could share ideas or frustrations. My only condition would be that in exchange for my visit, the office would present an action initiative they pledged to undertake. In the end, I was unable to establish a quid pro quo, but I did begin to spend more time visiting buying offices; and typically the office would brief me on local change initiatives. Colleen Preston, my colleague in the Defense Department, began to spend lots of her time the same way. Frontline procurement people had never seen so much of political appointees. And whenever I gave speeches, I centered them around a suggested list of activities listeners could undertake to improve the system.

Another thought I had was to get the National Contract Management Association more involved. A few months after FASA was passed, the organization signed a pledge to encourage chapters to take a reform initiative of special interest and work on its implementation in their area. They also agreed to open a section of their monthly magazine to a feature called "Reinventing Acquisition." The chapter pledge petered out; a number of chapters did choose an area to work on, but I never heard any follow-up. However, the feature flourished, publishing articles by frontline people about initiatives they were undertaking. I fiercely resisted the tendency of staff offices such as ours to populate the feature with our policy statements. I wanted to showcase frontline people doing things.

In a similar vein, Preston and I established a Frontline Procurement Professionals Forum. We solicited nominations of a nonsupervisory contracting employee from each cabinet department and military service. The group met once a quarter in the Indian Treaty Room in the White House complex. The Frontline Forum provided a new voice for employees in reform. I worked to get forum members invited as conference panelists; one member testified at a congressional hearing; and the forum made public comments on the proposed changes to the *Federal Acquisition Regulation*.

Another way to hit at the feather pillow was training. An entire industry exists to train people in contracting. We shared an interest in getting the word out about new approaches. For us, it helped spread our message; for them, it was a business opportunity. Soon after reform was initiated, I began seeing training advertisements for courses in areas of reform, such as past performance and buying commercially. I sent out letters to training vendors, urging them to include certain material in their courses. In addition, the Office of Federal Procurement Policy began, for the first time, publishing best-practices guides, giving nonregulatory suggestions for implementing new policies. In 1996 the reinventing government office also set up a procurement reform website (this was well before websites were everywhere), called Acquisition Reform Net, featuring training materials and a chat room capability for people to discuss ideas online. The Defense Department established an Acquisition Deskbook on the Internet that offered suggestions and best practices.

Positive Feedback and the Creation of Successful Experience with Procurement Reform: Evidence

The first way positive feedback can help consolidate support for change is by helping people achieve successful experience with a change, independent of the "inherent" quality of the experience. This in turn promotes increased support for the change.

Two ordinary least-squares regression models were developed to test the influence of feedback mechanisms on successful experience.[3] In the first model, first experience was the dependent variable.[4] It was suggested at the end of the last chapter that early experience with a change effort is a dangerous time, during which initial support for change might get extinguished by negative feedback rather than promoted by positive feedback. In the second, the respondent's report (reflecting a judgment as of the time of the survey) on whether reform "has empowered me," was used to represent overall experience.[5] Looking at overall experience is important to see whether positive feedback mechanisms continue to function over a longer period, so as to continue a path toward change consolidation and keep support for a change on track against setbacks in terms of actual experience that otherwise might threaten consolidation. Specification of the models appears in appendix A, which also discusses how asymmetric effects were tested using quadratic terms.

Tables 8-1 and 8-2 present results predicting first and overall experience. Most feedback mechanisms tested had an impact. These mechanisms are important for understanding experience with a change; they explain (leaving out the control variables) a large percentage of variance in experience (R^2 of .29 for first experience and .30 for overall experi-

TABLE 8-1. Feedback Effects in Explaining First Experience

Variable	Standardized coefficient	Nonstandardized coefficient
Performance-promoting personality and demographic characteristics		
Drive to succeed	.06*	.07
Impact	−.04	−.04
Self-confidence	.08**	.11
Work late	.01	.01
Education	.29****	.32
Job level	.30***	.31
Job level × education	−.37**	−.08
Leader and co-worker behavioral facilitation		
Supervisor attitude	.05+	.06
Local office head attitude	.06+	.14
Most-respected co-worker attitude	.13***	.16
Percentage of workgroup in change vanguard	.10**	.70
Self-fulfilling prophecy		
Initial attitude	.27****	.24
Control variables		
Job autonomy	.15****	.01
Job burdens	−.05+	−.05
Timeliness	.05+	−.48
Distortion	−.19****	−.01

Adj. R^2 = .32
N = 1,100

Source: Frontline Survey.
+ ≤ .10   * ≤ .05   ** ≤ .01   *** ≤ .001   **** ≤ .0001

ence).[6] Significantly, most started generating positive feedback through mere initiation of the change process. However, none showed a prochange asymmetry (that is, values for the variable that enhanced the likelihood of successful experience did not have a greater positive impact on experience than ones inhibiting successful experience had a negative impact). These results thus provide no confirmation, in the case of procurement reform, for the suggestion in the last chapter that one way to avoid having negative feedback dominate at the beginning of a change process could be through prochange asymmetries allowing feedback to be positive, even if mean values for some feedback mechanisms would have hurt change consolidation.

Of the mechanisms generating negative as well as positive feedback, operation of the self-fulfilling prophecy generated the strongest feedback

TABLE 8-2. Feedback Effects in Explaining Successful Overall Experience

Variable	Standardized coefficient	Nonstandardized coefficient
Performance-promoting personality and demographic characteristics		
Drive to succeed	.11****	.14
Impact	.10**	.10
Self-confidence	.52**	.76
Self-confidence quadratic	−.53**	−.10
Work late	.03	.03
Education	.15*	.16
Job level	.24**	.25
Leader and co-worker behavioral facilitation		
Supervisor attitude	.07**	.11
Local office head attitude	−.07**	−.19
Most-respected co-worker attitude	.18****	.10
Mean workgroup attitude	.10**	.01
Training	−.23*	−.75
Training × initial experience	.30**	.02
Self-fulfilling prophecy		
Initial experience	−.26	−.28
Initial experience quadratic	.33+	.05
Perceptual confirmation		
Distortion	.13****	−.008
Distortion quadratic	−.05+	−.0001
Control variables		
Job autonomy	.03	.002
Job burdens	−.01	−.01
Timeliness	.05*	.05
Adj. R^2 = .31		
N = 1,593		

Source: Frontline Survey.
+ ≤ .10   * ≤ .05   ** ≤ .01   *** ≤ .001   **** ≤ .0001

effects. Its overall impact was neutral for respondents' first experience but began on balance generating positive feedback just thereafter. The most important mechanism generating negative feedback during people's first experience was the operation of perceptual confirmation; furthermore, even at the end of the process, perceptual confirmation was still not generating positive feedback on balance.

Leader and Co-worker Behavioral Facilitation

Both proreform supervisors and local office heads in the change vanguard promoted successful experience with change. The impact of supervisors stood in contrast to their lack of ability to influence people attitudinally to join the reform coalition. However, even here, their impact was surprisingly weak: the effect size for supervisor impact was small,[7] half the size of that for one's workgroup. Given the ability of a supervisor to structure the work environment, this suggests that the positive impact was counteracted by a negative attitude many had toward their immediate supervisors.

As for co-worker facilitation, having a most-respected co-worker who was proreform had a large impact on successful experience, one of the largest in the model. A respected co-worker may have been the best source of informal training. This finding adds to the argument in the diffusion-of-innovation literature on the importance of opinion leadership in promoting support for change, which emphasizes its direct role influencing attitudes, by showing the role trusted co-workers also play in behavioral facilitation. The impact of a workgroup with a high percentage of change vanguard members was also positive, though the effect size was smaller than for the most-respected co-worker.

Leader and co-worker behavioral facilitation was likely to have created positive feedback from the beginning. If one form of aid from supervisors or co-workers is creating a psychologically safe environment from which to innovate, these mechanisms have the potential to generate negative feedback (from opponents who discourage such a feeling of safety) as well as positive. At the beginning of the change process, both leader categories already had proreform majorities, while proreform most-respected co-workers may have been a large minority rather than a majority.[8] Given that other forms of behavioral facilitation would be expected to create only positive feedback and, additionally, that majorities or large minorities of these groups were proreform, it seems probable that behavioral facilitation provided positive feedback from the beginning.

Personality and Demographic Traits

People with some of the personality traits encouraging successful performance—self-confidence and a drive to succeed at one's job—were more likely to have a successful experience. Effect sizes were fairly modest. Working late and believing one had an impact on mission success were not significant.[9]

Self-confidence and the drive to succeed can create negative as well as positive feedback.[10] However, a majority believed they possessed these performance-promoting traits: the sample mean value for both was above the midpoint of 3 for neutral effect—3.88 for self-confidence and 4.29 for success orientation—meaning on balance they created positive feedback.[11]

Both higher education and higher job level promoted successful experience. But there was an interesting interaction between the two variables: the lower one's job level, the stronger was the impact of higher education on successful experience (and the lower one's education, the stronger the impact of high job level).[12] The nonstandardized coefficient for education at the lowest job level was .24, the highest effect size in the model. One may speculate that people with an anomalous education for their job level (or the reverse) might be trying to prove something to themselves or to others. Highly educated people at low job levels would be trying to gain a promotion and thereby encouraged to try hard to be successful on the job; poorly educated people at high job levels would be trying to show they were competent to perform well despite their lack of education. (One thinks, somewhat analogously, of the special success that well-educated, low-status minorities such as Jews and overseas Chinese have often had.) These considerations constituted an overlay on the impact of cognitive and experiential resources as demographic traits serving as sources of positive feedback for successful experience.[13]

The Self-Fulfilling Prophecy

Except for the impact of education at the lowest job level, the self-fulfilling prophecy had the biggest effect size in the model.[14] As with performance-promoting personality traits, the self-fulfilling prophecy can create negative as well as positive feedback. In this model, there was no asymmetry, implying a mean value for initial expectation greater than neutral was required for perceptual confirmation, on balance, to generate positive feedback.[15] The mean sample value for this variable was 3.01— basically, the neutral value of 3.0—meaning that on balance, based on recall data, the self-fulfilling prophecy at the beginning of the change process had neither a positive nor negative impact on experience.[16] However, as noted in chapter 7, the mean value for recalled first experience was positive (3.65). Thus after respondents' very first experience, the self-fulfilling prophecy began generating on balance positive feedback, because expectations going into subsequent experiences were positive.

Perceptual Confirmation

Perceptual confirmation had the next-strongest effect size in the model, after operation of the self-fulfilling prophecy. For reasons discussed in appendix A, the mean value of the variable measuring perceptual confirmation as of the time of the survey cannot be used to answer whether perceptual confirmation produced on balance negative or positive feedback during people's first experience.[17] The closest guess is that, since the mean sample value for initial attitude was about neutral, the overall feedback effect of perceptual confirmation was probably about neutral as well.

However, even had perceptual confirmation produced stronger negative feedback on balance, it is likely that the mechanisms in the model producing positive feedback—such as the influence of most-respected co-workers, education and job levels, and performance-promoting personality traits—would have added up to outweigh by a significant margin negative feedback from perceptual confirmation. The effect size of perceptual confirmation was .17, and the total of the effect sizes for mechanisms producing positive feedback was much larger. (The effect size for one's most-respected co-worker itself was nearly as large as for perceptual confirmation.) Any calculation of the impact on successful first experience of the positive feedback–producing variables, given their sample mean values, minus any plausible negative feedback from perceptual confirmation, would produce the conclusion that all the feedback mechanisms, taken together, produced on balance positive feedback, promoting successful first experience with reform, despite any negative feedback from perceptual confirmation.

Overall Experience

The overall experience model, reflecting long-run feedback effects, showed that feedback mechanisms generally continued to exert a positive impact on experience through the duration of the change process. There were a few twists. There were several instances of antichange asymmetries—situations where the negative effect of having a value for the mechanism that discouraged successful experience was stronger than the positive effect of having a value that encouraged success. By contrast, there was only one example of a prochange asymmetry.

Asymmetric feedback effects were tested in the first place in the context of the possibility, presented at the end of chapter 7, that negative feedback might dominate positive feedback early in a change process, causing feedback mechanisms to extinguish rather than promote change. However, the discovery of a number of antichange asymmetries raises interesting issues about limits to the spread of support as a change effort continues for a long time, to which I return at the end of this chapter.

Three of the four performance-promoting personality traits were significant in all the overall experience models. Believing one's actions had significant mission impact, which did not explain successful initial experience, did help explain long-run experience, suggesting that as experience accumulated, reform's impact on mission became more apparent and thus also its ability to promote successful experience among those who cared about mission accomplishment. Working late was again insignificant (p = .17). However, one of the personality traits, self-confidence, showed an antichange asymmetry: lack of self-confidence hurt successful overall experience more than high self-confidence helped it, though the net effect of self-confidence on successful experience was positive, since more of the people in the sample were self-confident than not.[18] Finally, there was a similar interaction between education and job level as in the earlier model.[19]

The impact of the local office head on successful experience varied by type of experience, with the results supporting, at quite a granular level, the influence of local office heads on experience with different aspects of reform. For example, the local office head influenced successful experience in being empowered, but the sign was the opposite from that for first experience; respondents whose local heads were most strongly proreform were *less* likely to report that reform had empowered them. The reason for this apparently puzzling result becomes clear when this model is run with the burden reduction and get-best-value measures of experience. For burden reduction, the coefficient for the local office head was significant (p = .08) and the sign was the same as for empowerment. With getting best value, there was a significant relationship (p = .01), but the sign of the coefficient was what would have been predicted—a more enthusiastic local head was associated with more successful experience.

The best explanation for these differences is the reform priorities of the most enthusiastic local heads, who were more likely to support the better-value agenda rather than only streamlining. Given these priorities, these local office heads were more likely to provide behavioral facilitation for changes designed to give the government better value, such as using past performance in awarding contracts—hence the positive coefficient for successful experience in getting better value. Less enthusiastic office heads (recall that none was downright antireform) would most likely emphasize streamlining. Hence respondents in those offices were more likely to report that reform had reduced burdens. Given that the most enthusiastic office heads were "imposing" priorities rather than allowing employees to choose them, it is not surprising that these respondents were less likely to report having been empowered by reform.[20]

The other leader-directed source of positive feedback, the ability to organize training, generally had an impact on successful experience as well, though somewhat differently for the different kinds of experience.[21] A proreform supervisor also promoted good experience, though again with considerably smaller effect size than co-workers supportive of reform. Co-worker effects were again large, most-respected co-worker's attitude having a greater influence than the workgroup as a whole on successful experience.

Operation of the self-fulfilling prophecy again had the strongest effect size.[22] Here there was a prochange asymmetry, so positive expectations had a much stronger effect in generating successful experience than did negative ones in producing bad experience.[23] This was the only variable in any of these models (including the one, discussed later, measuring the influence of organizational feedback on support of change) that displayed prochange asymmetry; the self-fulfilling prophecy is a mechanism for which a theoretical case is made in chapter 7 for why prochange asymmetries might exist.

Perceptual confirmation again was related to successful experience, with quite large effect size. In explaining experience with empowerment, perceptual confirmation showed an antichange asymmetry, though this was not present for explaining burden reduction or for getting best value.[24]

The mean value for the perceptual-confirmation variable was essentially neutral, that is, for the sample as a whole there was a balance between situations in which perceptual distortion acted to favor positive experience and those in which it favored negative experience.[25] Since, as noted in appendix A, the mean value of the perceptual-confirmation variable can be presumed to have fluctuated up and down during the course of the change process, this should be seen as reflecting the situation at the time of the survey only. About all that can be said is that, five years into the change process, the operation of perceptual confirmation was having an approximately neutral impact on successful experience or, where there was antichange asymmetry, a slightly negative impact; this mechanism was either not promoting successful experience or actually decreasing it.

TABLE 8-3. Effects of As-Time-Goes-By Support on Successful Experience

Variable	Standardized coefficient
Job easier	.04
Empowerment	.14****
Get best value	.09****
Too close to contractors	.09****
Success stories	.15****
As-time-goes-by support	.08***
Control variable	
Distortion	.33****
Initial attitude	.10****
Adj. R^2 = .43	
N = 1,593	

Source: Frontline Survey.
+ ≤ .10   * ≤ .05   ** ≤ .01   *** ≤ .001   **** ≤ .0001

As-Time-Goes-By Feedback Influences on Reform Support: Evidence

A variable in the survey presented respondents with the statement, "The more I try new ways of doing my job, the more I'm convinced they make sense." Respondents were actually more likely to agree with this statement than that reform had made their lives easier or had empowered them.[26] It is not possible, using questions in the Frontline Survey, to test separately for all hypothesized explanations for as-time-goes-by support. However, this question can be used to test for their combined impact.[27]

Table 8-3 displays the results of adding this variable to the model of the impact of successful experience on reform support presented in table 7-2. With all the substantive reasons why one might like reform more the more one tried it already in the model, this new variable may be seen as measuring as-time-goes-by support—the extent to which a respondent liked the changes the more they were tried, *just because* they had been tried more, controlling for successful actual experience. As can be seen, people did like reform more the more they tried it, controlling for experience. The effect size was larger than for burden reduction and about equal to getting better value and customer service.[28] Thus a higher score on this variable predicted greater support, independent of successful experience. These results are, to my knowledge, the first evidence for the impact of these mechanisms outside the laboratory.[29]

As noted, two of these mechanisms (mere exposure and commitment) would be expected to operate in the same way for both early supporters

TABLE 8-4. Predictors of Reform Support among Initial Skeptics and Fence-Sitters and Initial Supporters[a]

Variable	Initial skeptics and fence-sitters	Initial supporters
Job easier	0.08*	0.06[+]
Empowerment	0.20****	0.17**
Get best value	0.12**	0.13**
Too close to contractors	0.11**	0.14***
Success stories	0.24****	0.05
As-time-goes-by support	0.11***	0.07[+]
Adj. R^2	.35	.20
N	728	438

Source: Frontline Survey.
a. Coefficients are standardized.
$^+ \leq .10$ $^* \leq .05$ $^{**} \leq .01$ $^{***} \leq .001$ $^{****} \leq .0001$

and skeptics or fence-sitters, while cognitive dissonance, and perhaps foot-in-the-door, would be expected to operate with greater force on skeptics and fence-sitters. To test this, the substantive experience variables and as-time-goes-by support were tested for their impact on reform support, with the sample divided into initial supporters and skeptics or fence-sitters (see table 8-4). Consistent with the prediction, as-time-goes-by support was more important for initial skeptics than for supporters; for initial skeptics, it had an effect size around the middle for these variables, while for initial supporters, the effect size was one of the smallest (and was only marginally significant). The higher coefficients for skeptics support the view that cognitive dissonance and foot-in-the-door exerted an impact on attitudes; the presence of at least some impact for as-time-goes-by support for initial supporters is consistent with the view that mere exposure and commitment were functioning as well.

How much of reform support do the various mechanisms of as-time-goes-by support explain? The unique variance[30] this variable adds in the model in table 7-2 is only an additional 1 percent of variance explained, but this result is excessively conservative.[31] Nonetheless, it is probably correct to state that while as-time-goes-by support contributed to spread of support for reform, it did so fairly modestly.

Organizational Feedback Influences on Reform Support: Evidence

To model organizational feedback influences on reform support (as well as both organizational and individual-level influences of early wins), an

TABLE 8-5. Organizational Influences on Attitudes toward Procurement Reform

Variable	Standardized coefficient	Nonstandardized coefficient
Co-worker variables		
Mean workgroup attitude	1.10****	2.90
Mean workgroup attitude quadratic	−.48*	−.01
Mean workgroup attitude standard deviation	.64****	3.45
Mean workgroup attitude × attitude standard deviation	−.60****	−.06
Most-respected co-worker attitude	.12****	1.38
Mean workgroup initial experience	−.00	−.27
Leader variables		
Local office head attitude	−.09	−4.71
Systemwide leader influence	−.10	−1.95
Deference	−.13*	−3.75
Systemwide leader influence × deference	.22*	.99
Same message	−.96	.03
Training	.02	.15
Driven to succeed	.24*	6.09
Driven to succeed quadratic	−.24*	−.79
External locus of control	−.03	−.57
Career enhancing	−.04	−.87
Go with a winner	−.03	−.51
Control variables		
Empowerment	.11****	2.22
Job easier	.04+	.92
Get best value	.10****	2.16
Initial experience	.15****	3.04
Distortion	.40****	.49
Adj. R^2 = .48		
N = 1,593		

Source: Frontline Survey.
+ ≤ .10   * ≤ .05   ** ≤ .01   *** ≤ .001   **** ≤ .0001

ordinary least-squares regression equation was created with reform support (measured by the 100-degree feeling thermometer) as the dependent variable. Specification of the model appears in appendix A.

Results appear in table 8-5. The model did a good job explaining attitudes. Eliminating the control variables, the model explained 24 percent of variance, somewhat less than the impact of successful experience on reform support presented at the beginning of chapter 7.[32] Again, this shows the strong importance of positive feedback for consolidating change support. Social influence, both from most-respected co-workers and the workgroup as a whole, was a huge source of positive feedback

TABLE 8-6. Nonlinear Impacts of Social Influence Variables on Support for Procurement Reform

Change in mean workgroup attitude	Mean workgroup attitude standard deviation			Actual sample value for increment[a]
	10	20	25	
From 45 to 35	−15.5	−10.0	−7.3	−7.0
From 60 to 70	+10.6	+5.1	+2.3	+4.8
From 85 to 95	+5.7	+0.2	−2.6	+2.6

Source: Calculated from table 8-5.

a. Actual mean values for workgroup attitude standard deviation were as follows: from 45 to 35, 25.4; from 60 to 70, 20.6; from 85 to 95, 15.5.

and a major source of reform support. Leaders exerted a moderate direct impact (although immediate supervisors did not), but the impact of direct personal benefit was minimal.

Social Influence

Social influence had enormous impact. The proportion of change vanguard members in the workgroup helped explain reform coalition membership, as found in chapter 4, and, generally, successful reform experience, as noted in this chapter. But effect sizes in other models were much smaller. In this model, on average, the nonstandardized coefficient for mean workgroup attitude was .59, meaning that a 10-unit change in average reform support in one's workgroup was associated with an enormous 5.9-unit change in one's own reform attitude on the 100-point feeling thermometer scale.[33] This was larger than the change associated with moving from lowest to highest values of *any* variable in *any* model. There was also a significant interaction between mean workgroup attitude and within-workgroup consensus: the impact of mean workgroup attitude was much greater on individuals in workgroups with high consensus over whatever attitude they had. Interestingly, though, workgroup attitude displayed an "antichange" asymmetry: an antireform workgroup depressed a respondent's own reform support more than a proreform workgroup increased it.

The impacts of these various complications on the effect of mean workgroup attitude on individual support for reform are shown in table 8-6. The table illustrates the impact of a 10-unit change in mean workgroup attitude (for example, from 45 to 35) on individual reform support.[34] The numbers are complicated, so we should note overall patterns. Mean workgroup attitude had a far larger impact on individual attitude at lower values for workgroup attitude than at higher values. For example, the move from a somewhat negative workgroup attitude (45) to the most critical workgroup attitude in the sample (35) was associated with a very large 7.0-unit decline in individual reform support.[35] In other words, a 1-unit change in workgroup attitude produced a .7-unit change in individual attitude. The effect of the mean workgroup view was considerably smaller when the workgroup was more proreform—an increase of only 2.6 units when mean workgroup attitude increased from 85 to 95. At the same time, the more unified the workgroup was, the greater was its impact.[36] However, workgroup support for reform was associated with greater consensus; as a result, the antireform asymmetry of mean workgroup attitude was mitigated by the impact of within-group consensus working in an opposite direction.[37]

Thus even with the antireform asymmetry of the operation of mean workgroup attitude, this variable on balance, and taken as a whole during the whole period of the change effort, generated substantial positive feedback encouraging consolidation of reform support. This reflected high average levels of workgroup reform support and the mitigating effects of within-workgroup consensus among proreform groups on the antireform asymmetry of this variable. Given the actual distribution values for mean workgroup attitudes, support for reform was an enormous 12.5 points higher than it would have been had the relationship between mean workgroup and individual support been linear and if workgroup attitude were having no net effect on individual support.[38]

Most-respected co-worker attitude also was an important source of positive feedback, much smaller than for workgroup attitude but larger than for any other variable.[39] Mean sample value for most-respected co-worker attitude, at 5.6 (on a scale of 1 to 8), was well above the neutral value of 4, generating on balance clear positive feedback.

The data available here allow detection only of the overall feedback effects of social influence for the change process as a whole. In a separate analysis, I conclude that both information receipt and persuasion (from most-respected co-workers and workgroup members of the change vanguard) provided positive feedback encouraging growth of reform support early in the change process.[40] Furthermore, there was evidence that trend spotters (the organizational equivalent of the fashion conscious) became reform supporters early in the process, before majority support existed, when they sensed a social trend in support of reform. So social influence did not function only through conformity effects late in the process.

Leader Influence

Compared with the striking impact of social influence, leader impact was rather modest. There was also a monotonic increase in leader influence based on level. Top leaders were most influential, followed by local office heads. Immediate supervisors (consistent with results in the models explaining early support for reform) had no impact on attitudes (p = .45). Because first-line supervisors did not serve as opinion leaders, some potential advantage for the change effort coming from strong supervisor support for reform was lost.[41]

The influence of both systemwide leaders and local office heads was greatest among the more deferent. For the most deferent, leader impact on reform support was very large.[42] By contrast, for the least deferent (a small percentage of the sample), leader reform support actually lowered an individual's support—the least deferent ran in the opposite direction from where leaders were going.[43] These results support the ironic hypothesis that deference encouraged reform support, even though the *content* of reform was to combat deference. This result is also fascinating in view of the finding in chapter 4 that when the change effort was beginning, greater deference was associated with lower reform support. This is dramatic evidence of a prochange impact of the mere passage of time a change effort continues.

The different impacts of leaders at different levels suggest that leaders exert influence in a change process by articulating an appealing vision. It might seem surprising that government-wide procurement leadership had the greatest influence of any leader category, since they were the most distant from respondents. They were exclusively in the vision business. By contrast, first-line supervisors, preoccupied with the here and now, seldom articulate a vision. Moreover, the variable measuring local office head attitude was coded in such a way as to separate the most enthusiastic (and long-standing) local leaders from the rest—and these were the local leaders who had articulated a vision of the significance of reform.[44]

While training was earlier found to have affected successful experience, it did not affect attitude.[45] Nor did an individual perception of mere leader persistence, believing that leaders were giving the same message on reform.

Personal Benefits and Going with a Winner

Personal benefit and "going with a winner" did little to promote reform support. Neither the view that supporting reform was career enhancing nor believing that proreform offices had higher status was associated with greater reform support.[46] There was no confirmation of the ironic hypothesis that respondents with an external locus of control might be more inclined to support reform because they thought that in doing so they would be going with a winner.[47] Being driven to succeed at one's job was significantly related to reform support, but it had an asymmetric effect such that strongly disagreeing one was driven to succeed depressed support considerably more than being driven to succeed promoted it.[48]

Early Wins

The guru literature argues that early wins directly increase individual support for change: an individual's own early wins might affect that individual's attitude. However, the literature especially emphasizes the impact of early wins that change-skeptical individuals observe within their workgroup.

In this model, an individual's own early wins had a strong impact on change support, controlling for their impact (through operation of the self-fulfilling prophecy) on successful experience. The coefficient for a respondent's own early wins was one of the largest in the model. Given the strong impact of early wins on successful experience seen earlier, these two results show clearly that the guru literature is correct to emphasize the importance of early wins. However, the mechanism by which the guru literature argues that early wins have their most important impact turned out not to have promoted support for change. The direct impact of workgroup first experience on individual support for reform—the impact of simply observing successful workgroup first experience—was insignificant (controlling for impact through increasing mean workgroup support for reform).[49]

Replacement Influences on Reform Support

People working in these offices at the time of the research, five years or so after reform had been launched, were not the same people who were working in these organizations when the effort began. Replacement seems generally to have contributed modestly to increasing support for reform and was quite important for increasing support among local office heads, who in turn influenced both successful experience and attitudes.

Available numbers suggest that replacement was fairly substantial. Staff downsizing had occurred in most offices, averaging around 15 to 20 percent.[50] However, even as people were leaving, others were entering: 15 percent of the sample started working in government procurement after reform began. Replacement thus involved both outflows and inflows.

The best data available to examine the impact of outflows are for local office heads. Ten of the nineteen local office heads at the time of the research had been appointed to their positions after reform started. All outflow came through retirement of the previous office head. In only one case was there any evidence that a prereform leader had been encouraged to retire or forced out because of insufficient support for reform.

Information was gathered on local leaders who were on the job when reform began but who left afterwards. Differences between them and others are quite dramatic, though numbers are small. Of the ten who left, six were characterized as having had a skeptical initial reaction to reform, with the rest mildly positive and none a member of the change vanguard. By contrast, of the nine local leaders who stayed,[51] seven (78 percent) were members of the change vanguard, and none had been skeptics. Of the ten people replacing those who left, half had been members of the change vanguard (though they were not local office heads at the time). Another two were early recruits.

Second, the Frontline Survey included respondent reports on their supervisor's reform attitude, allowing comparison between respondents who still had the same supervisor as at the beginning of reform (that is, supervisors who stayed) and those who had gotten a new supervisor (to some extent, supervisors who had left). Although there are issues with interpretation of these data,[52] they do show a modest difference in reform support—42 percent of the outflow (leavers) were reported to have been "enthusiastic," compared with 48 percent of those who stayed, while 8 percent of the outflow and 2 percent of the inflow were described as "critical."

Third, the impact of outflows on frontline employees can be estimated by comparing reform attitudes of older respondents still in their organizations with their younger counterparts. Most, though not all, of

TABLE 8-7. Influence of Replacement on Attitudes toward Procurement Reform[a]

	Age of respondent		Tenure of respondent		Tenure of supervisor	
Attitude	Over 55	Under 55	Before 1994	New hire after 1993	Before 1994	After 1993
Reform attitude						
Percent	63.9	68.6*	69.2	68.9	74.1	71.9
N	93	532	1,280	254	110	47
Support for "reinventing government"						
Percent	3.16	3.07	3.06	2.92+	3.00	2.75
N	67	340	783	123	83	28

Source: Frontline Survey.

a. Separate variances method used to calculate p values for reform attitude and support for "reinventing government" for pre- and post-1993 hires. For others, equal variances method was used.

+ $\leq$ .10 level, two-tailed t test   * $\leq$ .05 level, two-tailed t test

those who left after reform started did so pursuant to authority that had been given to agencies, as part of downsizing, to offer financial incentives for older employees to leave ("buyouts"). A test of the extent to which those who left were more skeptical of reform than those who remained is therefore to observe attitude differences between older and younger employees in the sample, since those who left were mostly older. This is a conservative test, because it is likely that older people remaining were more willing to accept the changes than colleagues of the same age who left. Table 8-7 compares mean values on reform support for respondents 55 or older (in 1993) with those under 55.[53] Among employees who stayed with their jobs, older ones were a bit less sympathetic to reform, suggesting, even using a conservative test, a statistically significant, though small, replacement effect from frontline outflows.

To look at the impact of inflows, attitudes of new hires can be compared with those who had been around before the change began.[54] The data in table 8-7 show that mean reform support among these two groups was indistinguishable, though mean initial sympathy for "reinventing government" was somewhat higher for new hires. As for supervisors, the data show that newly appointed first-line supervisors in the sample had lower mean support for reform than those in the sample who had been supervisors before the change began (and who stayed in the organization), though the difference was not statistically significant. This may reflect the fact that new supervisors were selected only to a modest extent based on their support for reform. A survey question asked respondents to agree or disagree with the statement, "My impression is that my current supervisor got his or her job a least in part because of their support for acquisition reform." Of those who had had a new supervisor in the previous two years, only 18 percent agreed.[55]

Consolidating Change Support: Self-Sustainment and Self-Limitation

One of the most dramatic findings of this chapter is that, in the case of procurement reform, the change effort was set on a path toward self-sustainment at the very beginning of the change process. This was the result of a confluence of three circumstance. First, social influence from a respondent's workgroup had a dramatic impact on the reform attitudes of individuals. Second, many of the hypothesized feedback influences promoted successful experience in trying reform for the first time. The combined size of positive feedback mechanisms was larger than the size of negative feedback from perceptual confirmation, meaning that on balance positive feedback predominated, producing a net positive impact on successful experience the first time individuals tried reform, which increased individual support for reform and thus mean workgroup support for reform as well. Third, positive feedback mechanisms continued to influence, on average, both successful experience and reform attitude during the change process as a whole, so these mechanisms did not stop exerting effects as the effort proceeded.

Combine these results with the finding (presented at the beginning of the last chapter) that mean first experience with reform was positive, and recall the conditions for generating self-sustainment (or extinction) of support for change presented at the end of the last chapter. These findings, taken together, produce the result that people's first experience with reform set these organizations on a path toward change consolidation, assuming nothing intervened to stop that journey.

This result might or might not apply to other change efforts; that is an empirical question. But since many of the mechanisms involve fairly general social and individual influences (workgroup influence, most-respected co-worker influence, individual personality traits), there is reason to assume that results would be similar for other change efforts as well, provided that these efforts start with some moderately significant level of individual and leader support. This is good news for the prospects for organizational change: absent countervailing factors (most significantly, poor actual experience with a change), there is a good chance that change efforts starting with at least some support can consolidate that support.

Self-sustainment can in principle continue indefinitely, producing ever-higher levels of support. Such growth will generally occur more slowly over time. With time, some sources of positive feedback are likely to decrease or disappear (such as, for example, impacts of the learning curve or foot-in-the-door). Self-reinforcement works more slowly as support levels get closer to the maximum feasible.

Furthermore, self-limiting forces may appear to arrest or even reverse the growth of support. A classic example in international politics is the balance of power. A nation's growing power first creates positive feedback, as uncommitted nations seek to attach themselves to it and rivals become more hesitant to oppose it. But later on, positive feedback may turn negative as the state's growing power creates fears of its domination, causing others to ally against it.[56]

For a number of variables in these models, antichange asymmetries were present, suggesting the possibility of self-limitation. Why do these arise? As support for change grows, the presence of influences encouraging support become likely to be taken for granted and stand out less in people's minds, making them less salient than influences encouraging opposition.[57] So in a proreform environment, people would be less likely to notice that their own workgroup or most-respected co-worker was proreform. As workgroup support for a change becomes more widespread, trend spotters may abandon it, since support no longer makes them distinctive. Georg Simmel argues that "as fashion spreads, it gradually goes to its doom. The distinctiveness which in the early stages of a set fashion assures for it a certain distribution is destroyed as the fashion spreads, and as this element wanes, the fashion is also bound to die. . . . Fashion as such can never be generally in vogue." In addition, strongly proreform workgroups might generate not just conformity but also reactance—resentment about being told what to do—among individuals.[58] Furthermore, as reform becomes a taken-for-granted part of the environment, reform-oriented bad news would most likely be more talked about and noticed than good news because it is more out of the ordinary. People would come to recall a bad workgroup experience more strongly than a good one.[59]

If this argument is correct, however, antichange asymmetries would not have operated earlier in the change process, when average support levels were lower. Recall that values for overall experience and overall reform support reflect all influences, past and present, on respondents. If some variables show antichange asymmetry, on average, and if such asymmetry is driven by effects late in the process, it can be deduced that late-stage antichange asymmetry was more dramatic than such asymmetry on average and that, in terms of impacts late in the change process, these results are underestimates. Perceptual confirmation, one variable showing this pattern, created mild negative feedback even on average. It is possible (though speculative) that, if late-stage impacts are isolated, feedback from other variables may have turned negative as well.

Thus many feedback effects that may have played a crucial role in getting change consolidated are likely to come over time to stop working so strongly or, at the extreme, even to start generating negative feedback, creating a self-limiting effect for further increase in change support. Actual experience—as opposed to feedback mechanisms—may start turning less positive, or even negative as well, an issue to which I return in chapter 11.

A Concluding Word

I close this discussion with a normative question. To the extent that positive feedback occurs independently of the inherent quality of individual experience with change, does change support spread through mechanisms whereby people come to support changes that are not necessarily delivering improvements?

Several responses may be given. One is that positive feedback mechanisms, taken together, by no means fully accounted for support for procurement reform. People's perceived experiences were important. Furthermore, almost all positive feedback mechanisms affecting the quality of a person's perceived experience actually did promote genuinely successful experience. Finally, positive feedback mechanisms from initiating and persisting with a change may be seen as serving, at least partly, to counteract forces for inertia and resistance that hurt the chances for success of justified reform efforts.

CHAPTER 9

From Attitude
to Behavior

Up to now, the discussion has focused on the consolidation of change in terms of creating increased attitudinal support for procurement reform. At the end of the day, however, consolidating change requires new behaviors as well. What are the determinants of behavior change?

Reform-oriented behavior change was measured in the Frontline Survey through a question asking, "In terms of the way you do your job every day, how much impact has acquisition reform had?" The four alternatives were "It has significantly changed the way I do my job"; "It has had some impact on the way I do my job"; "It has had little impact on the way I do my job"; and "It has had no impact on the way I do my job." Responses to this question represent the dependent variable in this chapter. As noted in chapter 1, the mean score for this question was 1.81, somewhat higher than "some impact."

One anchor for this discussion is the link between attitude and behavior. Common sense suggests that a positive attitude toward procurement reform should, more or less automatically, get translated into reform-oriented changes in behavior, just as people who like apple pie are likely to eat it. Indeed, most of the guru literature on organizational change conflates change in attitude and change in behavior, assuming that convincing people to develop a positive attitude toward a change equates to generating changed behavior.[1] If common sense is correct, no separate discussion of attitude and behavior is necessary—the demonstration of attitudinal support for change suffices to predict change in behavior.

However, common sense may not be correct. Indeed, there was a time when the conventional view among scholars doing research on the relationship between attitude and behavior was that any connection between the two was minimal, even nonexistent. The less attitude translates simply into behavior, the more one needs to look at factors other than attitude that have an influence on behavior.

The evidence presented in this chapter strikes something of a blow to the commonsense view. An important reason people undertook reform-oriented behavior change was indeed simply that they liked procurement reform. But the story is more complicated. Factors other than attitude influenced behavior change, including ones such as education and job level, discussed earlier in the context of positive feedback mechanisms promoting attitudinal support for change.[2] This means that the impact of positive feedback on consolidating change is stronger than presented in chapter 8, because these mechanisms not only promote attitudinal support, and thus indirectly change in behavior, but also because they promote behavior change directly.

Second, one issue strangely ignored in the psychology literature on the relationship between attitude and behavior is the impact of material incentives on behavior. Shock-and-awe prescriptions for consolidating change are based on the view that such incentives encourage the behavior being incentivized, a view shared by academic economists and behaviorist psychologists. There is evidence that the relationship between incentives and behavior change is not straightforward, because of a countervailing negative impact of material incentives on intrinsic motivation to perform a behavior, a finding that sounds a caution about shock-and-awe prescriptions for consolidating change.

The Relationship between Attitude and Behavior

Skepticism about the relationship between attitude and behavior posited by common sense was inaugurated by a study appearing in the 1930s showing little tie between responses restaurant proprietors gave to a letter querying their willingness to serve Chinese patrons and their actual behavior when a Chinese couple showed up.[3] Over the following two decades, studies reaching similar conclusions proliferated, leading to a number of discussions on the link between attitude and behavior, whose provocative headline was that attitude poorly predicts behavior.[4]

The general tone of the skeptical research presented an unflattering view of human behavior, seeing a weak relationship between attitude and behavior as suggesting that people were either hypocrites or pawns. Some skepticism expressed in scholarly form the adage, "Talk is cheap"; one of the leading articles expressing skepticism about the attitude-behavior link had the expressive title, "Words and Deeds."[5] Since talk is cheap, the argument went, expressed attitudes mean little. They may merely express socially desirable responses—what one believes others expect one's attitude should be, rather than one's actual attitude. Just because people say they do not have prejudiced attitudes does not mean they can be counted on to behave in nonracist ways. Additionally, people may, if asked, express attitudes that in reality they do not have, or that they hold only weakly, simply from embarrassment to state that they lack any opinion on the subject.[6] A person's expressed attitude may thus in fact be, to use a phrase coined by Philip Converse, a "non-attitude."[7]

The other consideration leading the skeptical to their conclusion was what they saw as the key importance of situational factors in explaining behavior, particularly pressure to conform.[8] In this view, if an individual's own attitude conflicts with social expectations, the latter will usually win out; individuals are seen as pawns of larger social forces rather than creatures able to command their own behavior based on their own attitudes.

Seen from the outside, something about the headline version of this literature went over the line from counterintuitive to surreal. So, for example, with respect to both the non-attitude and socially acceptable reported attitude, the problem is drawing conclusions about behavior from *measured* attitudes, not real ones, since in the former case no real attitude exists and in the latter the measured attitude is not the same as the real one. This suggests a measurement issue, not a theoretical reason why attitude and behavior are not related. Surely people who genuinely like apple pie must indeed, on the whole, be more likely to eat it than those who do not. If attitude were hypothetically the only determinant of behavior, could it really be true that behavior would be random, as the theory implies? One is inclined to reply as the philosopher G. E. Moore did, when asked to prove the world around him actually existed, that he believed in the existence of the world more deeply than in any argument that could be given on the statement's behalf.

Skeptical iconoclasm is no longer in vogue. Richard Hill, reexamining earlier literature reviews and noting that the modal correlation found between attitude and behavior was about .3, comments that "this is about as good—or as bad—as we frequently observe when we examine relationships between social variables."[9] In a recent review, Icek Ajzen states, "Pessimistic conclusions regarding the predictive validity of attitudes, which in the late 1960s culminated in calls to abandon the attitude construct, have given way to the recognition that attitudes, properly assessed, can and do predict behavior."[10]

The postskeptical literature asks under what circumstances attitudes are more, or less, related to behavior. So, for example, attitudes less subject to the effects of social acceptability or social influence are likely to predict behavior better than those for which such factors are a big issue. The stronger one's attitude, the more likely it is to influence behavior, both because the attitude is more likely to be genuine and because it may motivate behavior more than a weak attitude. Greater personal experience with the situation about which one is expressing an attitude increases the influence of attitude on behavior.[11] Finally, the newer literature also notes what Ajzen calls the "principle of compatibility": "attitudes correlate strongly with behavior when they are assessed at the same level of generality or specificity."[12] Many studies showing low attitude-behavior relationships examined attitudes toward a general object—a politician, labor unions in general, children in general—and very specific behaviors—donating money to the politician's campaign, attendance at union meetings, support for specific child-rearing techniques.

Beyond suggesting that the skeptical literature overstates the case against the influence of attitude on behavior, it is also possible to portray nonattitudinal influences on behavior in a less unflattering light than that arising from the emphasis on pressure to conform, which sees individuals as pawns of social situations that easily override their personal views. For example, the performance-promoting personality and demographic traits discussed in chapter 7 in the context of the role of positive feedback in successful change experience may influence the extent of behavior change as well. Take the link between one's attitude toward the desirability of losing weight and one's dieting behavior. Dieting is hard. It is plausible to believe individual personality traits, over and above attitude—such as perseverance or self-confidence—would have an impact on dieting behavior, independent of and controlling for attitude. (Alternatively, there may be an interaction between these traits and attitude in predicting behavior. For example, perseverance is likely to predict dieting behavior only among those who believe they need to lose weight. Curiously, the literature on the attitude-behavior link, large as it is, has seldom looked at interaction effects between attitude and other factors.)[13]

If people who, for example, persevere are more likely to adopt a new behavior than those who do not, this reduces the strength of the attitude-behavior link, since such variables "compete" with attitude to explain behavior: the more important they are, the less attitude predicts behavior. But these nonattitudinal factors do not present an unflattering view, since they suggest that people who are more able to take charge of their lives generate more behavioral results than those who less able to do so. Furthermore, if there are interaction effects between attitude and nonattitudinal factors in explaining behavior, the strength of the attitude-behavior link also becomes more understandable; in circumstances in which we can reasonably expect a strong link, it is present, while the link declines where it is more difficult to translate attitude into behavior.

Individual and Organizational Influences on Behavior Change

In this section I discuss, and in the next section test, a number of possible individual and organizational influences on the extent of behavior change, including many already discussed in chapters 7 and 8 as feedback influences on successful experience or attitudinal support for reform. Two points should be noted. First, successful experience is not the same as extent of behavior change. The first measures quality, the second quantity. A person might have had a small number of highly successful experiences, producing reports of successful experience but only a small amount of behavior change, or a large number of mixed experiences, producing significant behavior change but less-favorable experience.[14] Second, since reform attitude is present in the regression model tested here, any influence of these variables controls for indirect influence on behavior change through increasing attitudinal support for reform. If positive feedback variables help explain behavior change here, this will constitute an additional source of positive-feedback explanation for change consolidation.

Individual-Level Influences

The skeptical argued that one reason for a weak attitude-behavior link is that attitudes may be weakly held. The flip side of this would be the expectation that the greater the intensity with which a person holds an attitude, the greater its impact on behavior. If this is the case, one would expect a kinked nonlinear relationship between reform attitude and behavior change—the slope of the relationship should be steep at low and high values for reform support and less steep in middle-range values.

In chapter 8, individual performance-promoting personality and demographic traits, such as self-confidence and job level, were examined for their impacts on successful experience with reform, which, in turn, promoted attitudinal support for reform. These might influence the extent of behavior change as well.

Organization-Level Influences

There are a number of ways leaders and co-workers might promote behavior change. First, as noted in chapter 7, supportive leaders and co-workers could help a person achieve more favorable experience by providing advice and modeling new behaviors. Such facilitation might make it easier to adopt a larger number of reform-oriented behaviors as well.

Second, as also noted in chapter 7, organizational production is often a group activity. The larger the quantity of reform-oriented group activities taking place, the more an individual may be "swept up" in them. However, the opposite is also possible, since free riding, or what psychologists call "social loafing," might occur.[15] Changing behavior takes effort. If one sees lots of changed behavior in the workgroup, one might conclude that one's own changes will not make much difference and become discouraged from making the effort.

Third, subordinates might change their behaviors because they are influenced by superiors in their views of how they should behave, just as they are influenced in their attitudes. As with attitudes, more-deferent subordinates might be more subject to such influence. Additionally, the basic feature of the employment relationship is that an employee gets paid in exchange for agreeing to take direction from superiors. Proreform superiors and local office heads may direct subordinates to undertake many reform-oriented activities. In chapter 8, training was found to have promoted successful experience with, though not attitudinal support for, procurement reform. A similar influence might be expected here.

Fourth, there are other possible sources of leader influence. Mere leader persistence in presenting the reform message did not increase reform support. However, it might affect the extent of behavior change, influencing what people show (behavior) rather than what goes on inside their heads (attitude). These factors were also found to have no significant influence on reform attitudes. However, as with mere leader persistence, they may have influence on behavior.

Finally, superiors can offer subordinates incentives for behaving as the boss wishes, although these are generally weaker in government than in firms. These include promotions, attractive work assignments, accommodation of special requests, recognition and praise, and, to a limited extent, salaries or bonuses. It is likely that the supervisors in this study used some incentives to influence the behavior of those working for them. Co-workers can also provide incentives, in the form of praise or criticism, to encourage adoption of behavior they favor, just as they do to encourage attitudes they favor. (Under the name "conformity pressures" rather than "incentives," these play, of course, a key role in skeptical theories about the attitude-behavior link.)

A fundamental tenet of economic theory is that incentives affect behavior—if you want more of something, provide rewards for supplying it, and if you want less of something, provide punishments.[16] Economists would therefore argue that crucial to producing more behavior change in the context of a change effort is to reward change and to punish failure to change.[17] The shock-and-awe prescription makes a similar suggestion, though with an emphasis on punishing resisters more than rewarding supporters.

There is, however, an entirely different hypothesis about the impact of incentives on behavior change. It grows out of social psychological research on the impact of offering extrinsic incentives to people who already have an intrinsic motivation to undertake the behavior.[18] The "undermining effect" hypothesis argues that extrinsic rewards have a negative impact on intrinsic motivation.[19]

"Intrinsic motivation is the innate, natural propensity to engage one's interests and exercise one's capacities."[20] In addition to the underlying interest in undertaking activities one enjoys, the opportunity to choose freely to do something and to demonstrate competence by doing it provides a basis for intrinsic motivation. The earliest experiments in intrinsic motivation—repeated in many different forms since—compared college students who were paid and those who were not paid for solving block-building puzzles.[21] The experiments found paid students were less likely to play with the puzzle during a free-choice period afterwards, when other activities were also available. Intrinsic motivation theory argues that such results show that extrinsic reward undermines intrinsic motivation. The extrinsic reward led the behavior to be experienced as having been externally controlled. This impression reduced intrinsic motivation to perform the behavior and hence its production when the reward was removed. A similar analysis is made for surveillance or performance pressure on individuals, argued to create a "controlling" situation and thereby reducing intrinsic motivation.[22]

It should be remembered—as the literature on intrinsic motivation seldom does—what the argument claims and what it does not. This literature generally treats intrinsic motivation, not overall behavior, as the dependent variable. If the dependent variable instead becomes overall behavioral response and not just the response induced by intrinsic motivation, the impact of extrinsic incentives becomes more complicated. The argument would be that extrinsic incentives have two opposite effects—incentivizing the behavior for everybody, as economists and behaviorist psychologists predict, and undermining it for the intrinsically motivated. In the context of procurement reform, one would therefore predict different effects of extrinsic rewards on reform critics and supporters. Critics lack any intrinsic motivation to undertake reform-oriented behavior, since they do not like reform in the first place. No undermining occurs; extrinsic rewards simply incentivize. However, for supporters, the two effects go in opposite directions. The incentivizing effect encourages behavior change, while the undermining effect discourages it. (Bruno Frey and Reto Jegen call this "crowding out.")[23]

This argument generates the prediction of an interaction between an individual's own reform support and the reform support of his or her superiors in predicting behavior change. Extrinsic rewards provided by superiors will generate larger changes in the behavior of critics than that of supporters. Rewards will incentivize behavior change in critics, who lack any intrinsic motivation for change. For supporters, though, the undermining effect of extrinsic rewards must be subtracted from the incentive effect, with net effect indeterminate; the empirical possibility exists that extrinsic rewards might actually reduce net behavior change, if the reduction in intrinsic motivation the rewards elicit is greater than their incentivizing effect. In such a case, one would find a crossover in the interaction—a level of reform support where the overall impact of increasing extrinsic reward would be to decrease behavior change.[24]

In contrast to monetary rewards, this literature argues that positive verbal feedback (praise) may promote intrinsic motivation.[25] Intrinsic motivation theory postulates that the opportunity to demonstrate competence is a source of intrinsic motivation. The more a reward provides information that a person is competent at doing something, the more it promotes intrinsic motivation.[26] Typically, the literature argues, with praise, the provision of information is more salient, while with monetary rewards, control is. Experiments do not always show praise increasing intrinsic motivation. When perceived as "controlling" or "pressuring," it has a negative impact. Thus positive feedback from adults does not promote intrinsic motivation among children the way it does in otherwise identical experiments with college students or other adults.[27]

An alternative explanation for why praise may not undermine intrinsic motivation focuses specifically on the role of money or other material benefits versus other rewards. Frey and Felix Oberholzer-Gee find people's self-declared willingness to accept siting of nuclear waste facilities near them decreased by half when compensation for accepting the facility was offered.[28] The falloff came from those previously willing to accept such a facility because of ideological support for nuclear power or a belief the siting decision process had been fair. Accepting a nuclear waste facility for a cash payment is not the same as accepting a nuclear waste facility because it is the right thing to do. The first is a package contaminated by selfishness, a force whose power most recognize but also deplore. It provides less utility, translated into less display of the corresponding behavior through a standard attitude-behavior relationship (since the attitude is less positive). This account is consistent with Richard Titmuss's argument that a society that pays for blood reduces the intrinsic motivation to give blood out of a sense of social solidarity and produces the counterintuitive result that less blood gets donated the more it is paid for; many value selling blood for money less than giving blood to help others.[29]

Intrinsic-motivation theory thus generates the possibility that supportive co-workers may have a different impact on behavior from that of superiors for reasons related to intrinsic motivation. By providing praise for behavior change, supportive co-workers may increase the intrinsic motivation of those who are proreform. If this occurs, the more proreform the workgroup (though not the more proreform the superiors), the greater the intrinsic motivation developed. By contrast, if intrinsic motivation is absent because a person does not have a positive attitude in the first place, praise will not increase it.

Finally, in terms of organizational influences, a classic argument is that while centralization (concentration of power at the top) hurts an organization's ability to generate innovative ideas, it helps for implementing them (assuming those at the top support the change).[30] In the case of procurement reform, given that the change involved empowering lower organization levels, there would an irony in such a relationship— a stronger hierarchy would favor spread of a change hostile to hierarchy. Also, pressure for change from strong central authority might be a source of performance pressure and thus subject to undermining effects on intrinsic motivation.

Testing for Explanations of Behavior Change

An ordinary least-squares regression model was developed to test for the influence of reform attitude, attitude strength, individual-level performance-promoting personality and demographic traits, and organizational influences on behavior change. The dependent variable was the four-point behavior change scale presented at the beginning of this chapter. Asymmetries were also tested for mechanisms that might generate negative as well as positive feedback.[31] For many variables, the model tested both for independent (main) effects and for interaction effects with reform attitude, to test for undermining effects. This model provides what may be the first opportunity to test undermining effects in a real-life setting, using survey data. Specification of the model appears in appendix A.

Results appear in table 9-1.[32] Table 9-2 displays the impacts, where there were significant interactions between organization-level variables and attitude in predicting behavior change, for critics (with a reform attitude of 40), those around the sample mean (reform attitude of 70), and strong supporters (reform attitude of 90).[33] The results show a strong impact of attitude on behavior. They also show strong leader influence on behavior, but in the context of a crowding-out effect of extrinsic incentives on intrinsic motivation.

Before specific results are discussed, the general observation should be noted that adding interactions and nonlinearities did improve the explanatory power of attitudes somewhat, mostly through the impact of the nonlinear relationship between attitude and behavior. A conservative estimate of the impact of moving from a model including main effects to one with only interactions (plus the reform support quadratic term) was to increase variance explained from .24 to .27.[34] This finding has implications for the scholarly study of the attitude-behavior relationship, sug-

TABLE 9-1. Personality and Demographic Influences Predicting Extent of Behavior Change

Variable	Standardized coefficient	Nonstandardized coefficient
Attitude		
Reform attitude	−0.57	−0.02
Reform attitude quadratic	0.32*	0.0001
Behavior-promoting personality and demographic traits		
Impact	0.03	0.02
Drive to succeed	0.03	0.03
Drive to succeed × reform attitude	−0.22	−0.001
Self-confidence	0.04	0.04
Work late	0.05*	0.03
External locus of control	0.28*	0.18
External locus of control quadratic	−0.23[+]	−0.03
Job level	−0.12	−0.08
Job level × reform attitude	0.23[+]	0.002
Education	0.07**	0.05
Leadership and co-worker variables		
Supervisor attitude	0.26**	0.28
Local office head attitude	0.03	0.06
Centralization	0.21*	−0.16
Central pressure	0.39****	0.25
Most-respected co-worker attitude	0.01	0.003
Mean workgroup attitude	−0.75*	−0.07
Mean workgroup attitude standard deviation	−0.99[+]	−0.19
Career enhancing	−0.48***	−0.36
Career enhancing quadratic	0.54****	0.06
Same message	0.07*	0.05
Training	0.12****	0.03
Leadership interactions with reform attitude		
Supervisor attitude × reform attitude	−0.39*	−0.0032
Centralization × reform attitude	−0.21*	0.002
Central pressure × reform attitude	−0.42**	−0.0028
Co-worker interactions with reform attitude		
Mean workgroup attitude × reform attitude	1.79[+]	0.001
Mean workgroup attitude standard deviation × reform attitude	1.45	0.002
Mean workgroup attitude × mean workgroup attitude standard deviation	1.02*	0.003
Mean workgroup attitude × mean workgroup attitude standard deviation × reform attitude	−2.02[+]	−0.00005
Control variables		
Distortion	−0.04	−0.002
Creative work	0.02	0.02

Adj. R^2 = .28
N = 1,593

Source: Frontline Survey.
[+] ≤ .10   * ≤ .05   ** ≤ .01   *** ≤ .001   **** ≤ .0001

TABLE 9-2. Coefficients for Organizational Variables Interacting
with Reform Support

Variable	Reform attitude			Crossover at reform attitude
	40	70	90	
Supervisor attitude	.150	.050	−.006	90
Mean workgroup attitude standard deviation				
Low	.020	−.010	.002	97
Medium	−.004	−.0078	−.010	
High	.002	−.0075	−.014	47
Central pressure	.130	.050	−.003	90
Centralization	.10	.03	−.01	84

Source: Frontline Survey.

gesting that studies should investigate possible interactions and nonlinear relationships (which is currently seldom done) to gain a better appreciation for how attitude affects behavior.

Results: The Influence of Attitude

Attitude strongly predicted behavior, accounting by itself for somewhere between around 10 and 16 percent of total variance in behavior change.[35] Since proreform attitudes strongly predicted behavior change, an important reason behavior change got consolidated is that attitudinal support for reform had become high. These data do not support the skeptical argument of little tie between attitude and behavior.

Literature on the attitude-behavior relationship suggests two reasons why the link would be high here. First, respondents had far more personal experience with the behavior toward which they were expressing an attitude—they had lived with procurement reform on the job for a number of years—than with many other objects in attitude-behavior research. Second, the level of generality of the attitude and behavior is similar: there are fewer steps between reform attitude and reform-oriented behavior than, for example, between liking a politician and giving him or her money.

In addition, a quadratic term for reform support was strongly significant and had an effect size larger by far than any other variable. Calculating the effect of attitude on behavior at different levels of attitude strength did not, however, show a kinked pattern whereby the relationship between attitude and behavior was strongest for strong supporters and strong opponents. Instead, among strong opponents, little relationship existed between attitude and behavior, while for strong supporters, there was a strong relationship. Loving reform made one much more likely to change behavior than merely liking it, but disliking reform produced only modestly greater resistance to behavior change than mere skepticism.[36] This suggests that support for reform was more salient to enthusiasts than opposition to reform was salient to critics. This finding has implications for positive feedback in organizational change processes. It suggests that as attitudinal support for a change increases over time, behavior change may increase disproportionately. (This counteracts tendencies toward self-limitation, discussed in chapter 8, with regard to increases in attitudinal support over time.)

Results: Individual-Level Performance-Promoting Personality and Demographic Traits

Many of the performance-promoting traits—self-confidence, job level, and education—that generated successful experience also had an independent impact on the extent of behavior change.[37] Working late was significant in this model: thus it was associated with a greater *quantity* of behavior change, though the insignificant results presented in chapter 8 showed it had not been associated with better *quality* (that is, more successful experience). The belief that one had an impact on mission was not significant. None of these variables showed an asymmetric impact.[38] Effect sizes for education and job level were greater than for personality traits.[39]

Interactions between reform support and performance-promoting traits in explaining behavior change were mostly insignificant, so having these traits promoted behavior change independent of one's attitude.[40] Only one, that between attitude and job level, was significant in predicting behavior change. Higher job level was associated with more behavior change for reform supporters, less change for reform critics. (The level of reform support where a crossover occurred was 49, essentially the neutral score of 50.) A higher job level allowed reform supporters more effectively to translate high support into behavior change, while giving critics the means to resist change.

Results: Organizational Influences

There are some particularly interesting findings here, from both practical and theoretical perspectives. Proreform co-workers did not promote behavior change, suggesting the presence of free-riding or social-loafing effects. Supervisors influenced behavior change, a result that, together with the results on supervisor influence presented in chapter 8, suggests that while supervisors had little impact on subordinates' hearts, they were able to influence their bodies. Third, findings regarding the impact of incentives support crowding-out theory. Finally, both mere leader persistence and the personal-benefit or going-with-a-winner variables, none of which affected attitudes, did affect behavior: these influences did not affect what was going on inside an individual's head but did influence behaviors displayed on the outside.

CO-WORKERS. The dog that didn't bark was the influence of co-workers. In dramatic contrast to the strong influences of one's work-group and one's most-respected co-worker on attitudes, co-workers did not directly affect behavior change at all.[41] The absence of impact here does not mean that co-workers did not influence behavior. They had a large impact, but it was exerted indirectly, by influencing attitudes (both through social influence and promoting successful experience). As discussed later in this chapter, there was a significant triple interaction involving workgroup attitude, workgroup attitude consensus, and individual reform support, and most of the coefficients for different cells of a matrix generated from this triple interaction were actually negative—the more proreform the workgroup, the less the behavior change. This is consistent with the presence of free riding: in strongly proreform workgroups, some individuals felt that their participation was unnecessary.[42]

These findings are particularly dramatic given the strong emphasis in the literature on the attitude-behavior link on the ability of conformity pressures to trump attitude in explaining behavior. They support an alternate view, that social influence strongly affects attitudes, which, in turn, strongly affect behavior.

LEADERS. Although it did have an impact on individual attitudes, the reform attitude of one's local office head did not help explain behavior change.[43] However, as with explaining successful experience but contrasting dramatically with the absence of influence on attitudes, supervisor attitude did explain behavior change, with a quite strong effect size.[44] As with successful experience (but not reform attitude), training had a positive impact on behavior change, with one of the larger effect sizes in the model.[45] In contrast to its lack of effect on attitude, mere leader persistence did promote behavior change, with a moderate effect size.

INCENTIVES. There is some good news and some bad news here for advocates of the impact of material incentives (economists and those prescribing shock-and-awe tactics) and for advocates of the view that extrinsic incentives depress intrinsic motivation. The results provide strong evidence that extrinsic incentives depressed intrinsic motivation. Consistent with the undermining-effects hypothesis, regression results show that the lower the respondent's own level of attitudinal reform support, the higher the effect of supervisor attitude on the respondent's own behavior.[46] In other words, a proreform supervisor influenced the behavior of critics more than the behavior of supporters. At very high attitudinal support, there was a crossover: the more proreform one's supervisor, the less the respondent changed behavior. Put another way, the strongest proreform respondents actually changed their behavior more if they had a hostile supervisor than a supportive one. This crossover occurred where the value for reform support was 87, meaning that for 22 percent of the sample, the more one's supervisor supported reform, the less one changed one's behavior. Operation of both the organization pressure variables, outside pressure and centralization, showed the same pattern. Both these extrinsic incentive variables had a greater positive impact on behavior change for critics than for supporters, and at very high levels of reform support, greater pressure was associated with less change.

One caveat about the generalizability of these findings is that they may be more dramatic for behavior change regarding procurement reform than other kinds of organizational change. To the extent that extrinsic incentives undermine creativity—which, evidence suggests, it does under some conditions[47]—the specific kinds of behavior change sought by reform, which included being more innovative, may be particularly subject to the undermining effect of extrinsic incentives.

A second prediction of the undermining-effects hypothesis is that workgroup praise might not undermine intrinsic motivation the way material rewards do, unless it were perceived as pressuring, in which case it would act, as an extrinsic incentive does, to depress intrinsic motivation. The regression model provides evidence for the differential impact of workgroup praise when experienced as nonpressuring and pressuring as well. It shows a significant ($p = .06$) triple interaction, involving the respondent's own reform attitude, mean workgroup reform attitude, and the standard deviation of mean workgroup attitude.[48] With the triple interaction, different effects of the reform attitudes of one's workgroup for individuals who were reform critics or supporters can be seen at different levels of consensus in the workgroup about those attitudes.[49]

The basic results are astounding. Identical changes in mean workgroup support for reform exerted opposite effects on individual behavior change for reform supporters and critics, based on the degree of workgroup consensus. For strong reform supporters, workgroup support had a much more positive impact on behavior change for people in high- than low-consensus workgroups. For critics, it was the opposite: workgroup support had a much more positive impact on behavior change in low- than high-consensus workgroups.

I can imagine only one explanation. In workgroups with high consensus on reform attitude, workgroup praise promoted intrinsic motivation, promoting behavior change more among reform supporters than critics. But where there was low workgroup consensus, the effect was the opposite, showing results like the one produced by extrinsic rewards, promoting behavior change more among critics than among supporters. In accordance with the distinction made in intrinsic-motivation theory between praise with and without "pressure," workgroup praise acted to reinforce the intrinsic motivation of proreform individuals in the first situation while undermining it in the second. At the same time, for reform critics, where workgroup praise exerted more pressure, thus acting as an extrinsic incentive, it had more behavior impact.

The story would appear to be as follows: When workgroup consensus about reform was high, there was little tension in the group about the issue. Advocates of views held by just about everybody in the group would not feel any need to pressure co-workers to adopt their views. If group reform support were high, praise to group members for undertaking reform-oriented behavior would come across to an individual as noncontrolling and nonpressuring. Group praise would thus strengthen intrinsic motivation among reform supporters. So where consensus was high, high levels of workgroup support for reform had a more positive impact on behavior change among reform supporters than among reform critics. By contrast, when workgroup consensus was low, much more tension over the issue occurred. In a workgroup with a high mean level of reform support but low consensus, there would be many strong reform supporters but also strong critics. Activities of supporters in this more conflictual environment would most likely come across to those on the receiving end as controlling or pressuring, as supporters pressed

176 FROM ATTITUDE TO BEHAVIOR

others to adopt their views. They thus acted as a source of extrinsic reward, depressing behavior change among reform supporters—but, at the same time, driving greater behavior change among critics. This is dramatic evidence for the view that group praise can either encourage or discourage intrinsic motivation, depending on how it is offered.[50]

There is, however, some good news in these data for proponents of extrinsic incentives, whether economists or shock-and-awe advocates. The key piece of good news for them is that, despite the undermining effect, the overall impact of supervisor attitude on behavior change (as shown by the positive coefficient for the main effect of this variable) is positive. Furthermore, given a crossover value for reform support at just under 87—where the influence of a proreform supervisor on behavior change turns negative—for 78 percent of the sample, the more proreform one's supervisor, the greater the behavior change. So, although extrinsic incentives did undermine intrinsic motivation, that indirect effect did not appear to outweigh the direct positive effects of these incentives, at least for the sample as a whole. Furthermore, the concentration of the impact of extrinsic incentives on critics is consistent with the emphasis in the shock-and-awe prescription for getting critics to change their behavior.

Caution should be expressed about the overall impact of extrinsic incentives on behavior change, however. First, it is plausible—the data cannot answer this question one way or the other—that proreform supervisors influenced behavior change not just by providing incentives but also through behavioral facilitation and direction of workplace activities. If proreform supervisors promoted behavior change for reasons in addition to providing incentives, this implies that the overall coefficient for the positive influence of supervisor attitude on behavior change overstates the impact of supervisor-provided incentives specifically, since the influence of incentives would have been overlaid on other supervisor influences. With the influence of incentives depressed, the crossover value for reform support, above which the net impact of a proreform supervisor on behavior change turned negative, would be lower, by an undetermined amount, and the positive effect of extrinsic incentives exaggerated.[51]

There is a second problem with a too-easy assumption that extrinsic incentives had a positive effect on behavior change overall. Table 9-3 displays correlation coefficients for the relationship between the variables for extent of behavior change (the variable measured in this chap-

TABLE 9-3. Correlation between Quantity of Behavior Change and Successful Experience at Different Levels of Reform Support

Variable	Critics[a]	Strong supporters[b]
Empowerment	−.23	.23
Job easier	−.05	.12
Get best value	−.05	.21
Customer service	−.18	.10
Success stories	−.17	.30

Source: Frontline Survey.
a. Reform support less than 50.
b. Reform support greater than 90.

ter) and successful experience measured in chapter 8, at different levels of reform support. The findings indicate that, for the strongest reform supporters, a larger amount of behavior change was associated with more successful experience. For reform critics, however, the pattern was the opposite—greater behavior change was associated with less successful experience. So the greater quantity of behavior change that extrinsic incentives were able to bring forth among critics may not have helped the cause of reform, by producing, to put it bluntly, botched change endeavors. Meanwhile, extrinsic incentives decreased or had only a minimal positive impact on changes in behavior among those whose additional behavior changes were likely to generate good results. Finally, the finding that centralization promoted behavior change supports the view—ironic, with regard to procurement reform—that centralization facilitates the implementation of organizational change, though such facilitation occurred mostly through centralization's effect on the behavior of skeptics.

PERSONAL BENEFIT AND GOING WITH A WINNER. Personal benefits and going with a winner did a bit more to promote behavior than attitude change, although on the whole their impacts were small. The belief that openly demonstrating support for reform would enhance their careers increased behavior change for some respondents (though this mechanism did not change their attitudes). The variable had an asymmetric effect that added to its impact.[52] However, being driven to succeed at one's job was, unexpectedly, associated with less change in behavior, not more. This result is most likely associated with a cagey strategy of prioritizing quality (successful change) over quantity—a cageyness generally characterizing these respondents.[53]

Finally, for lacking control over one's life, there was an asymmetric effect of a fascinating sort. Respondents at both extremes—both those who strongly believed they lacked control over their lives and those who strongly disagreed—had the lowest behavior change. Strongly agreeing that one controlled one's own destiny appears to have reduced behavior change by giving people an independent streak that may have discouraged from participating in behavior change most of those around them were doing. Strongly believing one was under the control of outside forces appears to have reduced behavior change by reducing a person's ability to direct those changes. So, interestingly enough, the greatest behavior change occurred among those in the middle—those with mixed feelings about whether they lacked control. On net, as with attitude change, these results did not favor the ironic hypothesis that in a proreform environment one would go along with reform more, the more one felt one lacked control, even though reform sought to give people greater control.[54]

CHAPTER 10

"Deepening" and Organizational Change

I use the term *deepening* to mean expansion over time of the extensiveness and character of new behaviors or beliefs someone supporting a change effort is willing to endorse. Partly, deepening may simply be a matter of numbers: someone originally willing to endorse only a small number of changes becomes willing to support a larger number. But deepening often involves a transformation in the nature of changes endorsed. From being willing to agree only to changes reflecting personal discontents, a person comes to accept changes reflecting an ideological agenda; from accepting only changes close to the familiar, a person becomes willing to accept ones that are more unfamiliar; from agreeing only to changes that ask little of them personally, a person comes to accept more demanding ones. Frequently, deepening involves endorsement of a broader agenda sought by change leaders from the beginning.

The Deepening Challenge

As discussed in chapter 4, most frontline employees who initially supported reform did so because of personal rather than ideological discontents with the traditional system. By contrast, reformers at the top, though supporting streamlining changes that did reduce job burdens, had primarily ideological goals, what I have called the better-value agenda. This ideological discontent was only to a modest degree shared on the front lines. Reform could be launched because it got tied to existing discontents. Absent deepening, significant weakening of the better-value thrust of the reformers' agenda might be the price paid for getting reform launched—perhaps (I noted at the end of chapter 6) a Faustian bargain for reform leaders.

The easier challenge for the reformers at the top involved the majority of frontline supporters interested in job autonomy because they valued creative work. For them, at least for those not supporting the better-value agenda from the beginning, what was required was to direct their desire for work involving creative thinking toward an embrace of innovative ways to do their jobs in order to achieve better-value goals. The harder challenge involved the minority (though not a negligible group) of initial frontline supporters who sought mostly an easing of personal work burdens—those who had initially seen reform as mostly about reducing burdens on contracting officials. (Henceforth I call these people "initial burden-reducers.") While procurement reform did promote reduction of paperwork and reviews, certainly by no means did all reforms make jobs easier. People using autonomy to be innovative might find their jobs more challenging; and elements of the reformers' better-value agenda required more work, not less. The two most prominent examples of this were using past performance in the awarding of contracts and decreased reliance on milspecs, the two signature better-value reform initiatives top leaders pushed. Evaluating vendor past performance takes time and effort, as does converting existing milspecs (which had simply been able to be pasted into new contracts) into new performance specs. Other examples of reform that generated more work included moving to performance-based service contracting, which also required replacing existing requirements with new ones, and doing more market research in advance of a procurement to learn about how commercial customers bought products or services the government would be buying. Reform leaders' advocacy of less adversarial relationships with industry, in order to create better value through customer-supplier partnership, might also create more work, such as additional meetings with industry.[1]

The analysis in this chapter focuses on initial burden-reducers, the hardest challenge for the reform leadership. It should be realized, however, that a milder version of this challenge was present with regard to many other reform supporters as well.

Deepening in the Literature on Social Movements and on Organizational Change

Deepening, both as an empirical reality and as something change leaders consciously promote, is familiar from social movements, though the term used here is new. I note in chapter 6 how early Christianity and many contemporary social movements got launched by appealing to people in ways close to supporters' existing beliefs rather than by fully reflecting what movement leaders had in mind. In early Christianity, the pagan features discussed in chapter 6 gradually disappeared.

> Familiar vernacular equivalents had to be found to express Christian concepts. Their very familiarity meant that they would have all sorts of non-Christian . . . connotations for those who used them. However, churchmen could contrive so to slant matters, by use and by teaching, that in the longer term only the Christian meaning would survive. In sum, words could be adopted and exploited, their range of meanings could be transformed, drained of secular content and appropriated to Christian ends. . . . Old high German (OHG) Geist had the primary meaning of "inner emotional arousal" or "possession (by a spirit)": Christian churchmen transformed its meaning into "spirit" or "soul." OHG Heil conveyed "material well-being, beneficence of the gods": after Christian treatment it became "holiness, salvation."[2]

Over time, the church also became more strict about doctrinal observance so that "rather more [came to be] required of the Christian laity than had been asked in the past."[3]

Bringing about deepening is often a conscious strategy of social movement leaders. Without deepening, Lenin has argued, workers would remain mired in mere "trade union consciousness" and be lost to revolution. "Socialist consciousness is . . . not something that arose with [workers] spontaneously. . . . The task of Social-Democracy is to imbue the proletariat with the *consciousness* of its position and the consciousness of its task. There would be no need for this if consciousness arose of itself from the class struggle."[4]

Although an important (if only infrequently analyzed) theme for movements for *social* or *political* change, deepening has received virtually no attention in literature on *organizational* change.[5] However, deepening efforts might constitute examples of a general concept about leadership discussed in the literature. Leader actions to create deepening would be examples of visioning. Also, to the extent that deepening involves leader efforts to reframe how organization members see situations they face, promoting deepening may be seen as an example of leader efforts at "sense-giving" or of leader efforts to unfreeze existing attitudes.[6] Like other examples of sense-making, promotion of deepening in a context of organizational change occurs in the context of shock or turbulence in an organization's environment.[7]

Did Deepening Occur in Procurement Reform?

A number of questions in the In-Person Interviews and the Frontline Survey addressed whether, five years after reform began, respondents had embraced the better-value agenda. The short answer is: to some extent. There is greater evidence for deepening in responses to forced-response questions, where respondents were asked to agree or disagree with aspects of the better-value agenda, than in responses to open-ended questions, where respondents stated spontaneously what was important to them.

One question in the In-Person Interviews was, "What do you see as the most important general goals associated with acquisition reform?" The question wording prompted responses directed toward policies underlying reform rather than changes in one's personal job, though respondents were free to give any answer that came to mind. Respondents could offer as many responses as they wished (and were prompted with the question, "Anything else?" to give additional answers until they ran out of goals they believed important). Table 10-1 presents the five most-mentioned categories and their frequencies for initial burden-reducers.[8] The table also presents percentages mentioning goals related to the better-value agenda. Such responses showed deepening, since none of these respondents mentioned failure to produce better value as an initial source of their discontent with the system.[9]

The most important result is the dominant view that better service for program offices, especially faster buying, was an important goal of reform, with a significant percentage mentioning burden reduction.[10] Only a modest percentage mentioned any element of better value as even one goal of reform, and no better-value goal was among the top five.[11] This is especially noteworthy since respondents were not limited

TABLE 10-1. General Goals of Procurement Reform

Goal	Percent[a]
Most important	
Faster service	27
Streamlining, simplification	26
"Government acts more like a business"	20
Reduce red tape, burdens	19
"Do more with less," cope with downsizing	17
Related to better value	
"Best value" versus low bid, quality, better mission support	16
Better communication with industry	4
More flexibility and innovation	8
Save money on what government buys, "better deal for government"	3
Pride in work, "do a better job," professionalism	4
Better government access to commercial items	3
$N = 98$	

Source: In-Person Interviews

a. Column total adds up to more than 100 percent because respondents could give multiple answers.

to one answer. At the same time, these answers do show some deepening had occurred: 16 percent mentioned "best value" as one goal, which none had mentioned as an original source of discontent, and other better-value goals were mentioned as well.

The last In-Person Interview question was, "How, if at all, have you personally been influenced by acquisition reform in terms of your own personal attitudes, approaches, or philosophies?"[12] This question specifically asked respondents to reflect on attitude change. Forty percent of respondents were coded as either reporting no attitude change or stating their attitudes had not changed but their ability to act in accordance with them had increased. From those reporting a change, by far the most common responses involved changed attitude toward one's own job. Twenty-six percent gave a general response coded as having become "more positive about change," and 14 percent "more positive about my job"; 20 percent reported they had become "more independent/more willing to take initiative/empowered/now believe 'if not prohibited, it's allowed.'"[13]

Two common responses did, however, reflect deepening. Fourteen percent gave responses coded as having become "more innovative/more likely to 'think outside of the box.'" Seventeen percent described themselves as "more oriented to customer service/trying to help the program," which might be related to better mission attainment though it might also have simply involved faster service. Responses directly related to increased appreciation for better value (coded as "greater appreciation of agency mission," "less adversarial with contractors," and "more expansive view of job") were the least frequently mentioned, by 3 percent. All in all, considering that 40 percent reported no attitude change and modest percentages reported changes tied to deepening, these responses do not provide evidence of much deepening.

However, in contrast with open-ended questions in the In-Person Interviews, the Frontline Survey, presenting forced-response questions about attitudes toward innovativeness in general and specific better-value contracting techniques in particular, provided evidence for significant deepening. The relevant questions (all answered on a five-point scale ranging from strongly agree to strongly disagree) sought to capture the following:

—whether change was just about burden reduction: The statement was, "Acquisition reform involves a lot more than just reducing the burdens on government contracting officials." This expressed the opposite view from the one asking respondents whether they had initially seen reform as involving mostly burden reduction. While the question is not specific about what else reform involves, and therefore does not imply endorsement of a better-value agenda, agreement does reject burden reduction as reform's only goal.[14]

—changes in innovation orientation: This variable was created from responses to two questions asking people about current attitudes toward some job-related statements and what their attitudes would have been five years earlier. Here, the statement was, "I like to come up on my own with ways to do my job better." The variable was created by taking the respondent's current attitude and subtracting the attitude of five years ago.[15] For those who saw themselves as having become more innovative during the reform period, the value would be positive; the closer the value to zero (or negative), the less the increase in innovativeness.[16]

—attitude toward reform-oriented innovation: The question was, "Acquisition reform isn't just a bunch of specific policy changes directed from the top. It's also an attitude encouraging individual contracting professionals to try out new ideas on their own."[17]

—support for better-value contracting methods: Support for changes designed to achieve better value, but that might make jobs harder, was measured with several questions. Most came from a section where respondents were given a list of eighteen reform-related changes and, for

TABLE 10-2. Mean Support for Better-Value Agenda
among Initial Burden-Reducers

Variable	Mean	N
Past performance	6.00	157
Milspecs	5.89	57
Performance-based service contracting	5.62	133
Cooperation with industry	5.36	156
Market research	60.50	158
Not just burden reduction	1.79	157
Reform about innovation	2.11	154
Change in innovation orientation	0.37	130
Less paperwork	6.34	154

Source: Frontline Survey.

each, asked "the extent to which you personally feel this is a good idea." Responses could range from 1 ("strongly disagree") to 7 ("strongly agree"). The changes were "past performance," "milspec reform," "performance-based service contracting," and "partnering with industry." Also included was the respondent's reaction to the idea of "spending more time on market research," a feeling-thermometer question with possible answers from 0 to 100 (50 was neutral). To compare with a nondeepening reform, views on "reducing the paperwork burden for government contracting professionals" were examined.

Table 10-2 presents mean values for these variables for initial burden-reducers. As can be seen, a majority supported each element of the better-value agenda, when these were presented as forced-response questions. Most agreed that reform was about much more than reducing burdens, suggesting deepening since these respondents had all reported that when they first heard about reform, they had thought it *was* mostly about burden reduction. Furthermore, these respondents on average saw themselves as having become more innovative over time, also suggesting deepening. Indeed, the mean increase in innovativeness, 0.37 unit, was much greater than for respondents who disagreed or were neutral on the question about initially seeing reform as being about burden reduction, for whom the mean increase was only 0.19. So initial burden-reducers had increased desire to innovate more than others. At the same time, mean support for reducing paperwork was higher than for any better-value reform.[18]

What can be made of the differences between data from the In-Person Interviews and those from the Frontline Survey, where the former provide far less evidence of deepening than the latter? Each provides important information. Open-ended questions have the advantage of giving a better view of which aspects of reform came spontaneously to the respondent, suggesting conscious endorsement—what can be called "active deepening." But strong agreement with forced-response statements supporting better value suggests that, though better value was not at the center of consciousness when these people thought about reform, it was something endorsed if asked—suggesting what may be called "passive deepening." That is not as powerful as active deepening, but it's better than nothing.

How Might Deepening Have Occurred?

Deepening might occur through several mechanisms. These include leader support for the better-value agenda; successful experience with innovative behavior or using better-value contracting methods; as-time-goes-by support, after repeatedly trying innovation or better-value contracting methods; and categorization.

As shown in chapter 8, both top systemwide leaders and proreform local office heads had an impact promoting general support for reform, though supervisors did not. Both local office heads and supervisors were more likely to embrace the better-value agenda than early reform supporters in general. Initial burden-reducers might have been responsive to leader messages supporting that agenda. If so, systemwide leaders themselves would help mitigate any Faustian bargain whereby gaining front-line support might have occurred at the price of losing parts of the content of reform important to them. This kind of direct leader influence would be most consistent with the concept of sense-giving or with literature suggesting the role of leaders in providing a vision. If local leaders were able to promote deepening, this would constitute another impact of the disproportionate presence of local leaders in the change vanguard.

As-time-goes-by support and successful experience may operate to promote deepening in the same way that they promote expansion of reform support in general. Given greater local leader support for the better-value agenda, many on the front lines might have been placed in situations where they were asked to be innovative or use best-value techniques, even though they would never personally have taken the initiative to do so, and received behavioral facilitation to be successful at these new activities. For the same reasons good experience with other elements of reform can be expected to produce positive attitudes, it is likely that if a person had successfully tried something innovative, or a better-value technique, that experience would make him or her more positive toward the better-value agenda. Attitude change might also occur simply by undertaking the new behavior, independent of good experience (as-time-goes-by support). Many efforts by organizers of social change or religious movements to involve converts through simple activities, with the hope of later gaining support for a broader agenda, have the feel of foot-in-the-door.

Deepening might also occur through categorization, by which is meant the transfer of general attitudinal approval of reform felt by initial burden-reducers into the willingness to support specific reform ideas, including better value, even though they do not reduce burdens. This may be seen as having two elements: establishment of a category called "procurement reform," including in the category a positive affect toward objects in the category, and transfer of that positive affect from already known to new instances of the category.

A category is a grouping of objects that highlights similarities. A category "exists whenever two or more distinguishable objects have been grouped together and set apart from other objects on the basis of some common feature or property characteristic of each."[19] Any category has features. These may include both descriptive ("a chair includes someplace one can sit") and attitudinal ones ("Italians are friendly").

We form categories all the time, because of the advantages doing so brings. "If an individual were to utilize fully his capacity for distinguishing between things and were to respond to each event as unique, he would shortly be overcome by the complexity and unpredictability of his environment. Categorizing is . . . a necessary way of dealing with the tremendous diversity one encounters in everyday life."[20] Category-based processing occurs in two stages. The first is to subsume an individual object into the category. The second is to use the features associated with the category to help process new, incomplete, or ambiguous information.[21]

In the context of deepening, the key point is that, by subsuming the individual case into a category with many features, categorization influences judgments—both cognitive and attitudinal—of individual objects.[22] Clifford Geertz argues that Churchill's "We shall fight them on the beaches" speech after Dunkirk was an example of the impact of creating a category where none had existed before.[23] Churchill's words placed fighting the Nazis into a category called "the British spirit." The categorization then influenced how people saw the fight against Hitler. For procurement reform, the argument is that those with a positive category called "procurement reform" will adopt a positive attitude toward specific reforms.

The impact of categorization on attitudinal judgments about people (rather than objects or stimuli) has been highlighted in discussions of the "halo effect."[24] In one experiment, most students who had heard a foreign-accented professor provide friendly answers in the classroom rated the professor's physical appearance as attractive, and just under half rated his accent as "appealing," while only 30 percent of those who had heard the professor provide cold answers rated his appearance positively, and just over 20 percent rated his accent as appealing. The warm answers appear to have triggered categorization of the professor as a warm person, which in turn prompted a general positive reaction.[25]

It would not be surprising for "procurement reform" people to become a category among people in buying offices. Living in an environment in which reform ideas and initiatives are salient is easier if one develops a category that allows the structuring of reactions to the changes. If one has had good experiences—or been persuaded that reform in general is good—the category will become positive.[26]

Explaining Active Deepening

After the question in the In-Person Interviews about whether the respondent had been "personally" influenced by reform, a follow-up question was asked to those stating they had been so influenced: "This is hard to do—to reconstruct in your own mind—but could you talk a little bit about how and why you changed your attitudes? Could you try as best you can to reconstruct the change process you went through?"[27] Table 10-3 displays frequency distributions for responses, though coding was challenging.[28] Answers to this question reflected consciously understood explanations for active deepening.

The most common reasons were coded as successful experience, leader influence—mostly involving local office heads, not systemwide leaders—and as-time-goes-by support. Two categories, "learning/persuasion" and "'in the air'/constant repetition," show elements of leader influence as well; taking these three categories together, leader influence was as important as successful experience. (Obviously, respondents would not mention categorization, a mechanism operating nonconsciously; some would also most likely fail to perceive the impact of as-

TABLE 10-3. Respondent Accounts of Why Attitudes Changed

Reason	Percent[a]
Successful personal experience	44
Leader influence	29
As-time-goes-by support	29
Learning, persuasion	10
"In the air," constant repetition	5
N = 41	

Source: In-Person Interviews.
a. Column total is more than 100 percent because respondents could give multiple answers.

time-goes-by support, though some answers were coded into this category.) The strong role for local leaders in active deepening stands in contrast with results for determinants of passive deepening, presented shortly, where local leaders had a more modest impact.

The following responses were coded as examples of change resulting from successful experience (note that responses did not exclusively involve successful experience with the better-value agenda):

Another change in policy was talking with industry. Now we can communicate more intelligently. Industry makes us aware in advance if what we are doing is technically wrong. It's so much better that you don't have to wait until you get a protest or a request from the inspector general. Now I feel differently about all this, because of the education I gained from my users. Once you participate and realize that this helps you do your job better and makes you feel more professional, you change your opinion.

I remember being petrified when they told us we had to use past performance in making contract awards. We rushed to get as many procurements as possible out before the deadline. We thought, "God forbid we fail somebody, we'll be protested." But our early experience wasn't negative. In fact, people started to think when they were going to training and told we should buy more like commercial market, and started to ask, how do you shop for something at home? I told people you could tailor the way we did this. They asked, "Could you change the sheet they gave us [to interview other customers about their experience with the contractor]?" I told them they could. People got better at doing questions and interviews. They learned to schedule the interviews, tell the people they were interviewing that we only needed fifteen minutes, and give the people they were interviewing the questions in advance.

It started a few years ago, when they began saying to us, "Let's do this, let's try that." I had a positive experience where we had to get a . . . clearance for the price we were trying to negotiate with [a contractor]. It used to be that the contractor would submit a cost proposal and we would have lots of questions, and the contractor and we would be way apart when we got the . . . clearance. Now, [the head of contracting] told us to sit down with the contractor before we went to [get the] clearance, and get so we were within 10 percent of each other. We got together with [the contractor], and we were able to get to where we were only 7 percent apart.

Gradually, my confidence in myself grew. Five years ago, I would have seen myself more as a mechanic. Now I view myself as being more of an adviser, or [in] a team member–type relationship. I could explain why you need this and do that. My role has mushroomed. I now get along very well with program managers, and they seek me out as being a person that has positive inputs.

Before, my goal was not to be the best I could possibly be to support the program but to be the best at contracting. I knew the choreography of contracting. Getting a good product was at most a by-product. It used to be that we had to follow a certain sequence of events. Now it's "get the product in the door." It's no longer step one, step two. Now it's "don't break the law, but get the product."

I started to change when I first had to write a performance spec. That made me think about how we do things. I looked at the sequence of events and said, "That doesn't make sense—good God!" No individual step was obscenely bureaucratic or counterproductive, but the accumulation produced total inertia. That gave me the opportunity for an "ah-ha." It allowed me to take the ideas of acquisition reform and apply them.

I was on one of the initial teams to try out [a new procurement approach involving procurement–end user teams]. I was brought up as "you're on your own, run it yourself." I was originally opposed to this new way, I thought the teams let the program office off too easily. It was initially a negative experience. I had fifteen people on the team, and [my boss] decided to make me the contracting officer, which I had never been before. There was lots of conflict within the team for the first few months. The program office said, "Hey, we're supposed to be empowered." As we got proposals and started jelling as a team, we started working well together. I felt involved. We awarded the contract in five months. I learned about leading a team and trying to get a team to work. I had never done that before. I was forced to try new things, and they worked.

The following responses were coded as involving leader influence:

Now, I think I can do anything. I can do it faster and smarter. I have to give [the local office head] lots of credit for what's happened. He has kept to the forefront of what's happening and fostered the idea that change is a good thing. He's pushed us to change. The message got repeated until it became engrained in our daily lives.

We were getting all kinds of complaints from customers about [a problem]. I went to see the commander to brief him on some initiatives to deal with the problem, and I told him there were lots of concerns that the changes we wanted would never happen. He looked at me and said, "You're right. It won't happen unless you do it. What are you waiting on? You waiting for a blessing from me?" The way he said it to me really made an impression. I realized that if you take the initiative, and it's logical and makes good business sense, nobody will stop you. The commander said to me: "Why are you here? If you're not going to make it happen, who will?"

I now have an expanded idea of what I do. I get to make good business decisions instead of just good contracting decisions—just following the regs and having good documentation. I changed because we had some leaders here who wanted you to think outside the box. And they got me to start talking with customers for the first time, and to have meaningful discussions with industry. I had never done any of that before.

I no longer see the concept of contracting as being here to write contracts, but that we're here to get x and y that somebody in [the agency] needs, and my job is to facilitate that.

These concepts were being thrown about, being there as a service. The fact that this was an emphasis being talked about from the top of the agency was important. This wasn't just for procurement. [Our whole agency] had to rethink its processes—our agency had a broader mission than just enforcing some regulations, we had a role in [achieving a mission].

The following responses were coded as involving learning from written materials, conferences, and speeches:

I used to be a lot more conservative in my interpretation of the [*Federal Acquisition Regulation*]. I was an inside-the-box thinker. Before, the attitude was, "Forget it, we set the rules, we tell them what to do." People had an attitude.

I was in the trenches when the word got out we were getting [procurement reform legislation] and that it meant big changes. The boss would leave out *Contract Management* magazine, and I'd thumb through it. Everybody was pushing teams and partnering. We had meetings and were told about it. I'm not sure how it happened. It got to the point where working-level people were pushing for this more than managers. I'm not sure how it happened—I guess I started listening to the stuff that was out there. It was in the air.

I learned that you need to be more liberal and more oriented to customer service. You need to move from being a policeman to being an enabler.

Previously, my automatic reaction to something new was, "We can't do that." Now it's, "Let's think about it. Is it possible? How can we do that?" I'm more open to looking at things in different ways.

I think it mainly happened as I was exposed more, literally hearing the phrase "acquisition reform," with all the training and hearing more and more, "Let's look at different ways." It was the repetitiveness and the push.

DEEPENING" AND ORGANIZATIONAL CHANGE 193

The following responses were coded as the impact of as-time-goes-by support:

> Having been here before reform, changing from entrenched ways of doing business was extremely difficult for me. Slowly it became more familiar, and I became more comfortable, less afraid of change, and soon it was part of the culture.

> Once you break out of that box and deviate from the [regulation] you thought was the gospel, it opens up other opportunities.

> It made me understand that drastic changes can be for the better and make an organization more effective.

Explaining Passive Deepening

The possible determinants of support for passive deepening were tested with Frontline Survey data using ordinary least-squares regression equations with the better-value variables discussed earlier (three involving innovativeness in general and four involving specific better-value contracting methods) as dependent variables.[29] The specification for the variables is presented in appendix A. Table 10-4 displays results for initial burden-reducers for the eight better-value agenda variables.[30] Across these variables, categorization and as-time-goes-by support were among the two most important predictors of passive deepening. What is noteworthy is that these are the two variables operating in the least conscious, or least self-conscious, manner; they are psychological mechanisms acting without people really being aware of them.

The factor most consistently associated with deepening was categorization, a significant predictor of greater support for the better-value agenda for six of the eight variables. For the specific better-value contracting methods, categorization was the only consistently significant predictor; for those two with the lowest visibility—performance-based service contracting and partnership with industry—it was essentially the only significant predictor.

Tied for next most important determinants (influencing four of eight variables each) were as-time-goes-by support and success stories. For those variables for which it was significant, success stories often had the largest effect size of any variable, typically larger than those for the less conscious influences.[31]

TABLE 10-4. Predictors of Passive Deepening of Attitudes toward Better-Value Agenda, Standardized Coefficients

Variable	Past performance	Milspecs	Performance-based service contracting	Cooperation with industry	Market research	Not just burden reduction	Reform about innovation	Change in innovation orientation
Categorization	0.31****	0.18*	0.41****	0.42****	-0.01	0.17*	0.14*	-0.12
Success stories	0.04	0.43****	0.05	-0.12	0.07	0.21*	0.37****	0.35***
As-time-goes-by support	0.29****	-0.01	0.10	0.12	0.22*	0.11	0.28**	0.16+
Leadership								
Systemwide leader influence	0.17*	-0.08	0.16**	-0.02	0.21*	-0.02	-0.09	0.01
Office head deepening	0.13*	-0.02	0.00	0.02	0.20**	-0.04	-0.12+	0.05
Supervisor attitude	-0.03	0.12+	-0.11	0.09	0.11	0.12	0.21**	0.19*
Control variables								
Idealism	0.04	0.21*	-0.08	-0.02	0.13	0.10	0.02	0.20*
Initial attitude	-0.08	0.01	0.04	0.09	-0.03	-0.03	0.00	0.04
Adj. R^2	0.27	0.27	0.26	0.23	0.14	0.09	0.31	0.26
N	156	106	135	156	156	156	156	156

Source: Frontline Survey.
+ $\leq$ .10   * $\leq$ .05   ** $\leq$ .01   *** $\leq$ .001   **** $\leq$ .0001

Leaders had some impact on promoting deepening, thereby contributing to mitigation of any Faustian bargain. As in other contexts, the influence of systemwide leaders was greatest, followed by local office heads and supervisors—again suggesting the importance of visioning as a form of leader influence.

Systemwide leaders influenced, with moderately strong effect sizes, attitudes on three specific better-value contracting methods—past performance, market research, and performance-based contracting—consistent with these having been concrete issues their leaders most strongly emphasized. However, they had no impact on views on milspec reform, which Defense Department leaders pushed strongly, or on broader attitudes toward innovativeness. Local office heads modestly promoted deepening, influencing support for two of the three specific methods for better-value contracting on which systemwide leaders had an influence.[32]

Supervisors may possibly have had a modest ability to promote support for the better-value agenda, though this is not certain—and, as becomes clear later in this chapter, they were not able to influence how far an office came in implementing better-value reforms. The coefficient for the influence of a proreform supervisor on support for two elements of the better-value agenda, milspec reform and market research, was positive; p values (.14 and .18, respectively) were somewhat short of significance, but this was probably a result of the small sample size and the consequent conservative nature of this measurement.[33] Supervisor attitude was significant and had a fairly strong effect size for whether respondents believed reform involved individual initiative as well as centrally driven reforms; it is plausible that a supervisor, through his or her actions, would communicate such a message, creating understanding of this part of the better-value agenda by deed rather than word.

Leaders indirectly influenced deepening as well. By persisting in reform efforts, top systemwide leaders helped create as-time-goes-by support that also influenced deepening. As discussed later in this chapter, leader success in reducing job burdens also helped create a positively valenced procurement reform category among initial burden-reducers. Local leaders helped create success stories. All these point to an indirect leader role in deepening, one going beyond the visioning role discussed in the literature.

Factors explaining passive deepening had a large impact on views of the better-value agenda. Table 10-5 compares predicted values on deter-

TABLE 10-5. Predicted Scores for Better-Value Variables at Minimum and Maximum Values of Deepening Predictors

Variable	Minimum	Maximum
Past perfromance	1.1	7.6
Milspecs	1.7	7.5
Performance-based service contracting	2.2	6.5
Cooperation with industry	2.5	6.1
Market research	38.8	74.5
Not just burden reduction	1.1	4.1
Reform about innovation	1.5	4.7
Change in innovation orientation	0.2	0.8

minant variables that were least and most conducive to deepening.[34] They show large differences in support from those factors.

What Causes Categorization?

Given the important role categorization played for (at least passive) deepening, it is important to ask what caused respondents to develop a positive "procurement reform" category. The intuitive answer is that the stronger one's support for reform, the higher the categorization. That turns out to be true: for initial burden-reducers, the first-order correlation between reform support and categorization was .29 (p = .0003). However, the story turns out to be more complicated than that. For initial burden-reducers, reform support was much more strongly associated with categorization when support was itself based on the view that reform had made the respondent's job easier.

This was tested inconspicuously by creating and then correlating two variables. The first expressed how close the relationship was at the individual respondent level between support for reform and the belief that reform had made one's job easier. A hypothetical regression line implying that reform attitude was perfectly predicted by views on whether reform had made one's job easier was first created.[35] Each respondent's value for the made-job-easier variable was then taken, and the deviation of the respondent's reform attitude from the score predicted using just the made-job-easier variable was calculated, indicating whether the respondent's reform support was higher or lower than it would have been had the made-job-easier variable completely predicted reform attitude.[36] A similar variable was then created expressing how close the relationship between reform attitude and categorization was, and a sim-

FIGURE 10-1. Explaining Categorization

Categorization deviations

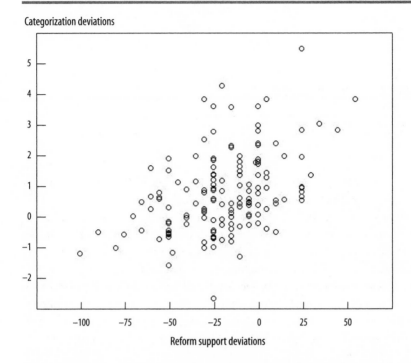

Reform support deviations

ilar calculation of the respondent's deviation (whether the actual value for categorization was higher or lower than predicted, given the respondent's value for predicted reform attitude) was made.[37]

I then computed the first-order correlation between these two variables. It was a very strong .48 (p = .0000, N = 148), stronger than the .29 correlation between reform support and categorization. What this means is that if a respondent's overall support for reform was based mostly on the respondent's view of whether reform had made the job easier, the degree of categorization closely tracked the respondent's overall reform support. By contrast, if factors other than believing reform had made one's job easier were driving the respondent to be positive toward reform,[38] then categorization was weaker than expected.[39] Similarly, if factors other than making the job easier were driving a respondent to be negative toward reform,[40] then categorization was greater than expected (see figure 10-1). In other words, the more support was based on the view that reform had made the respondent's job easier, the more strongly related to overall support for reform was categorization. Put negatively, if

TABLE 10-6. Deepening: How Far Have Offices Gotten?

Variable	Mean perception of progress[a]	N
Less paperwork	6.2	1,484
Past performance	5.6	1,367
Milspecs reform	5.1	969
Performance-based service contracting	4.8	1,141
Cooperation with industry	4.7	1,390

Source: Frontline Survey.
a. Based on responses on a seven-point scale, from "just getting started" (1) to "all the way there" (7).

factors other than reform making one's job easier influenced reform support, support was less likely to produce categorization.[41]

Why might that be? The answer is that support need not equal emotional attachment. During the Clinton presidency, commentators noted that many liked Clinton's policies without liking Clinton. Somebody might support reform without feeling "warm and fuzzy" about it. For initial burden-reducers, many factors could produce overall reform support. But satisfaction of their original desire for burden reduction produced stronger emotional attachment, creating a positive category that, in turn, extended the nature of changes they were willing to support.

Behavior Change in Support of the Better-Value Agenda

As with change consolidation in general, the ultimate test of the success of deepening comes not just from attitudinal deepening but from behavior change on behalf of the better-value agenda. No data available from the surveys allow determination of the extent to which initial burden-reducers (or other respondents) translated attitudinal support for the better-value agenda into personal behavior change. However, the section of the Frontline Survey presenting reform ideas such as past performance (used in the data analysis in the previous section) also asked, "For each idea, please indicate how far you personally believe *your office has come* in making the policy part of the way contracting professionals routinely do their jobs, *independently of whether you personally feel the policy is a good idea or not.*" Allowed responses ranged from 1 ("just getting started") to 7 ("all the way there").[42]

Table 10-6 shows mean responses among all respondents (not just initial burden-reducers) for four better-value variables compared with

TABLE 10-7. Role of Leader Attitude in Deepening Behavior

	Better-value variables				
Variable	Past performance	Performance-based service contracting	Milspecs	Partnership with industry	Paperwork reduction
Local office head	0.29****	0.15*	0.48****	0.34****	0.11
Mean workgroup supervisor	0.18*	0.02	0.14	−0.02	0.19
Adj. R^2	0.25	0.04	0.25	0.28	0.03
N	64	64	59	65	65

Source: Frontline Survey.
$+ \leq .10$ $* \leq .05$ $** \leq .01$ $*** \leq .001$ $**** \leq .0001$

responses for a question involving burden reduction ("reducing the paperwork burden for government contracting professionals"). Results show that people believed their offices had made greater progress on burden reduction than on the better-value agenda. For better value, they saw greater progress on the two issues addressed most by systemwide leaders: past performance and milspec reform. However, for each better-value variable, the mean response was higher than the middle response (4), suggesting that respondents, though perhaps reflecting a view more optimistic than reality, perceived their offices were somewhat closer to being "all the way there" than "just getting started." As with attitudinal deepening among initial burden-reducers, the glass may be seen as either half-empty or half-full: offices had made progress on the better-value agenda, but less than their progress in burden reduction.

What about the influence of local leadership on better-value behavior change? Table 10-7 presents results from a simple regression equation where the dependent variable was mean workgroup perception of how far the office had come in implementing these changes.[43] Predictor variables were the attitude of local office heads and the mean workgroup perception of first-line supervisor reform support.[44] There was a clear difference between the impacts on better-value policies and on burden reduction. Having a local office head categorized as a strongest supporter of reform had a much larger effect on behavior change for the former than the latter.[45] Given that local office heads coded in the lower-support category were not opponents of reform, these results should be interpreted as supporting the view that both strongest and more lukewarm supporters promoted burden reduction, producing less difference between the two groups, while members of the change vanguard promoted the better-value agenda as well as burden reduction. The data suggest little impact from having a more proreform supervisor, though the measure was noisy.[46] Coefficients for the different changes were about the same (close to zero for two of the better-value variables, performance-based service contracting and partnership with industry). Supervisors did have an impact on progress on past performance, which systemwide leaders promoted strongly.

That local leadership, particularly local office heads, was disproportionately sympathetic to the better-value agenda thus also had a direct impact on the ability to achieve change in frontline behavior in support of that agenda. In this way, as with some elements of attitudinal deepening, local leaders helped avoid the worst of any Faustian bargain.

CHAPTER 11

Consolidating Change:
Implications for Theory and Practice

Five years into the change effort, procurement reform had produced significant changes on the front lines of the system. It had won the battle for the hearts and minds of those on the front lines, and proreform attitudes had gotten significantly translated into behavior. Reform had become reality. Furthermore, although reform as practiced included a larger dose of streamlining than the leaders at the top would have chosen—reflecting the influence of those at the bottom—it also included a bigger dose of better-value changes than people at the bottom would have brought about on their own—reflecting influences of both the local change vanguard and deepening support over time.

The underlying argument in guru prescriptions for inducing attitude change is that people need to be shown that change works: the many skeptics a change effort faces will be brought around only by success. Certainly, the evidence presented here shows the importance of successful experience in generating reform support. Early wins, an important part of the conventional prescription, were important, but not for reasons the guru literature suggests. Early wins acted through the operation of the self-fulfilling prophecy and through direct effects on the attitudes of those personally experiencing the wins, not by creating support among skeptical members of a workgroup who saw the wins occur around them.

Shock-and-awe prescriptions to reward supporters and punish opponents receive mixed support. The strongest version of the shock-and-awe prescription—firing change opponents—was hardly tried. A separate paper growing out of this research provides evidence that downsizing, the closest the system came to shock-and-awe tactics by creating a crisis that might produce incentives for change, reduced both attitudinal support for the change and, independently, reform-oriented behavior change.[1] More natural employee replacement processes (the outflow of people leaving and the inflow of new local office heads, supervisors, and frontline employees to replace them) generally had small, albeit positive, effects, with the departure of a large number of reform-skeptical local office heads and their replacement by new ones producing a quite dramatic increase in reform support among local leaders. Finally, as demonstrated in chapter 9, material incentives did increase behavior change among reform critics. However, the negative impact of extrinsic incentives on intrinsic motivation show a downside to shock-and-awe prescriptions that its advocates do not acknowledge.

Most important, the guru prescriptions miss the role of positive feedback in consolidating change. John Kotter argues that the successful quality of early wins must be "unambiguous"—"there can be little argument over the call."[2] Certainly, success helps, and of course support will not continue to spread if faced with ongoing failure. However, many of the mechanisms of positive feedback—especially various elements of as-time-goes-by support—are set in motion simply by early action, even if such action is not unambiguously successful. So the findings in this book add to conventional prescriptions for consolidating change. By stressing the role of positive feedback, they emphasize the importance of leader persistence and energy injection in enabling positive feedback to help consolidate change support.

Positive Feedback and Organizational Change

I have identified eighteen feedback mechanisms—independent of a person's inherent experience with the change—that can encourage growth of both attitudinal support for an organizational change and the extent of behavior change. Some (such as operation of the learning curve and some personality or demographic traits that promote changes in attitude or behavior) begin with mere initiation of a change process and have only, or almost only, positive feedback effects. Other mechanisms with only positive feedback effects (such as mere exposure and foot-in-the-door) kick in with the mere passage of time a change effort persists. Still others (such as social influence, operation of the self-fulfilling prophecy, and perceptual confirmation) can create negative as well as positive feedback and do not necessarily generate positive feedback on balance. The data analysis supports the influence of virtually all the feedback effects discussed, and, except for the operation of perceptual confirmation, all ended up creating on balance positive feedback.[3]

Most of these mechanisms grow from general features of individual psychology or organization life rather than specific features of organizational change in procurement. These results should therefore be seen as generalizable to other change efforts until shown otherwise.

Positive feedback mechanisms shed light on the link between initial support for reform and the consolidation of support. In chapter 4 I note the strikingly high degree of initial reform support among local formal leaders (supervisors and office heads) and opinion leaders (most-respected co-worker and people who reported that they received an above-average number of requests for advice). The analysis of the consolidation of change shows that leaders' views were important feedback mechanisms.

Implications of a Positive Feedback Approach to Organizational Change

A positive feedback approach has three particular implications for studying organizational change. First, positive feedback provides a reason for a "bias for action" different from that enunciated by Thomas Peters and Robert Waterman.[4] This bias favors quick action when introducing new practices or changing existing ones, as opposed to developing a comprehensive plan before starting. Peters and Waterman argue for a bias for action, because gaining experience provides a way to figure out what works and what does not, so that adjustments can be made based on what has been learned.[5] By contrast, the reason for a bias for action suggested by a positive feedback approach is that, once change gets started, there will be forces encouraging the process to spread, just because it has gotten started.

Second, this approach improves the understanding of the role of formal and opinion leaders in organizational change. These leaders provided a number of the sources of positive feedback. They also were important in a different way, not captured in the models, by establishing a context in which feedback mechanisms could exert influence. The positive-feedback approach argues that the longer a change effort continues, the more change will become consolidated. The context provided by leaders is persistence and continual injection of energy into the system—keeping the effort going to allow positive feedback to operate until change has been consolidated. This takes time. It also takes continual injection of energy into the system.[6] As administrator of the Office of Federal Procurement Policy, I sought on an ongoing basis to establish both to persuade people to support reform (the results of which are measured with the systemwide leader influence variable in the models in chapter 8) and to send the message that reform was continuing.

The guru literature is forthright in the view (perhaps partly owing to the literature's audience) that leaders are crucial to sustaining change. Like some of the discussion in the present volume, this literature sees the leader role as, in part, influencing frontline attitudes.[7] Otherwise, the literature sees the leader role in sustaining change as similar to how it sees it in initiation—to make sure, by demonstrating commitment, that reluctant people understand that the effort is serious. Leaders are the only ones able "to compel the compliance of all parties involved." Communication of the leader's change message "must be relentless," not to persuade people (or at least this is not mentioned as a reason) but because "stopping [the message] could be interpreted as the end of executive commitment."[8] Kotter and others discuss the importance of the leader's nudging out (or firing) opponents and promoting supporters.[9]

Research on personality traits of successful leaders identifies persistence as one such trait.[10] The importance of leader persistence in achieving successful organizational change is frequently recognized, but it is generally seen as important for making opponents realize they cannot "wait out" the change.[11] ("Secretaries . . . come and go while the career services stay on. . . . Career officials can fight an unpopular order or change with the oldest and most lethal weapon in the arsenal of the public bureaucracy: delay.")[12] Here, instead, persistence allows positive feedback mechanisms to function.

One reason persistence is not often seen in change efforts in government is that senior political appointees usually have short tenures.[13] By contrast, I stayed at the Office of Federal Procurement Policy for four years and was replaced by a successor who shared my approach; Colleen Preston stayed three years and also was replaced by a like-minded successor. Similarly, a study of successful organizational change in the Environmental Protection Agency's Superfund program in the

1990s (and also part of reinventing government) notes that leaders of the effort stayed on the job for six years.[14]

A related important difference between procurement reform and many other change efforts in government is that the top leaders of the effort, Colleen Preston and I, had no other responsibilities.[15] Other top leaders have operating organizations to run. This makes it difficult for them to devote large blocks of time over sustained periods to an organizational change. The odds are high that something will come up to preoccupy the attention of a leader in charge of running an organization with ongoing operating responsibilities other than a change effort he or she might have launched. Preston and I were able to display a persistence that is hard for others to show. The contrast between us and the director of the Office of Personnel Management, operating in another area (civil service reform) where reinventing government had announced initiatives analogous to procurement reform, is instructive. The operating responsibilities of the head of that office included government hiring policy and running civil service pensions. He could not focus on civil service reform the same way we could focus on procurement reform. And unlike in procurement reform, legislative wrangling, owing to the partisan nature of union-management issues in civil service, prevented adoption of legislation, so new laws were unavailable to signal that civil service reform was more than a "flash in the pan."[16]

Third, a final implication of the existence of positive feedback in an organizational change process is that it creates the possibility that a version of so-called path dependence might occur. Path dependence is the idea that, because of positive feedback, "small and often accidental differences between two actors at an early stage can lead to enormous divergences later on."[17] Students of path dependence often find instances where the flow of events is strongly influenced by some unpredictable detail—such as the size of Cleopatra's nose, which, had it been different, might have made her less attractive to Marc Antony and thereby changed the course of history.

Most dramatically, in terms of explaining the ultimate success of an organizational change effort in one situation and its failure in another, an explanation based on path dependence would state that change succeeded in one situation and failed in another simply because it happened to have gotten started one place and not another. Explaining ultimate success would then simply be a matter of explaining successful initiation. Somewhat less dramatically, path dependence (and this has often been noted in the context of contagion models) suggests that relatively modest differences in initial conditions—such as small differences in what proportion of an organization consisted of early supporters—can produce large differences in final results. (It has, for example, been suggested that if a modest number of people had decided not to go out on the streets in East Germany in early 1989, mass demonstrations would never have been seen later that year.)

A strong version of path dependence would go too far in explaining the consolidation of procurement reform. Actual successful experience played a strong role in the spread of support. But the path dependence approach is a good antidote to the supposition that large end-state differences imply equally large going-in differences. As Robert Jervis puts it, "Looking back after the pattern is established, we may overestimate the degree of determinism involved."[18]

Perhaps the most important implication for practitioners of findings about positive feedback is the argument they provide for a bias for action. Chances for success are greater than one imagines. Leaders contemplating initiating a change effort might be disheartened to observe the large difference between their organizations and those that have successfully renewed themselves. A positive-feedback perspective should not lead practitioners to assume that the differences are unbreachable. These data also suggest that systemwide leaders, though far removed from the front lines, can nonetheless have a surprisingly large impact on frontline attitudes.

Extrinsic Incentives, Intrinsic Motivation, and Behavior Change

The message to be careful in using extrinsic incentives—something of a critique of shock-and-awe prescriptions—may apply especially in the context of government. First, compared to firms, government agencies typically can offer relatively weak incentives, and many are "engagement-contingent" rewards people get just for showing up, which the literature regards as most strongly depressing intrinsic motivation. If the net effect of extrinsic incentives to the intrinsically motivated is incentivizing minus undermining, the results will depend on the size of extrinsic incentives available: to quote the title of one article, "Pay enough or don't pay at all."[19] If undermining partly reflects unease at behaving for selfish reasons, it may be greater for government employees, given empirical evidence, presented in a different context in chapter 3, that government is more likely to attract those who seek to serve others and thus would tend be more upset with themselves about undertaking behavior for selfish reasons.[20]

Given the need for caution, what prescriptions might be offered about how leaders should try to influence employee behavior? One suggestion is for leaders to work to influence underlying attitudes, either directly or by encouraging successful experience. Attitudinal change produces behavior change without extrinsic incentives. Evidence presented in chapters 4 and 8 suggests that first-line supervisors had little direct influence on attitudes, probably because they were not respected as supervisors. One study shows a dramatic difference between how young employees in federal government offices and those in Fortune 500 firms evaluated the quality of the supervision they received.[21] Improving the quality of supervision may increase the chances of successful organizational change in government.

Second, the data show a clear positive impact of incentives for skeptics. It is plausible to believe—though no studies seem to exist on this— that supervisors tend to spend more time with those who are sympathetic to what the supervisor is trying to do than with critics. Doing so would respond to a natural tendency to prefer the company of others who are "like us" and reduce the number of unpleasant situations one experiences. So the advice is to fight this tendency and instead concentrate supervisory attention on skeptics and critics.[22]

What about influencing supporter behavior? It is not feasible (and would not be just) for supervisors to refrain from giving extrinsic rewards to intrinsically motivated high performers, squirreling them instead for skeptics.[23] Given the competence-affirming impact of establishing performance standards, which enhances intrinsic motivation, managers would be wise to look for opportunities to establish such standards. Second, studies of the impact of praise on intrinsic motivation show that relatively small changes in the wording of feedback can have large effects on whether praise encourages or undermines intrinsic motivation.[24] Chapter 9 reports dramatic differences in the impact of work-group praise on intrinsic motivation based on whether it was given in a pressuring or nonpressuring environment. The most important advice is therefore for the manager, when providing the intrinsically motivated with extrinsic rewards, to pay attention to the words surrounding those rewards. The supervisor might, for example, take pains to note verbally that the supervisor knows the employee is not "doing it for the money" but because it is the right thing to do and that the money (or promotion or praise) is simply a signal that others recognize and value the employee's competence. If part of the reason extrinsic rewards undermine intrinsic motivation is that they cause behavior to become associated with selfishness, leaders should also take pains to emphasize the importance of the organization's public purpose and make statements to the effect that "the most important reward is to serve the public."[25]

Deepening of Support

Leaders of change movements with an agenda for promoting the public good (or, in a private sector context, the greater organizational good) face the additional challenge of achieving deepening among supporters whose initial backing was based on a personal agenda. This was a challenge reform leaders faced. The results presented in chapter 10 suggest that those leaders enjoyed some success. One lesson is that deepening was the way those seeking personal benefits paid back their leaders, without realizing themselves what they were doing, for delivering the benefits of reform they had hoped for.

There were important limits to what deepening did occur. The quantitatively more significant deepening was passive, not active—people were not consciously aware it had occurred. It resulted significantly from categorization and as-time-goes-by support, the two sources of deepening least involving conscious processes and hence explicit awareness, compared with, for example, having been persuaded of the importance of the better-value agenda by leaders. In this sense, deepening was less a choice made *by* people and more something happening *to* them.

The extent to which deepening occurred through leader visioning and sense-giving—of the kind discussed in the literature on leadership—varied depending on whether deepening was active or passive. Leaders, especially local leaders, played a more important role in promoting active than passive deepening, where less conscious factors were more important. However, leaders also influenced deepening indirectly, rather than through visioning or sense-giving. By persisting in the change effort rather than losing interest and moving to other things, systemwide leaders continued long enough for as-time-goes-by support to encourage deepening. Furthermore, proreform local leaders played a modest role in promoting successful experience with reform, which, in turn, was found here to promote deepening. These differences in leader influence between active and passive deepening, and the alternative routes for leader impact, refine existing theories emphasizing visioning and sense-giving as sources of leader influence during a change process.

Ference Marton and Shirley Booth describe learning as the ability to discern "aspects of the phenomenon other than those [a learner] had been capable of discerning before. . . . When this occurs, the learner's awareness of the phenomenon has changed, and it appears different from before."[26] A good deal of deepening seems to have involved less awareness; and in this sense learning, for these people, was less significant than it might have been. One would also suspect that less awareness of changes occurring inside oneself would, in turn, mean less translation of new attitudes into new behavior. In this regard, leader influence, which (certainly with regard to local leaders) had a more important influence on active than on passive deepening, may have produced converts fewer in number but higher in quality.

Ten Years After

As discussed at the end of chapter 8, forces may appear late in a change process that limit or even reverse the operation of positive feedback in promoting the growth of change support. Additionally, one can easily imagine that substantive experience with a change might start getting worse, also acting to halt or reverse change support. Generically, this might happen for two reasons. First, top leaders might start promoting inappropriate changes, producing experiences more negative than earlier ones. This might occur because leaders introduced the most promising changes early, so that after a while the most beneficial changes have been "taken," leaving only more doubtful ones. Leaders might also become "giddy with success," believing successful experience with earlier changes suggests that more marginal, risky ones might produce good experience as well.[27] Furthermore, as James March writes, "Individuals are normally elevated to positions of decision-making authority by virtue of their ability to handle future events," leading them to underestimate the risks of failure in actions they undertake.[28] Given psychological forces acting on successful leaders, avoiding giddiness with success is easier said than done.

Second, as Christopher Hood argues, every approach to public management that emphasizes one side of an issue—such as, in the case of procurement reform, a focus on mission accomplishment more than abuse—will tend to produce problems as the other side gets ignored. This will occur because "'blind spots' built in to any one approach are likely to become more severe the more entrenched it is" or because "resistance from those who espouse alternative preferences about how to organize are likely to increase as any one form of organization becomes dominant." Problems appearing along the neglected dimension will encourage the view that change has started producing less-successful experience. This is at the root of the idea of "pendulum swings."[29]

There is an additional challenge to any change effort the longer it goes on. Institutionalizing a change within an organizational system does not mean an end to history. External political pressures—whether systematic or appearing randomly—influence what goes on inside agencies. A change may succeed in consolidating itself inside an organization, but this does not ensure its survival if new winds buffet it from the outside. The laws of chance suggest that the longer a change effort continues, the greater the chances that a shift in political winds will at some point occur.

In the years after Bill Clinton left office, political winds around procurement began to shift toward greater attention to abuse. Partly, this occurred for random reasons. The Bush administration's priority procurement issue had nothing to do, one way or another, with issues procurement reform had addressed. Instead, the focus was on increasing the use of job competitions between government employees and private contractors to decide who should perform government work. This was made the chief job for the new Office of Federal Procurement Policy administrator, so senior political interest in the health of the procurement system itself subsided dramatically in favor of attention to these job competitions. Furthermore, the person the administration named to run the procurement office was a young lawyer who, like many procurement lawyers, was a proponent of the traditional system. Her appointment had nothing to do with her views on procurement reform (she had strong family ties to President Bush). But she immediately announced an approach she dubbed "back to basics," by which she meant seeking a return to the traditional focus on controlling abuse rather than newfangled ideas about mission support and better value. While new political leadership in the Defense Department sought to continue reform, overall the new administration's interest in procurement management declined dramatically, at best leaving the system to its own devices. Moreover, during the Bush administration (mainly owing to increased defense and homeland security spending), total dollars spent on procurement increased by half, after remaining stable throughout the 1990s, while the size of the procurement workforce, already downsized, remained the same (it actually declined very slightly). This put workload strains on employees, increasing the chances that contracting errors would make the system perform worse, thereby reducing the benefits reform had realized.

The most serious challenge to reform came from a move to use procurement abuse, real or alleged, as a partisan political issue. From the perspective of the procurement system, the emergence of procurement as a partisan issue was random, in the sense that the system itself did not generate it.

The political system had never lost interest in abuse. But now abuse took on a partisan edge. Partly, this came as an unintended consequence of the effort to increase public-private competitions for jobs held by government employees. The understandably vociferous opposition of federal employee unions to this shift created a situation in which an important organized group developed a vested interest in a procurement system that worked badly (or appeared to work badly), since a bad procurement system could not be trusted to manage contracts with private sector winners of these job competitions. So unions began to oppose procurement reform, which had been trying to improve the system, and to play up allegations of abuse that made the system look bad. Democrats, in opposition, toed the unions' line. Then, in the run-up to the 2004 presidential campaign and debates over Iraq policy, Democrats discovered an issue in allegations that Halliburton, the company formerly headed by Vice President Richard Cheney, had illegitimately received large Iraq contracts and was cheating the government under the contracts. Virtually every expert dismissed these claims. But the accusations brought procurement abuse to the center of attention.

Some of reform's wounds were self-inflicted, a version of becoming giddy with success. Reform leaders avoided one manifestation of this problem, which would have been pursuing new reforms of marginal or negative value: my successor wisely made her priority "implementation" of existing reforms rather than adding new ones. However, leaders were guilty of another kind of giddy-with-success failure, the problem of blind spots Hood discusses. In their eagerness to switch the system's focus from abuse to mission accomplishment, reformers (including me) were insufficiently vigilant about abuse problems that, though they should not have been the system's focus, should form the boundaries inside which mission goals may be pursued.[30] Reports thus started emerging of instances of abuse of government-provided credit cards by government employees and of contracts awarded using streamlined procurement vehicles where there was only one bid. In a situation especially toxic because it involved the Iraq war, the Army was discovered to have procured private interrogators for Iraqi prisons by improperly using a contract intended for buying information-technology services, and some of the interrogators were among those found, in the context of a broader scandal involving the military's behavior in Iraq, to have tortured prisoners.

The renewed attention to abuse had two effects. First, it caused at least some on the front lines to revise their views of how successful experience with reform had been, which would, of course, affect support for change. More important, it created a situation where attention was directed to the issue central to the traditional system, not to the reformed one. Not surprisingly, attention to abuse produced demands for a "crackdown," along with suggestions that reform had gone too far in eliminating controls and in becoming oriented to satisfying program customers, thereby promoting abuse.

Reformers were mistaken not to have acted more forcefully from the beginning to tend the condition of the system's boundaries. There is a broader lesson here for debureaucratizing change efforts, since many of them share with procurement reform the basic feature of attempting to reorient abuse-oriented systems to results-oriented ones. The lesson is that attention to an ongoing battle against abuse is important for long-run political sustainability. Civil service reformers in the Bush administration did a better job on this than procurement reformers had, emphasizing vigilance against hiring abuse ("protecting the merit system") from the beginning.

As of this writing (spring 2005), more than a decade after procurement reform was launched, its fate at the hands of the political system was, then, uncertain. Virtually all the specific changes reform had brought were still intact. Furthermore, despite many real or alleged "scandals," reform had become rooted enough that it had not, as a result of the scandals, simply been swept away like a house of straw: in the era of the traditional system, so focused on abuse, the huff and puff of a lone scandal was enough to blow the house down, generating additional rules and hierarchy. The strongest continued support for reform came from procurement officials and program customers, testimony to the institutionalization of reform inside the system. However, reform also had political defenders, including members of Congress and staff involved in the original effort and many in the information-technology industry and other nontraditional vendors whose relationship with government had been improved by reform.

A number of crucial elements of reform, such as using past performance in selecting bidders, Defense Department use of commercial rather than milspec items, and performance-based contracting (interestingly, all part of the better-value agenda), had survived attack and seemed certain to endure. It appeared unlikely that agencies would again be willing to accept waiting six months for a desktop computer or two years to hire a company to develop a new software application. But the spirit of frontline empowerment and innovation had dissipated, largely replaced by caution and fear. Furthermore, increased workload pressures made it more difficult for people to find time for innovation, and the number of new contracting approaches the system generated had dramatically declined.

The interested reader may wish, on finishing this book, to see what is going on in procurement at the time he or she reads it. However procurement looks, it is hard to imagine it will not be different from how it would have looked had reform never renewed the system.

Specifying Models and Determinants

Specifying a Model Explaining Support for Job Autonomy

Desire to Choose or Exercise Judgment

Desire to choose or exercise judgment: This was measured by the statement, "I prefer work that requires original thinking."*

Education and job level: Two questions asked respondents to indicate the highest level of schooling attained, from high school to a doctoral degree,[1] and their job level, from "purchasing agent" (the lowest job category) through "contract specialist," "nonsupervisory contracting officer," and "supervisor."

Affluence: Respondents were asked their age. The link between age (logged) and desire for original work tested for the postmaterialism hypothesis.

Venturesomeness or risk tolerance: A scale consisting of four questions measured venturesomeness or risk tolerance. The questions were "I like to explore a strange city or section of town by myself, even if it means getting lost";* "When I go on a trip, I like to plan my route and timetable fairly carefully"; "I generally like to stick with the same brands of food or other consumer products I buy"; and "I can't

---

*Here and in subsequent models, an asterisk (*) after the measure indicates the variable was reverse coded to make interpretation of results more intuitive.

understand people who risk their necks climbing mountains"* (alpha = .47).[2]

Deference: A scale was developed from three questions: "It is easy for me to take orders and do what I am told"; "I believe in showing respect for people in authority by my attitude and manner"; and "I'm the kind of person who never acts without proper authority"* (alpha = .56).

Self-confidence: This was measured using the statement, "When I make plans, I am almost certain that I can make them work."*

In addition, the model tested variables that might lead a person to wish to exercise choice or judgment and thus be indirectly linked with desire for autonomy, by testing for whether they predicted higher desire for a job with original thinking. These included the results-orientation variables discussed below, as well as education and job level.

Desire for Burden Reduction

High job burdens: If people feeling overworked and stressed on the job show a greater desire for autonomy, it may be inferred they seek autonomy to reduce overwork. The measure of workload and stress came from two questions, part of a larger series where respondents were asked to agree or disagree with statements about their jobs and were also asked to recall what their attitudes had been five years earlier. The statements were "The workload is very high on my job"* and "My job is very stressful."* Responses to the two recall questions were combined to form a scale (alpha = .70).

Desire to work less: If people seeking to minimize work done on the job show a greater desire for autonomy, one may infer they seek autonomy to avoid controls to make them work harder. The desire to minimize work was measured by the statement, "I'm very strongly driven to succeed at my job,"* where lack of orientation toward success meant a desire to minimize work.[3]

Desire to Produce Better Organizational Results

The variables tested, both for direct links to a desire for autonomy and for links mediated through the desire to choose or exercise judgment, included reasons to be interested in producing better organizational results.[4] If interest in generating better results was associated with desire for autonomy, it can be inferred that the respondent seeks autonomy to generate better results:

Impact: This was measured by the statement, "How I do my job has a big impact on how well our agency performs its mission."*[5]

Desire to innovate: This was measured with a statement about another on the list of job features discussed above (in the context of job burdens), "I like to come up on my own with ways to do my job better."* In contrast to the question about liking a job with original work, this directly measured interest in applying the desire to choose specifically to developing innovative ways to do one's job, rather than just to exercise judgment in the context of existing ways of doing business.

Interest in substantive goals promoted by greater autonomy: This was measured with two other statements from the list of job features, "We generally get procurements or mods [contract modifications] accomplished in a timely manner," and "We generally get contractors who end up performing well."[6]

Idealism: Idealists care about creating a better world and thus might be expected to be interested in producing better value for the government. An idealist who values job autonomy would presumably agree that a less bureaucratic system would yield a better world. Idealism was measured with the statement, "I would rather be called an idealist than a practical person."*

Drive to succeed: The same question about being driven to succeed at one's job used to test for association between the desire to avoid work and a desire for autonomy was also used to test the opposite hypothesis. If the relationship between success orientation and desire for autonomy were the opposite of the one presented earlier, this would suggest an opposite conclusion.*[7]

Abstraction ability: The model tested for a direct path between support for autonomy and both education and job levels, to see whether effects of these two factors occurred through greater ability to develop an abstract conception of the public good. A direct relationship between these variables and desire for autonomy would then reflect the impact of a desire for better organization results.

Other Variables Explaining Support for Job Autonomy

Psychological traits: Venturesomeness or risk tolerance, deference, and self-confidence might be directly related to support for autonomy, as well as indirectly through the desire to exercise choice or judgment because they affect the cost of autonomy (so that, controlling for benefits autonomy might provide, one becomes more or less inclined to seek it). For example, as noted in chapter 2, rules and hierarchy provide an excuse for failure ("I followed the rules"). One would therefore expect risk-averse people to be more inclined to worry about autonomy.

Commitment to traditional system values from long exposure: Many factors promoting support for the traditional system's values (in this case, lack of autonomy) increase the longer one has been exposed to them. Exposure was measured using the number of years of experience (logged) the respondent had been working in procurement for the government.[8]

Specifying Determinants of Reform Coalition Membership

The following variables, a number of which are the same as in the models explaining the desire for job autonomy in chapter 3, were used to specify the determinants of membership in the reform coalition.[9]

Sources of Discontent with the Traditional System

Desire for job autonomy: The variables measuring desire for job autonomy and dislike of rules were used.

Support for total quality management and customer service: Two questions were used. First, the traditional system was hostile toward the program customer, and so support for the traditional system was measured by the question, "The most important job of the contracting professional is to make sure that program people follow the rules." A higher value therefore reflected greater support for the alternate philosophy TQM represented. Second, since a person accepting TQM was likely to be sensitive to program customers' criticisms that the system was too slow, the question used to measure the impact of customer-service orientation was the timeliness variable, used earlier, measuring the extent to which the respondent was discontented with the timeliness of service the system provided.[10]

High job burdens: The job burden variable, used earlier, tested for the influence of job burden and stress.

Discontent with the ideology of the traditional system and support for better value from contracting: A number of variables were used to measure support for a better value from contracting ideology. The most important were the idealism and the dissatisfaction-with-poor-contractors variables, used earlier. Also, the traditional system's emphasis on rules and hierarchy was based on distrust (of contractors and program people, and by external overseers of procurement people, as well). Procurement reform, which tried to move to an emphasis on mission rather than compliance, assumed that people were somewhat more worthy of trust. It was therefore hypothesized that the extent to which an individual had an underlying trust of people in general might predict ideological opposition to the traditional system. The model therefore included a scale with four questions on trust.[11]

On the view that idealism or trustfulness might be more likely to be translated into change vanguard membership among those with greater abstraction ability—making it easier to conceive of an abstract ideological alternative to the existing system—the model tested for an interaction (multiplicative) effect between idealism and job level (also education) in predicting change vanguard membership. The same interactions were tested for the trust scale.

Early-Adopter Variables

Venturesomeness or risk tolerance: The venturesomeness scale, used earlier to measure interest in job autonomy, here measured something else—the willingness to take the risk of signing up to a new, untried organizational change.[12]

Abstraction ability: Job level and education both tested for the impact of an ability to think about states of the world that do not yet exist. In both cases, the worry existed that these variables would not just test for abstraction ability but might also reflect (going in the other direction, toward support of the traditional system) reward by and (in the case of people gaining a government-paid education) gratefulness to the traditional system.

Cosmopolitanism: This was measured through three factors: the question, "I try to keep up with the statements being made about acquisition issues by the top acquisition leadership of my agency and the White House";*[13] whether the respondent read *Federal Contracts Report*, the main weekly covering procurement, thus a measure of exposure to outside procurement-related media; and whether the respondent was a member of the National Contract Management Association, the professional association for people in government contracting. In addition, a sociability scale, with statements measuring whether a respondent was a loner versus liking socializing with his or her workgroup,[14] tested whether reform coalition members were "strangers" or deviants, orienting to the outside world because they did not fit in with the local one.

Self-efficacy: This was measured with two variables. Everett M. Rogers discusses whether an individual feels efficacious achieving outcomes for personal decisions.[15] The self-confidence variable, used earlier, was used to test for this. However, since what was at stake here was support for changing *organizational* practices, the model also measured whether a respondent felt efficacious assisting a *collective* effort—the ability, as it is often phrased, to "make a difference." The question measuring collective self-efficacy was, "No matter how wonderful the ideas you are trying to get across may be, you cannot do a thing unless you have the powers that be on your side." A higher value showed greater belief that one could make a difference.

Finally, two possible early-adopter personality traits not appearing in the diffusion-of-innovation literature were also tested:

Rebelliousness: This was measured by the statement, "I am by nature a rebellious person."*[16]

Idealism: In addition to measuring support for a better-value ideology, those considering themselves idealistic might be more willing to join the change vanguard because of willingness to support "lost causes."[17]

Personality, Attitude, and Demographic Factors Creating Resistance to Change

General resistance to change: One recall question asked respondents to agree or disagree with the statement, "The first times I tried out some of the new acquisition reform ideas I felt very uncertain about whether I was doing them the right way."* This question was used to capture influence of all the sources of resistance to change discussed in chapter 2, controlling for specific sources of resistance discussed below.[18]

Job longevity: Support for the traditional system might come from having been exposed to it longer, measured by the job longevity (logged) variable.[19]

Impact of authority and power relationships: One source of support for an organizational status quo comes from the positions of authority that supporters of a traditional system enjoy. One would expect that the more deferent a respondent felt toward authority, the stronger his or her support for the traditional system would be. The models therefore included the deference scale, discussed earlier. One would also expect the more a respondent cared about career advancement, the greater his or her support for the traditional system, which those controlling advancement upheld. The model therefore included the question about being strongly driven to succeed at one's job, with the "at one's job" part of the question emphasized here, as compared with the "driven" part in the job autonomy model in chapter 3.

Fear of external criticism: One source of resistance to changing bureaucracy in government is the protection that rules and hierarchy provide against criticism. The recall questions on job characteristics included the statement, "I feel a high level of anxiety about the potential of critical reports from the IG [agency inspector general] or other auditors or investigators."* Such fear might promote support for bureaucracy and hence resistance to change.

Leader Influence Variables

Local office head reform attitude: A variable measuring this was developed based on information gathered from the In-Person Interviews and other sources; it took either the value 1 (local office head a member of the change vanguard) or 0 (everybody else); that value was assigned to each respondent in the office.[20]

Immediate supervisor reform attitude: Respondents were asked, "Which of the following statements *most closely* describes the overall attitude of *your immediate supervisor* towards acquisition reform?"* Alternatives were "enthusiastic," "somewhat supportive," "somewhat skeptical," and "critical."[21]

Social Influence Variables

Most-respected co-worker reform attitude: Respondents were asked, "Please think about the person (nonsupervisor) whom you respect most in your organization for his or her skills as a procurement professional. Which of the following statements *most closely* describes *that person's* attitude towards acquisition reform?"* There were eight possible responses, ranging from "an early enthusiast and evangelist for acquisition reform" to "a vocal critic."[22]

Size of the change vanguard in one's workgroup: At the workgroup level, a value was calculated representing the percentage who were members of the change vanguard, which was assigned to each respondent in the workgroup.[23]

Testing for the Burning-Platform Theory

Some version of a "crisis" occurred just before reform began in some buying offices but not in others, allowing a test for the hypothesis that people need to experience a "burning platform" to be willing to embrace change. After the end of the defense buildup in the late 1980s, a gradual downsizing of the Defense Department procurement work-force began in 1990, through attrition.[24] No downsizing had occurred in civilian agencies. Defense Department downsizing was modest, so one cannot speak of a severe crisis. Nonetheless, the model included a dummy variable for whether the respondent worked for Defense Department (1) or a civilian agency (0). Second, in 1992 the Defense Logistics Agency, two of whose offices were in the sample, ceased to receive appropriated funds and became dependent for resources on orders from Defense Department customers (who paid a fee to order through them). These offices' traditional source of revenue thus disappeared. So a dummy variable was included measuring whether the respondent worked for the Defense Logistics Agency.[25]

Specifying a Model Explaining Feedback Influences on Successful Experience

Leader and Co-worker Behavioral Facilitation

Supervisor attitude[26]
Local office head attitude[27]
Most-respected co-worker attitude[28]
Percentage of workgroup in the change vanguard[29]

Performance-Promoting Personality and Demographic Characteristics

Personality traits: drive to succeed, self-confidence, working late (measured by response to the question, "I often work late"*), and mission impact.[30] All four were assumed to create negative as well as positive feedback.

Demographic characteristics: Education and job level were tested to see the impact of competence in success at learning new behavior (the latter since people at higher job levels had probably demonstrated greater ability to perform tasks). People at higher job levels would also have gotten more experience performing nonroutine tasks, giving them greater experiential resources as well.

The Self-Fulfilling Prophecy

In the first-experience model, expectation was determined by the variable measuring initial reform attitude (did the respondent try it only because asked).*[31] In the overall-experience models, the following survey question was used to measure expectation based on first experience: "My first experiences trying out acquisition reform ideas were quite negative."*

Perceptual Confirmation

Perceptual confirmation was measured by the distortion variable presented in chapter 7, where values greater than zero represent a tendency of prochange people to distort experience in a prochange direction, while values less than zero represent a tendency of antichange people to distort experience in an antichange direction.[32]

Testing for Variables Where Impact on Experience Can Be Both Positive and Negative

For feedback mechanisms generating negative as well as positive feedback, it can be calculated whether, given actual distribution of values in the sample, the mechanism, empirically, on balance generated positive feedback. This involves testing for asymmetries and their impact on the balance of positive or negative feedback. Asymmetries can be tested for by seeing whether the relationship between the predictor and the dependent variable is nonlinear. If the impact of the variable is symmetric, the relationship between it and the dependent variable will be linear (the effect of the variable will be the same at all its values). If it is asymmetric, the variable will have a larger impact on the dependent variable at lower than at higher values, or vice versa, which would appear as a nonlinear relationship. Nonlinearity exists if there is a statistically significant quadratic—that is, squared—term. For all variables in these models where feedback might be negative as well as positive, the model therefore tested for a quadratic term.

If asymmetry promotes, for the sample as a whole, successful experience (or, in the model later in chapter 7, reform support), the variable will improve mean experience or attitude at a mean sample value less than the variable's neutral value. If asymmetry worsens change experience or attitude, a sample mean value greater than the neutral value would be needed.[33] For an asymmetric variable, it is possible to calculate, given the actual distribution in the sample of values for the variable, whether the variable's overall effect is to increase or decrease successful experience and reform support, compared with a hypothetical linear model where the variable had a neutral effect.[34]

Control Variables

There are alternative explanations for a connection between expectation and experience which must be controlled for. First, one would expect that how a person values the substance of a change will influence his or her experience: racists are less likely to experience exposure to an integrated environment as positively as the unprejudiced, since they regard mixing across racial lines negatively. In the procurement reform context, people desiring autonomy, or other substantive reform ideas, would be expected to experience changes enhancing these values differently from those who did not. Since support for autonomy, fast customer service, and reduced job burdens also influenced expectations, a potential omitted variable bias is created.[35] So the model included job autonomy, dissatisfaction with untimely customer service, and job burden and stress as controls.[36] It also included the dummy variable for working in the Defense Department, since this was associated with a negative initial reform attitude, controlling for these other factors (see chapter 4).[37] Finally, the distortion variable also controlled for distortion in self-reports for supervisor and most-respected co-worker attitude.

Overall Experience as the Dependent Variable

This model was similar to the one predicting initial experience. The only variable added measured the extent to which the respondent had received training that might have facilitated development of skills in turn promoting successful experience.[38] This was constructed using survey questions asking whether the respondent had received training that might be relevant to reform. Six possible training sources were listed (such as "off-site courses," "off-site conferences," and "the Internet or CD/ROMs"). For each type of training, the respondent was asked to identify whether he or she had received "acquisition training generally" or "acquisition *reform* training specifically" (or both). Four of the six forms of training were selected for inclusion in a scale representing how much training an individual had received.[39]

Also, the variable measuring the percentage of workgroup members in the change vanguard was replaced by a mean workgroup reform attitude variable measuring the mean current reform attitude of the respondent's workgroup.[40]

Specifying a Model of Organizational Feedback Influences on Reform Support

Social Influence

Mean workgroup reform attitude

Intragroup attitude consensus: One view is that the greater the level of agreement within a group (what David Chan calls "climate strength"),[41] the greater the peer influence. This was measured by calculating the standard deviation of the workgroup's reform attitude around the mean attitude.[42] To test whether greater consensus had an effect, an interaction between mean attitude and consensus was tested.

Most-respected co-worker attitude

In discussing influences on successful experience, it was argued that the mechanisms presented above could only generate positive feedback—that it was unlikely an unsympathetic most-respected co-worker would sabotage successful experience, only fail to help produce it. However, for attitude influence, these mechanisms are also assumed to be able to generate negative as well as positive feedback.

Leadership Variables

Supervisor attitude
Local office head attitude
Systemwide procurement leadership influence

In addition, the model tested for interactions between deference toward authority and leader attitudes, to see whether deference increased leader effects. As with peer influence mechanisms, leader influence was assumed to be capable of generating negative as well as positive feedback.

Training

Mere leader persistence: The following question was used: "We have been getting a consistent message from our leadership about acquisition reform for a long time now."* This allows testing for influence of mere leader persistence, controlling for influence through the content of what leaders are saying.

Personal benefits and "going with a winner": These were measured with three questions: "I'm very strongly driven to succeed at my job,"* "Being seen by my supervisor as 'pro-acquisition reform' is good for my career,"*[43] and "In this department, the organizations with the highest status are generally the ones people think have gone the furthest with acquisition reform."*

External locus of control: This was measured using the question, "Sometimes I feel that I don't have enough control over the direction my life is taking." As with the impact of deference, this is an ironic hypothesis, since, as a policy, reform sought to give people more control over their lives; it would be ironic if those less inclined to see themselves as in control become stronger supporters of reform.[44]

Early Wins

The impact of a respondent's own initial experience was measured through the first-experience variable. The impact of workgroup early wins on individual attitude was measured by developing a value for mean workgroup first experience, the same way analogous variables had been developed for mean workgroup reform attitude, which was assigned to each individual in the workgroup.[45]

Control Variables

Successful experience: A number of the variables in this model also appeared in the model explaining overall experience. The experience variables (empowerment, burden reduction, and getting best value) were therefore included as controls. Thus the model tests for direct impact of organizational feedback variables on attitude, over and above any indirect effect through explaining successful experience.

Distortion: This was included to control for any tendency to interpret the most-respected co-worker's or supervisor's attitude to be consistent with one's own, as well as for any similar influence regarding consistent message perception and career-enhancement perception.

Self-confidence: This was included as a control for impact of locus of control.

Testing for Asymmetries

All variables expected to generate negative as well as positive feedback were tested for significant quadratic terms.

Specifying a Model Explaining Influences on Behavior Change

Individual Attitudes and Personality Traits

The individual-level influences tested were the same as in the initial and overall experience models in chapter 8. These were self-confidence, drive to succeed at one's job, how much the respondent felt work had a significant impact on agency mission accomplishment, the extent the respondent worked late, education, and job level.

The model also included both reform attitude (using the 0–100 feeling thermometer) and attitude strength (measured by a reform support quadratic term to test for a curvilinear relationship).

Organizational Influences

Many of the same variables used to test for organizational influences on attitude were used to test for influence on behavior. To test for undermining effects or the effects of nonmaterial workgroup incentives, interactions with the respondent's own reform attitude were tested for the following variables: supervisor attitude, local office head attitude, mean workgroup attitude, most-respected co-worker attitude, headquarters pressure, and centralization. A triple interaction between mean workgroup attitude, workgroup consensus, and respondent's own reform attitude was also tested.

Central Pressure and Centralization

Central pressure: The following question was used: "I don't perceive any pressure from outside this office to pursue acquisition reform aggressively."

Centralization: The following question was used: "Regulations and policies promulgated at department headquarters have a very strong influence over how I do my job."*

Control Variables

Distortion: As earlier, this was used to control for perceptual confirmation, whereby reform supporters might perceive their behavior had changed a great deal while opponents might perceive few changes as having taken place.[46]

Creative work: People liking jobs involving creative work might, in a reform environment encouraging innovation, change behavior more. Since this attitude is correlated with attitudinal support for reform, as well as with a number of other variables in the model, this variable was included to control for the impact of that personality trait.

Also, the reform attitude variable controlled for the effect of the various organizational influences through their impact on attitude.

Specifying Determinants of Deepening

Leader Support for Better Value

Systemwide procurement leader influence

Local office head deepening activities: To examine whether local office heads had attempted to get a "deepened" message about the meaning of reform across to employees, I asked them the following question in the In-Person Interviews: "My data show that in many organizations, some working-level people see acquisition reform mainly in terms of awarding contracts faster and making their jobs easier. Yet you can certainly interpret acquisition reform much more broadly than that. Have you at all noticed that in your organization? If so, is there anything you've done to encourage your people to see the goals of acquisition reform more broadly?"

Some attempting to get a "deepened" message across gave these answers:

I have noticed that this is a problem. What you try to do is to get them to see beyond this and ask them why are they doing this in the first place. The answer is that it's to make sure the war fighter has the best equipment. We're in business to keep these folks alive and so that the U.S. will be victorious in any conflict.

I work to get that message across through a family day every year, where we bring in soldiers to demo equipment to contracting people, and their parents and families and kids. Our people can hear the soldiers say, "This stuff works for us." After Desert Storm, I brought in some people to say to our folks, "Here's what you bought, here's how it helped us." And I send some people to the National Training Center to see how soldiers are using our equipment. At every town meeting, I run a short Army film showing the Army in action, films where they're using our equipment. The message is, we're not just here writing contracts, what we write has an effect on the people protecting their country.

If you go back to what most of us see as the goals of reform, acquisition reform makes your job harder. You have to be willing to assimilate a lot more information—judgmental factors, information you must obtain and evaluate. We've spent a lot of time facilitating people adapting to that.

Neither "easier" nor "faster" is a primary objective. My stated objectives have been to make the business of government more businesslike and to enrich people's jobs.

Using responses to this question, a variable was constructed. Three of the nineteen offices were coded 3, signifying strong efforts by local office heads to promote reform goals going beyond burden reduction, eight were coded 2, for moderate efforts, and eight were coded 1, for no efforts. This value was assigned to each individual in the office.

Immediate supervisor reform attitude: Since a proreform supervisor might not have supported the better-value agenda—the supervisor may have been strongly proreform but only to gain autonomy or reduce burdens—results are conservative.[47]

Successful Experience

The success stories question was used to test successful experience. This was not specifically for "success stories" related to innovativeness or better-value contracting; the respondent may have experienced only successes involving reform elements that had been empowering or made the job easier. So this did not exactly test the specific impact of successful experiences with better-value elements of reform. These results should thus be regarded as a conservative test.[48]

As-Time-Goes-By Support

The variable for as-time-goes-by support was used. For the same reasons as with the success stories variable, this does not provide an exact test of the impact of as-time-goes-by support, and the results should be seen as conservative.

Categorization

It was a challenge to create a variable measuring development and strength of a positive category "procurement reform," given that people would not be consciously aware of its existence. The strategy used was to create a variable based on the questions asking respondents about different reform ideas such as past performance and milspec reform. Before being asked whether they "personally feel this is a good idea," respondents had been given the same list of eighteen ideas, with the following instructions: "Here is a list of various ideas. For each idea, indicate the extent to which you associate the idea with acquisition reform, independently of whether you personally feel the idea is a good one or not."[49]

The categorization variable was created by comparing similarity of responses on questions about the centrality of the various ideas with questions about the respondent's personal opinion about them. Thus a respondent might personally "strongly disagree" that using past performance was a good idea (code 1 on that question) but believe it was central to reform (code 7 on that one). A respondent's value for categorization was the mean absolute value of differences between the respondent's personal opinion regarding each of the eighteen ideas and the respondent's view of how central each was to reform. Thus (to oversimplify the case of two ideas), if a respondent's personal opinion on past performance was 7 and view of centrality was also 7, while the respondent's opinion on milspec reform was 5 and view of its centrality 3, the respondent value for categorization would be 1.[50]

This variable unobtrusively measures the presence or strength of a positively valenced category "procurement reform." When people have categories available, they use bits of information about particular instances to place them into categories. Once such categorization has occurred, it triggers knowledge structure–based processing for thinking about the instance. If a person had a positive attitude toward a procurement-related idea and had developed a positively valenced category "procurement reform," the person would be likely to use the information ("this is a procurement-related idea I like") to classify the instance as an example of the category ("procurement reform," consisting of good procurement-related ideas). The result would be high correspondence between liking a procurement-related idea and viewing it as central to reform.[51] Absent the underlying category, there is no reason to believe there should be anything but a random connection between one's personal opinion of, say, past performance and how central one thought the idea was to reform. Presence of correspondence provides evidence for existence of the category. Thus the lower the value of categorization (reflecting high correspondence between personal agreement and perception of centrality), the greater the positively valenced category "procurement reform." As the value of categorization increases, positively valenced categorization strength decreases; very high values suggest a negatively valenced category—the more one likes a policy, the less one associates it with reform.[52] To make results more intuitive, the variable was reverse coded.

Control Variables

One reason for variance in current support for the better-value agenda would be variance in early support for that agenda. Another might be variance in propensity to embrace better-value goals after learning about them. There was evidence from the Frontline Survey and the In-Person Interviews that early support for better value was associated with idealism. To measure both sources of variance in support for the better-value agenda, the model therefore included the idealism variable. One's initial overall reform attitude might also affect both how successful one regarded one's experiences as having been and, possibly, the dependent variable. Initial reform attitude was therefore also included as a control.

Methodological Considerations Involved in Using Only One Case

The data on which this study is based come from one case. An alternate research design would have been to look at many organizations that varied in how successful they had been in implementing debureaucratizing change or organizational change more generally. This alternative was rejected for many reasons. There were, first of all, important practical considerations. It would have been a daunting, probably impossible, challenge to gain the cooperation of many different organizations, compared with the easy access I had for procurement-related research because of my work in the government. In particular, gaining access to organizations that had *unsuccessfully* attempted change would probably have been impossible. Second, because of differences in the nature of efforts in different organizations, it would be difficult for results to measure the same thing. Many other organization-level variables, such as specifics of top-leader behavior with regard to the change effort, would have been very complicated to measure.

One might think that most of the problems with having only one case would relate to generalizability, that is, the ability to apply results from the one case to other cases. Actually, the more important problem is that with only one case it is difficult to establish accuracy. Inferences about how something is possible based on a successful case cannot be drawn without data about unsuccessful cases. This is a concern that Laurence Lynn has forcefully and cogently voiced about "best practices" research common in academic (and practitioner-oriented) management literature.[1] Best-practices studies typically look at various features of how an organization that has succeeded at something is structured or how its leaders behave and then conclude that such features explain success. The methodological problem is that such research typically presents no data about whether *failed* programs or organizations might not have had the same features as successful ones. Variance in the outcome (program or organizational success) is needed to explain success. Best-practice research lacks such variance.

The most important way this study seeks to avoid this problem is by taking *individuals* as the predominant unit of analysis, even though I am trying to explain successful *organizational* change. When one focuses on individual attitudes and behaviors, there is considerable variance to be explained. Five years into reform, most frontline employees had come to support reform, and considerable behavior change had taken place. But some were more enthusiastic than others, and a considerable number were critical. Some who were attitudinally supportive had changed their behavior a great deal, others less so; some who were attitudinally skeptical changed their behavior considerably. Light can be shed on why many did change by comparing them with those who did not.

Looking at the individual as the unit of analysis does not mean that explanations need be found only in individual-level variables. Individuals' attitudes may be influenced by their workgroup, local leaders, and agency- or government-wide leadership. The degree of individual change in behavior might be influenced by how many opportunities for change are made available by supervisors or by leaders and co-workers providing advice, training, and cooperation on performing new tasks. Since I know the buying office, and larger agency, where each respondent worked, I can assign various organization-level variables to individual respondents and thus examine "the effect of higher-level characteristics on lower-level processes."[2]

This approach toward establishing accuracy with only one case resolves most of the difficulty but not all. Problems arise in two situations. The first involves influences on individual attitudes or behavior that do not vary in the sample. An obvious example is the impact of efforts of the systemwide reform leadership on individuals. While the sample contained nineteen local office heads, who varied in attitudes toward reform, there was only one set of systemwide leaders and thus no variance. Without variance, the impact of that factor cannot be established.

My strategy for dealing with this problem is to find something that does vary as a way to capture the influence of something that does not. So, to take a hypothetical example (not one I actually pursued): that rules in the traditional system were a source of power for procurement employees might be hypothesized to serve as an obstacle to the willingness of these employees to abandon the traditional system. The presence of rules was a feature of the system that did not vary across individuals. However, the extent to which people value having a position of power does. So I might have measured the extent to which individual respondents seek power and then reasoned as follows: If you do not seek power, the ability of rules to provide power will be irrelevant. It is potentially relevant to those seeking power. But it might or might not have an effect among such people as an explanation for views on debureaucratizing the system. By seeing whether opposition to reform was greater among those with a taste for power than among those lacking it, I could see whether the (nonvarying) factor of a rule-rich system was affecting those whom it might potentially influence, namely, those who care a great deal about exercising power. If people who care about power think the same as those who do not, the ability of rules to generate support for the traditional system by conferring power would be presumed to have no effect.

Sometimes, however, it is not possible to use this strategy, and then the influence of systemwide influences on individuals becomes impossible to demonstrate. For example, some literature attributes enormous importance to top-leader behavior in explaining success or failure in organizational change. The advice this literature gives top leaders goes far beyond "support the change" to include many specifics about how leaders might be more persuasive and what steps they should take beyond persuasion. A single case, in which top leaders have displayed one set of behaviors, does not permit testing such hypotheses.

With regard to generalizability, my own view is that until more evidence is gathered, perhaps through analyses of other cases or quantitative analysis of large numbers of organizations, the assumption should be that findings presented here are generalizable—that is, that similar relationships exist between explanatory variables presented here and attitudes or behavior regarding debureaucratizing organizational change efforts specifically, and, more speculatively, organizational change efforts generally. In other words, I believe the rebuttable presumption should be that if a given factor increases or decreases attitudinal or behavioral support for change among frontline employees in procurement, it will do the same for people in other government organizations. The assumption underlying this presumption is that people in general and U.S. federal employees in particular are likely to react to similar influences in a similar way. This may not always be the case—indeed, there are examples in this study where the relationship between some variable and a respondent's attitudes or behavior regarding reform differed depending on whether the respondent worked for the Defense Department or a civilian agency. Absent further evidence, however, I believe this should be the presumption.

The greater challenge to generalizability is likely to come from organization- or system-level variables omitted from this one case. To take one important example, the kind of change involved here is debureaucratization. It is certainly plausible—especially given the role frontline dissatisfaction with bureaucracy plays in the story of the success of procurement reform—that other kinds of organizational change would be harder than debureaucratizing change. Similarly, other organization-level variables not apparent in the procurement case—such as whether employees are covered by civil service—might vary across organizations and have an impact on the success of change efforts.

Notes

Throughout these notes, I make numerous references to "Technical Footnotes." This is a separate document (available at ksghome.harvard.edu/~skelman/technicalfootnotes.pdf) that addresses the underlying scholarly literatures and methodological points in greater detail. The technical footnotes are keyed to the notes in this volume by chapter and note number.

Chapter 1

1. Paul C. Light, *Government's Greatest Achievements* (Brookings, 2002).

2. Council for Excellence in Government, "American Attitudes toward Government," 1997 (www.excelgov.org/usermedia/images/uploads/PDFs/juy97full-report.PDF).

3. Steven Kelman, *Procurement and Public Management: The Fear of Discretion and the Quality of Government Performance* (Washington: AEI Press, 1990).

4. Sara L. Rynes, Jean M. Bartunek, and Richard L. Daft, "Across the Great Divide: Knowledge Creation and Transfer between Practitioners and Academics," *Academy of Management Journal* 44 (April 2001): 340–55.

5. Federal Procurement Data Center, *Federal Procurement Report* (U.S. General Services Administration, 2004). Information on the size of the discretionary budget for fiscal year 2003 appears in "The Budget for Fiscal Year 2005: Historical Tables," table 8.1, "Outlays by Budget Enforcement Act Category:

1962–2009," 2004 (www.whitehouse.gov/omb/budget/fy2005/pdf/hist.pdf). I would like to thank Dana Vader, of the Office of Federal Procurement Policy, for providing me with this information.

6. Donald F. Kettl, *Sharing Power: Public Governance and Private Markets* (Brookings, 1993).

7. Donald F. Kettl, *Reinventing Government: A Fifth-Year Report Card* (Brookings, 1998).

8. "Cookie Mix, Dry," *Harper's Magazine*, October 1985, pp. 25–26.

9. Michael Barzelay, *Breaking through Bureaucracy* (University of California Press, 1992); David Osborne and Ted Gaebler, *Reinventing Government: How the Entrepreneurial Spirit Is Transforming the Public Sector* (Reading, Mass.: Addison-Wesley, 1992); Martin A. Levin and Mary Bryna Sanger, *Making Government Work: How Entrepreneurial Executives Turn Bright Ideas into Real Results* (San Francisco: Jossey-Bass, 1994); Jonathan Boston, John Martin, June Pallot, and Pat Walsh, *Public Management: The New Zealand Model* (Oxford University Press, 1996); David Osborne and Peter Plastrik, *Banishing Bureaucracy: The Five Strategies for Reinventing Government* (Reading, Mass.: Addison-Wesley, 1997); Sandford Borins, *Innovating with Integrity: How Local Heroes Are Transforming American Government* (Georgetown University Press, 1998).

Chapter 2

1. Max Weber, "Bureaucracy," in *From Max Weber: Essays in Sociology*, edited by H. H. Gerth and C. Wright Mills (Oxford University Press, 1946), pp. 196–98.

2. In formal organization theory, extensive use of rules is sometimes called "formalization," and hierarchy "centralization."

3. By no means everything to be discussed here, including the various rules, was eliminated by procurement reform. However, for the sake of consistency, all references in this section are kept in the past tense.

4. In government contracting jargon, *bidder* refers only to a firm bidding on a sealed-bid procurement, where low bid is the only factor taken into consideration, while a firm bidding on a procurement with factors other than price evaluation is referred to as an *offeror*. However, the lay term *bidder* is used here.

5. These committees were Government Reform (formerly Government Operations) in the House and Governmental Affairs in the Senate as well as Armed Services Committees in both houses.

6. Henry Mintzberg, *The Structuring of Organizations* (Englewood Cliffs, N.J.: Prentice-Hall, 1979), p. 84. For a more detailed discussion of the problems with bureaucracy, see Steven Kelman, *Procurement and Public Management: The Fear of Discretion and the Quality of Government Performance* (Washington: AEI Press, 1990).

7. Thomas J. Peters and Robert H. Waterman Jr., *In Search of Excellence: Lessons from America's Best-Run Companies* (New York: Harper and Row, 1982); Rosabeth Moss Kanter, *The Change Masters* (New York: Simon and Schuster, 1983); Thomas J. Peters, *Thriving on Chaos: Handbook for a Management Revolution* (New York: Knopf, 1987); Michael Hammer and James Champy, *Reengineering the Corporation: A Manifesto for Business Revolution* (New York: HarperBusiness, 1993).

8. Peters, *Thriving on Chaos*, pp. 377–78, 459.

9. John E. Chubb and Terry M. Moe, *Politics, Markets, and America's Schools* (Brookings, 1990); Kelman, *Procurement and Public Management*; Michael Barzelay, *Breaking through Bureaucracy* (University of California Press, 1992); David Osborne and Ted Gaebler, *Reinventing Government: How the Entrepreneurial Spirit Is Transforming the Public Sector* (Reading, Mass.: Addison-Wesley, 1992).

10. James G. March, Martin Schulz, and Xueguang Zhou, *The Dynamics of Rules* (Stanford University Press, 2000), pp. 3–4, 186; Arthur L. Stinchcombe, *When Formality Works: Authority and Abstraction in Law and Organizations* (University of Chicago Press, 2001).

11. Kelman, *Procurement and Public Management*, chap. 2; Susan Rose-Ackerman, *Corruption and Government: Causes, Consequences, and Reform* (Cambridge University Press, 1999), esp. pp. 59–68; Robert Klitgaard, Ronald MacLean-Abaroa, and H. Lindsey Parris, *Corrupt Cities: A Practical Guide to Cure and Prevention* (Oakland, Calif.: ICS Press, 2000), esp. chap. 2.

12. Kelman, *Procurement and Public Management*, pp. 6–7.

13. Ibid., p. 34.

14. Center for Strategic and International Studies, *Integrating Commercial and Military Technologies for National Strength: An Agenda for Change* (Washington: CSI Press, 1991), p. 20.

15. In some cases, commercial firms established separate production lines for runs of products just for the Defense Department, so that their extra costs of doing business with the government would not hurt their commercial business. This deprived the government of economies of scale.

16. This is an argument analogous to a view among public-choice scholars that government interventions each sought by one group can add up to a system whose costs outweigh its benefits for everybody; see, for example, Barry R. Weingast, Kenneth A. Shepsle, and Christopher Johnsen, "The Political Economy of Benefits and Costs: A Neoclassical Approach to Distributive Politics," *Journal of Political Economy* 89 (August 1981): 642–64.

17. Alvin W. Gouldner, *Patterns of Industrial Bureaucracy* (New York: Free Press, 1954), chap. 9; Gareth Morgan, *Images of Organization* (Newbury Park, Calif.: Sage, 1986), pp. 36, 38.

18. Mintzberg, *The Structuring of Organizations*, p. 346. An analogous argument may be made about hierarchy. If ideas developed by people at lower

levels are subject to endless second guessing, why bother to develop them in the first place?

19. Keki R. Bhote, *Strategic Supplier Management* (New York: American Management Association, 1989).

20. Paul C. Light, *The Tides of Reform: Making Government Work, 1945–1995* (Yale University Press, 1997), pp. 36–42.

21. Albert Gore, *From Red Tape to Results: Creating a Government That Works Better and Costs Less* (U.S. Government Printing Office, 1993).

22. Ibid., pp. 2–3.

23. Kelman, *Procurement and Public Management*.

24. Robert K. Merton, "Bureaucratic Structure and Personality," in *Social Theory and Social Structure* (New York: Free Press, 1968), pp. 249–60; Michel Crozier, *The Bureaucratic Phenomenon* (University of Chicago Press, 1964); Karl E. Weick, *The Social Psychology of Organizing*, 2nd ed. (New York: McGraw-Hill, 1979).

25. Michael T. Hannan and John Freeman, "The Population Ecology of Organizations," *American Journal of Sociology* 82 (1977): 929–64; Michael T. Hannan and John Freeman, "Structural Inertia and Organizational Change," *American Sociological Review* 49 (1984): 149–64.

26. Jeffrey L. Pressman and Aaron B. Wildavsky, *Implementation* (University of California Press, 1973), pp. 126–27.

27. Quoted in Jeffrey Pfeffer and Robert I. Sutton, *The Knowing-Doing Gap* (Harvard Business School Press, 2000), p. 74.

28. Robert B. Cialdini, *Influence: Science and Practice*, 4th ed. (Boston: Allyn and Bacon, 2001), p. 54. See also Pfeffer and Sutton, *The Knowing-Doing Gap*, pp. 73–74.

29. A. R. Allgeier, D. Byrne, B. Brooks, and D. Revnes, "The Waffle Phenomenon: Negative Evaluations of Those Who Shift Attitudinally," *Journal of Applied Social Psychology* 9 (1979): 170–82.

30. Albert A. Harrison, "Mere Exposure," in *Advances in Experimental Social Psychology*, edited by Leonard Berkowitz, vol. 10 (San Diego: Academic Press, 1977), pp. 39–83, 40; David G. Myers, *Social Psychology*, 6th ed. (New York: McGraw-Hill, 1999), pp. 431–33.

31. Robert F. Bornstein, "Exposure and Affect: Overview and Meta-Analysis of Research, 1968–1987," *Psychological Bulletin* 106 (1989): 265–66.

32. Charles A. Kiesler, *The Psychology of Commitment* (New York: Academic Press, 1971), pp. 66–74.

33. Steven Kelman, *Making Public Policy: A Hopeful View of American Government* (New York: Basic Books, 1987), p. 169.

34. Shelley E. Taylor, *Positive Illusions: Creative Self-Deception and the Healthy Mind* (New York: Basic Books, 1988), pp. 8, 10–11, 39–40.

35. Robert A. Katzmann, *Regulatory Bureaucracy: The Federal Trade Commission and Antitrust Policy* (MIT Press, 1980).

36. Weick, *The Social Psychology of Organizing*, p. 7.

37. Dorothy Leonard-Barton, "Core Capabilities and Core Rigidities: A Paradox in Managing New Product Development," *Strategic Management Journal* 13 (1992): 111–25.

38. Jeffrey Pfeffer, *New Directions for Organization Theory* (Oxford University Press, 1997), pp. 116–26.

39. Barry M. Staw and Jerry Ross, "Behavior of Escalation Situations: Antecedents, Prototypes, and Solutions," in *Research in Organizational Behavior*, edited by L. L. Cummings and Barry M. Staw, vol. 9 (Greenwich, Conn.: JAI Press, 1987), pp. 39–78.

40. Gerald R. Salancik, "Commitment and the Control of Organizational Behavior and Belief," in *New Directions in Organizational Behavior*, edited by Barry M. Staw and Gerald R. Salancik (Chicago: St. Clair Press, 1977), p. 36.

41. John Child, "Technological Innovation and Organizational Conservatism," in *New Technology as Organizational Innovation*, edited by Johannes M. Pennings and Arend Buitendam (Cambridge, Mass.: Ballinger, 1987).

42. To be sure, there might be winners from power changes as well as losers. However, as Machiavelli first noted, and as has been extensively discussed in the literature on behavioral decisionmaking, losers tend to act with more determination to prevent losses than do potential winners to achieve gains. See, for example, Daniel Kahneman and Amos Tversky, "Prospect Theory: An Analysis of Decisions under Risk," *Econometrica* 47 (1979): 263–91. "The innovator makes enemies of all those who prospered under the old order, and only lukewarm support is forthcoming from those who would prosper under the new. . . . Men are generally incredulous, never really trusting new things unless they have tested them by experience." Niccolo Machiavelli, *The Prince* (London: Penguin Books, 1961), p. 19.

43. Karl Weick, *Sensemaking in Organizations* (Thousand Oaks, Calif.: Sage, 1995), p. 4; see also James A. Galambos, Robert P. Abelson, and John B. Black, eds. *Knowledge Structures* (Hillsdale, N.J.: Lawrence Erlbaum, 1986).

44. See "Technical Footnotes."

45. John Van Maanen, "On the Understanding of Interpersonal Relations," in *Essays in Interpersonal Dynamics*, edited by Warren Bennis (Homewood, Ill.: Dorsey Press, 1979), p. 19.

46. William H. Starbuck and Frances J. Milliken, "Executives' Perceptual Filters: What They Notice and How They Make Sense," in *The Executive Effect*, edited by Donald C. Hambrick (Greenwich, Conn.: JAI Press, 1988), p. 40.

47. Charles R. Schwenk, "Linking Cognitive, Organizational, and Political Factors in Explaining Strategic Change," *Journal of Management Studies* 26 (1989): 179.

48. Shelley E. Taylor and Jennifer Crocker, "Schematic Bases of Social Information Processing," in *Social Cognition: The Ontario Symposium*, edited by E.

Tory Higgins, C. Peter Herman, and Mark P. Zanna, vol. 1 (Hillsdale, N.J.: Lawrence Erlbaum, 1981), p. 90.

49. Mark Snyder, E. D. Tanke, and E. Berscheid, "Social Perception and Interpersonal Behavior," *Journal of Personality and Social Psychology* 35 (1977): 656–66.

50. Weick, *The Social Psychology of Organizing*, p. 135.

51. Snyder, Tanke, and Berscheid, "Social Perception and Interpersonal Behavior."

52. Perceptual confirmation has received attention in scholarly literatures in many different contexts. In national security, it has been discussed with reference to the failure of Israeli intelligence to take seriously information suggesting an Egyptian attack in 1973, because of the preexisting view of Israeli intelligence that Egypt was unlikely to attack. Avi Shlaim, "Failures in National Intelligence Estimates: The Case of the Yom Kippur War," *World Politics* 28 (1976): 348–80. More recently, it has been discussed in suggestions that American analysts interpreted intelligence data from Iraq in accordance with a preexisting view that Saddam Hussein possessed weapons of mass destruction. For another national security example, see Scott A. Snook, *Friendly Fire: The Accidental Shootdown of U.S. Blackhawks over Northern Iraq* (Princeton University Press, 2000), pp. 80–94. For an example from the literature on voting behavior, see Bernard R. Berelson, Paul F. Lazarsfeld, and William N. McPhee, *Voting: A Study of Opinion Formation in a Presidential Campaign* (University of Chicago Press, 1954), pp. 220–22.

53. Weick, *The Social Psychology of Organizing*, p. 156.

54. Ibid.

55. Jerald Hage and Michael Aiken, "Program Change and Organizational Properties: A Comparative Analysis," *American Journal of Sociology* 72, no. 2 (March 1967): 503–19, 512.

56. Fariborz Damanpour, "Organizational Innovation: A Meta-Analysis of Effects of Determinants and Moderators," *Academy of Management Journal* 34, no. 3 (March 1991): 555–90, 571, 576.

57. Quoted in Victor A. Thompson, "Bureaucracy and Innovation," *Administrative Science Quarterly* 10, no. 1 (March 1965): 2.

58. Michel Crozier, *The Bureaucratic Phenomenon* (University of Chicago Press, 1964), p. 195.

59. James Q. Wilson, *Bureaucracy: What Government Agencies Do and Why They Do It* (New York: Basic Books, 1989), p. 127.

60. This argument is commonly taken to the additional step of arguing that organizational crisis is necessary for or promotes change, a view that is more controversial than the argument just presented. I discuss this issue in some detail later in this chapter and in Steven Kelman, "Downsizing, Competition, and Organizational Change: Is Necessity the Mother of Invention?" unpublished, Harvard University, 2005.

61. Rosabeth Moss Kanter, *The Change Masters* (New York: Simon and Schuster, 1983), p. 233.

62. Graham Allison and Philip Zelikow, *Essence of Decision: Explaining the Cuban Missile Crisis,* 2nd ed. (New York: Longman, 1999), pp. 303–04.

63. Donald P. Warwick, *A Theory of Public Bureaucracy* (Harvard University Press, 1975), p. 174.

64. Peter Cappelli, *The New Deal at Work: Managing the Market-Driven Workforce* (Harvard Business School Press, 1999), chap. 3.

65. Quoted in Peter Hennessy, *Whitehall* (London: Secker and Warburg, 1989), p. 595.

66. Robert D. Behn, "The Dilemmas of Innovation in American Government," in *Innovation in American Government: Challenges, Opportunities, and Dilemmas,* edited by Alan A. Altshuler and Robert D. Behn (Brookings, 1997), p. 15.

67. Edward P. Lazear, *Personnel Economics for Managers* (New York: Wiley and Sons, 1998), pp. 452–60; see also Frederick Schauer, *Playing by the Rules* (Oxford, U.K.: Clarendon Press, 1991), p. 153.

68. Warwick, *A Theory of Public Bureaucracy,* pp. 84–85.

69. Wilson, *Bureaucracy,* p. 133.

70. Herman Finer, "Administrative Responsibility in Democratic Government," *Public Administration Review* 1, no. 4 (Summer 1941): 335–50, 335.

71. Ronald C. Moe, "The Importance of Public Law: New and Old Paradigms of Government Management," in *Handbook of Public Law and Administration,* edited by Phillip J. Cooper and Chester A. Newland (San Francisco: Jossey-Bass, 1997), pp. 42–44.

72. Quoted in Warwick, *A Theory of Public Bureaucracy,* p. 70.

73. Weber, "Bureaucracy," p. 224.

74. For a discussion, see Steven Kelman, "Remaking Federal Procurement," *Public Contract Law Journal* 31 (Summer 2002): 581–622.

75. Wilson, *Bureaucracy,* pp. 315–17.

76. Ibid., p. 316.

77. Ibid., p. 321.

78. Michael Hammer and Steven A. Stanton, *The Reengineering Revolution* (New York: HarperBusiness, 1995), p. 284.

79. For a summary and meta-analysis, see Damanpour, "Organizational Innovation."

80. Martin A. Levin and Mary Bryna Sanger, *Making Government Work: How Entrepreneurial Executives Turn Bright Ideas into Real Results* (San Francisco: Jossey-Bass, 1994); Olivia Golden, "Innovation in Public Sector Human Services Programs: The Implications of Innovation by 'Groping Along,'" in Altshuler and Behn, *Innovation in American Government,* pp. 146–76; Sandford Borins, *Innovating with Integrity: How Local Heroes Are Transforming American Government* (Georgetown University Press, 1998).

81. There are exceptions: see, for example, Levin and Sanger, *Making Government Work,* chap. 6; Borins, *Innovating with Integrity,* chaps. 4 and 8.

82. Kurt Lewin, "Frontiers in Group Dynamics," *Human Relations* 1, no. 1 (1947): 33, 35; Dennis A. Gioia and Kuman Chittipeddi, "Sensemaking and Sensegiving in Strategic Change Initiation," *Strategic Management Journal* 12, no. 6 (1991): 433–48, 434; Edgar H. Schein, "Personal Change through Interpersonal Relationships," in *Essays in Interpersonal Dynamics,* edited by Warren G. Bennis (Homewood, Ill.: Dorsey Press, 1979), pp. 129–62.

83. An additional advantage of a focus on the front lines of the system is that it moves the analysis away from my own activities at the top of the system.

84. Missing values were imputed, using methods described in J. L. Schafer, *Analysis of Incomplete Multivariate Data* (London: Chapman and Hall, 1997). For each model, I analyzed thirty imputed data sets, combining the results. I used an overall list of about twenty variables to impute the missing values, along with any additional variables present in the model being specified. Values for interaction and quadratic terms were imputed separately. For further discussion of issues related to these surveys, see Steven Kelman, "Sampling Issues, Survey Administration, and Data Analysis," 2004 (ksghome.harvard.edu/~skelman/MS/SamplingIssues.pdf). My colleague Alberto Abadie and my research assistant, Chris Hans, helped me choose a method for dealing with missing values in the data.

85. Specifically, they circled a number between 1 and 5, representing "agree strongly," "agree somewhat," "mixed feelings," "disagree somewhat," or "disagree strongly." Respondents were also given the alternative of circling a box marked 0 for "don't know"; some respondents also simply left questions blank.

86. The five-point agree-disagree questions were considered interval variables for the purpose of ordinary least-squares regression analysis.

87. The first is what Campbell and Stanley call internal validity, the second external validity. Donald T. Campbell and Julian C. Stanley, *Experimental and Quasi-Experimental Designs for Research* (Chicago: Rand-McNally, 1963), pp. 5, 13–24.

88. Richard L. Daft and Selwyn W. Becker, *The Innovative Organization: Innovation Adoption in School Organizations* (New York: Elsevier, 1978).

89. See, for example, Everett M. Rogers, *The Diffusion of Innovations,* 4th ed. (New York: Free Press, 1995).

Chapter 3

1. While it is possible for those who support change in how work is performed to make a few changes on their own, many decisions affecting how people in organizations behave apply to the organization as a whole. Except for the

simplest procurements, individual employees cannot evaluate bidder past performance or change a milspec to a commercial specification by themselves. Even for actions a person theoretically could undertake individually, few would begin to behave in new ways absent movement of some significant number of coworkers in a similar direction. Finally, many policies, such as required local levels of hierarchical review, are established by the buying office as a whole. For these kinds of situations, there will need to be a process to make collective decisions about what the organization should do.

2. The view of organizational change as a political process is not entirely absent from the literature, though it is seldom presented as it is here. One place where politics appears in the literature on organizational change is in a strand of research, labeled as being about "innovation" more than "organizational change," that, criticizing an approach centered on top leadership, emphasizes the role of politics in general and frontline change advocates in particular in initiating innovations. Rosabeth Moss Kanter, *The Change Masters* (New York: Simon and Schuster, 1983), chap. 8; Sandford Borins, *Innovating with Integrity: How Local Heroes Are Transforming American Government* (Georgetown University Press, 1998); Andrew Van de Ven, Douglas Polley, Raghu Garud, and Sankaran Venkataraman, *The Innovation Journey* (Oxford University Press, 1999), chap. 2; Jane E. Dutton, Susan J. Ashford, Regina M. O'Neill, and Katherine A. Lawrence, "Moves That Matter: Issue Selling and Organizational Change," *Academy of Management Journal* 44 (August 2001): 716–36. Borins's study of innovations that were at least semifinalists in an awards program for government innovation has found that about half were initiated by career civil servants, the largest source of innovations in his sample. "I consider this result so unexpected—and significant," Borins writes, "that I incorporated it in the title of the book" ("Local Heroes"). Borins, *Innovating with Integrity*, p. 38. Some of this literature explicitly discusses political tactics used by frontline innovation advocates. However, this literature differs from the theory presented here because it generally focuses on discrete decisions for an organization to pursue a specific innovation (a new product or program) and the role of frontline advocates in getting such decisions made, rather than on behavior change at an organization's working levels. Also, this literature generally sees these decisions as made at higher levels, with advocates building political support for such decisions, rather than highlighting political decisionmaking on the front lines itself. Political tactics this literature discusses are generally advocacy methods used to persuade peers and superiors about why an innovation is a good idea. This literature may therefore be seen as a private sector counterpart to public sector literature on "bureaucratic entrepreneurship"—for example, Graham Allison and Philip Zelikow, *Essence of Decision: Explaining the Cuban Missile Crisis*, 2nd ed. (New York: Longman, 1999), chap. 5; Richard N. Haass, *The Power to Persuade* (Boston: Houghton Mifflin, 1994)—rather than as addressing issues cen-

tral to this research. Political processes in organizational change are also discussed in work coming out of a research tradition whose primary focus is not organizational change but power in organizations; Andrew Pettigrew, *The Awakening Giant: Continuity and Change in Imperial Chemical Industries* (Oxford, U.K.: Basil Blackwell, 1985), chap. 2. Jeffrey Pfeffer, sounding like what I argue here, states that "change in large organizations is often the result of a political process." But when one reads the argument, it becomes clear that the political disagreements he has in mind are structural ones among different organizational subunits, such as product development and finance, rather than disagreements among individuals within a unit, of the kind that is the focus here. Jeffrey Pfeffer, *Managing with Power* (Harvard Business School Press, 1992), p. 336.

3. Kurt Lewin, "Group Decision and Social Change," in *Readings in Social Psychology*, edited by Eleanor E. Maccoby, Theodore M. Newcomb, and Eugene L. Hartley, 3rd ed. (New York: Holt, Rinehart and Winston, 1958), pp. 197–211.

4. Lester Coch and John R. P. French Jr., "Overcoming Resistance to Change," *Human Relations* 1, no. 4 (1948): 512–32.

5. John P. Kotter, *Leading Change* (Harvard Business School Press, 1996), chap. 3.

6. Ibid., pp. 44, 46.

7. Michael Hammer and Steven A. Stanton, *The Reengineering Revolution* (New York: HarperBusiness, 1995), p. 34.

8. These and all data presented in this chapter include only respondents who were working in a buying office as of the beginning of 1993; for the Frontline Survey, this excludes 15 percent of the sample. See also "Technical Footnotes."

9. This is because they involve recall of the past, which generally biases responses in favor of current attitudes (which were, at the time of the survey, more favorable to reform than initial attitudes when reform began), and because the sample excludes people who were working for these organizations when reform began but had left by the time of the survey five years later. Furthermore, it is likely that those selected to participate in the In-Person Interviews were not a random sample of local buying office employees but were more proreform than the employees as a whole. At the same time, there is evidence from internal analysis of the Frontline Survey that these biases do not render the results of these recall questions meaningless or artifactual. See my discussion, "The Impact of Sample Attrition and Retrospective Recall Bias on Frequency Distributions and Coefficients Discussed in Chapter Three," 2005 (ksghome.harvard.edu/~skelman/MS/SampleAttrition.pdf).

10. Respondents who were characterized as members of the change vanguard both disagreed with the statement that they had first tried reform only because their bosses made them and checked the first box describing their overall atti-

tude toward reform ("This is something I was hoping for for a long time"). Those characterized as early recruits also disagreed that they had first tried reform only because their bosses made them do so and checked any but the first box as describing their overall attitude toward reform. Fence-sitters were respondents who gave the middle response to the first question and any response for the second question other than the first box. A respondent was categorized as a skeptic or critic if he or she agreed with the first question and also checked any box but the first on the second question.

11. To see whether anything analogous might have existed at policymaking levels in Washington as well, I examined all issues of the weekly trade publication *Federal Contracts Report* for 1991 and 1992, the two years before reinventing government was launched. The results are discussed in Steven Kelman, "The View from Washington on the Eve of Procurement Reform," 2005 (ksghome.harvard.edu/~skelman/MS/tvfw.pdf).

12. Edward E. Lawler III, *The Ultimate Advantage: Creating the High-Involvement Organization* (San Francisco: Jossey-Bass, 1992), p. 28. Also see J. Richard Hackman and Edward E. Lawler III, "Employee Reactions to Job Characteristics," *Journal of Applied Psychology* 55, no. 2 (1971): 259–86, 267.

13. In discussions of job design, where the concept of autonomy is frequently used, there is sometimes confusion between autonomy, on the one hand, and participation, on the other. Participation, however, involves more the ability to have one's voice heard in the collective establishment of workplace policies. Participation is analogous to political democracy, while autonomy is analogous to individual choice. They may be joined as two features of job redesign, but they need not be. Procurement reform was significantly about autonomy but not really about collective participation. Similarly, though the concepts are often conflated, autonomy is not necessarily the same as job enrichment, although the latter involves debureaucratizing highly specialized jobs and frequently involves, as autonomy always does, less reliance on rules and hierarchy.

14. Dan Ciampa, *Total Quality: A User's Guide for Implementation* (Reading, Mass.: Addison-Wesley, 1991), chaps. 6, 9.

15. Of course, rules that are good decision tools can significantly reduce work burdens. Compare the situation of an aircraft maintenance worker who needs to decide himself what maintenance to perform and how to do it with one who can follow an instruction manual.

16. This technique is commonly used in survey research. D. F. Alwin, "Feeling Thermometers versus Seven-Point Scales: Which Are Better?" *Sociological Methods and Research* 25, no. 3 1997): 318–40. A number of questions in the Frontline Survey involved the feeling thermometer, including the central question measuring overall current attitude toward procurement reform. Instructions for the section of the survey with the feeling thermometer questions were as follows: "The following is a list of concepts for you to rate on a 'feeling thermome-

ter.' A 'feeling thermometer' has 100 degrees. Ratings between 50 degrees and 100 degrees mean that you feel *favorable and warm* toward that concept. Ratings between 0 degrees and 50 degrees mean that you *don't feel much* for the concept. If you don't feel particularly warm or cold towards the concept, you would rate the concept at the 50 degree mark."

17. "Don't know" responses were excluded. These questions asked people about their views as of the time of the survey, not as of the time just before the beginning of reform. At the time of the survey, of course, reform had been under way, promoting "empowerment," for a number of years, and it is hard to know how different views on these questions would have been before reform got started. However, though some movement toward greater support for job autonomy almost surely occurred, it is hard to imagine that attitudes on such an elemental question as the approach to one's job, and to some extent to life in general, would have dramatically shifted for a large group of people over this period.

18. Joel Feinberg, "Autonomy," in *The Inner Citadel: Essays on Individual Autonomy*, edited by John Christman (Oxford University Press, 1989), pp. 41–43.

19. Thomas Nagel, *The Possibility of Altruism* (Princeton University Press, 1970), p. 29; E. J. Bond, *Reason and Value* (Cambridge University Press, 1983), pp. 11–12, 36.

20. Philosophical literature on liberty and autonomy makes similar distinctions. Isaiah Berlin's distinction between "two concepts of liberty" closely tracks the distinction between seeking autonomy (liberty) for burden reduction and for an opportunity to choose or to create a better result. "Negative liberty," or "freedom *from,*" is "not being interfered with by others." This corresponds to seeking autonomy to reduce burdens. An alternate concept is "positive liberty," or "freedom *to,*" namely "deciding, not being decided for, self-directed and not acted upon by external nature or by other men." Isaiah Berlin, *Two Concepts of Liberty* (Oxford: Clarendon Press, 1958), pp. 8, 16. This corresponds to seeking autonomy for the opportunity to choose, including the opportunity to create better results. Historical and sociological research on factory work discusses resentment at being forced to do things one would have preferred to avoid, engendering a desire for burden reduction autonomy. E. P. Thompson's *The Making of the English Working Class,* about early decades of the industrial revolution, discusses artisans-turned-factory-workers resenting being forced to arrive at work at the same time every day, compared to a person working at home who "could do it at his leisure." E. P. Thompson, *The Making of the English Working Class* (New York: Vintage Books, 1963), p. 305. Frederick Engels has written that before the advent of factories, an artisan weaver had "as many" leisure hours "as he chose to take, since he could weave whenever and as long as he pleased. . . . They did no more than they chose to do." Frederick

Engels, *The Condition of the Working-Class in England in 1844* (London: Allen and Unwin, 1952; originally published 1845), chap. 2. One sees similar findings over a hundred years later in Alvin Gouldner's work in a gypsum plant. Gouldner describes the plant's traditional management, before the appearance of a new boss who instituted many rules, as "lenient." "A crucial part of 'leniency' was that 'your free time is your own,' and that there is 'no constant check-up on you' by the foreman." The new rules involved "increased restriction of the worker, closer supervision and less 'free time.'" Alvin W. Gouldner, *Patterns of Industrial Bureaucracy* (New York: Free Press, 1954), pp. 46–47, 68. In their research on employee reactions to job characteristics, Richard Hackman and Edward Lawler measure the correlation of various characteristics with employee job satisfaction at different levels of what they call "higher-order" need strength. Most of their higher-order needs involved aspects of a desire to exercise judgment, such as how highly the respondent valued "the opportunity for personal growth and development on my job," "the opportunity for independent thought and action on my job," and "the opportunity to do challenging work." J. Richard Hackman and Edward W. Lawler III, "Employee Reactions to Job Characteristics," *Journal of Applied Psychology* 55 (1971): 269. They find that, for people with great higher-order need strength, the correlation between autonomy provided by the job and satisfaction with the job was .43, while for those with less such need strength, it was only .29. This suggests both the desire for exercising judgment and the desire for burden reduction contributed to the relationship between autonomy and satisfaction, since even those with low levels of higher-order needs liked autonomous jobs significantly more. (Hackman and Lawler do not discuss this interpretation of their findings.) See also "Technical Footnotes."

21. Philip E. Converse, "Attitudes and Non-Attitudes: Continuation of a Dialogue," in *The Quantitative Analysis of Social Problems,* edited by Edward R. Tufte (Reading, Mass.: Addison-Wesley, 1970), p. 213.

22. James P. Walsh, "Managerial and Organizational Cognition: Notes from a Trip down Memory Lane," *Organization Science* 6, no. 3 (1995): 299–300.

23. Ronald Inglehart, "The Silent Revolution in Europe: Intergenerational Change in Post-Industrial Societies," *American Political Science Review* 65, no. 4 (1971): 991–1017; Ronald Inglehart, *Culture Shift in Advanced Industrial Society* (Princeton University Press, 1990).

24. Abraham H. Maslow, *Motivation and Personality*, 2nd ed. (New York: Harper and Row, 1970; originally published 1954).

25. Surprisingly, arguments that increased education and affluence increase interest in autonomy have been infrequently presented in academic literature and have received virtually no empirical testing. (I consulted a number of scholarly experts in this area to seek out literature references, including Richard Hackman, Rosabeth Moss Kanter, Edward Lawler III, Greg Oldham, and my

colleague the late Susan Eaton.) In one survey asking employees to indicate which job features were most important, for white-collar workers "I have an opportunity to develop my special abilities" was the second most common response. For blue-collar workers, two of the top three features were "the pay is good" and "the job security is good." Developing "special abilities" was not among the top five desired features for blue-collar workers, while pay and security were not among the top five for white-collar ones. (These findings could be driven either by higher education or affluence of white-collar workers.) J. Richard Hackman and Greg R. Oldham, *Work Redesign* (Reading, Mass.: Addison-Wesley, 1980). A study of preference for rules among public and private sector managers has found that more highly educated managers were less likely to see a need for more rules. Barry Bozeman and Hal G. Rainey, "Organizational Rules and Bureaucratic Personality," *American Journal of Political Science* 42, no. 1 (1998): 163–89. In support of the view that affluence increases support for postmaterialist values, Inglehart uses age as a proxy for affluence and presents evidence showing a shift to such values in the baby-boom generation growing up in the affluent era after World War II compared with their parents. Ronald Inglehart, *The Silent Revolution: Changing Values and Political Styles among Western Publics* (Princeton University Press, 1977), chap. 2.

26. See "Technical Footnotes."

27. A *dependent variable* is the phenomenon to be explained. A *predictor variable* is one that may help explain the dependent variable.

28. So, for example, to test for the influence of education on the desire for job autonomy, both its direct connection to disliking rules or hierarchy (controlling for other variables in the model) and its influence on the desire for autonomy mediated through its effects on other variables that themselves have a direct connection to a dislike of rules or hierarchy, such as job level or interest in work requiring judgment, would be tested. These paths are hypothesized a priori. A structural equation model can establish that the hypothesized paths are consistent with the data, but they do not establish these paths causally. It is also possible to make inferences about mediated paths using ordinary least-squares regression, which I will sometimes do in subsequent analyses, but there were so many mediated paths of interest here that a structural equation model was more appropriate. I used the computer program EQS. I am grateful to my colleague Keith Allred, as well as to Professors Peter Bentler and Eric Wu, for answering various questions about using EQS.

29. Statistical significance refers to the probability that an effect observed in the sample owes only to chance. Conventionally, for a result to be considered statistically significant, there should be no more than a 5 percent probability that the observed result owes to chance (marginal statistical significance would be a 10 percent chance). Subsequently in the text, I use the word *significant* or *significance* to refer to statistical significance. Also, in examining results, I am

interested not just in significance but also, more important, in *effect size*—that is, how much of a change in the dependent variable is produced by a one-unit change in a predictor variable. Effect size indicates how powerful the association is between a predictor variable and a dependent variable. I generally present effect size as a standardized coefficient. This means the coefficient shows the impact of a change of one standard deviation in a respondent's answer to a predictor variable on the dependent variable. Standardized coefficients ease comparison by putting variables measured in different ways—age, education level, and agreement with a five-point scale question—into a common metric, thus facilitating comparison of effect sizes. See also "Technical Footnotes."

30. Rebelliousness was insignificant in relation to disliking rules, and it mildly predicted *less* desire for job autonomy overall (perhaps because rebels were less anxious to take the responsibility required by greater discretion).

31. The link between desire to produce better organizational results and support for autonomy might occur in two slightly different ways. One can imagine people believing they have an obligation to produce good organizational results and thus seeking autonomy to produce such results—even if a job involving original thought provided no personal satisfaction at all (and might indeed be personally painful). To give specific examples, one might wish for the opportunity for autonomy to increase the chances that good decisions get made, even if one did not personally relish making choices; one might even prefer that others make the decisions, if only convinced those decisions would be right. One might like choosing and exercising judgment even if this were unrelated to achieving better organizational results. One might, for example, enjoy developing ingenious contractual clauses or complex military specifications for the sake of complexity, though they serve little public purpose and might even unnecessarily harm the value the procurement system delivered. Alternatively, one might like choosing and exercising judgment even if this were unrelated to achieving better organizational results. The link between the desire for better organizational results and the desire for autonomy might also occur somewhat more indirectly: seeking better organizational results might create a desire to exercise judgment or choose, which in turn creates a desire for autonomy.

32. Of the six better-value variables, dissatisfaction with poorly performing contractors and liking to come up with innovative ideas on the job were not significant. (In chapter 4 I discuss reasons for skepticism with the relationship between dissatisfaction with the poorly performing contractors variable and dissatisfaction with the traditional procurement system.) Orientation to mission results was barely significant at the .1 level for job autonomy and just over .1 for dislike of rules. The two significant better-value variables, being driven to succeed (which might have involved strong performance with traditional procurement duties) and dissatisfaction with slow customer service, were less associated with the better-value agenda. Being driven to succeed had a large effect on

support for autonomy (though there are reasons to believe it may be exaggerated), dissatisfaction with slow service a modest one. It is also plausible that part of the connection between education and job level and the desire to exercise judgment and choose, as well as directly to support autonomy (noted later in this chapter), reflected greater interest by those with higher education or job level in the abstract idea of better value from contracting. The impact of idealism, another variable closely connected to the reformers' agenda, was complex. Idealism predicted desire for creative work in both models, and its effect size was quite large, so the desire to achieve a better world promoted a desire to exercise choice or judgment, in turn promoting the desire for autonomy. However, the *direct* link between idealism and attitude toward job autonomy went in the opposite direction. Controlling for the desire for creative work, the more idealistic one was, the less one sought job autonomy. What would appear to be occurring was that there were two types of idealists. One embraced an ideology in line with reformers', seeking jobs involving creative work to allow them to come up with ways to get better value for the government. The other believed rules and hierarchy promoted the public good by preventing favoritism and keeping contractors from cheating the government.

33. Deference had an additional impact through strongly predicting values for venturesomeness or risk tolerance.

34. Controlling for education, job level had weak or no effects. A higher job level was a significant direct predictor of dislike for rules (again, with a small effect size), though not for the general desire for job autonomy. For dislike for rules, job level was not a significant predictor of the desire for creative work; for job autonomy, it was significant at the .1 level (with modest effect size), but the association may be exaggerated by reverse causality.

35. Age did not significantly predict dislike of rules. This probably reflected the fact that any postmaterialism effect was counteracted by insecurity some young people felt about making job-related decisions without guidance from rules. Such insecurity seemed not to have created a desire for hierarchy, perhaps because young people believed that their supervisors were less wise than the rules.

36. Probably for the same reason that made age insignificant, years of government contracting experience was significant in neither the desire-for-autonomy nor the dislike-of-rules model.

37. If the cultural climate was driving the desire of younger respondents for job autonomy, this might create a secular trend over time, as do increased affluence and education levels over time, toward increased dissatisfaction with bureaucracy, assuming the cultural climate continues. Another possibility would be that age was related to desire for autonomy through life-cycle effects, according to which younger people in general (whether born in an affluent or poor era) care more about noneconomic values and start paying more attention to "prac-

tical" considerations with age. However, for this sample, a life-cycle explanation seems dubious: in 1993 only 1.5 percent of respondents were 25 or under and 7 percent 30 or under, the period in a life cycle where such effects would be expected.

38. Linda Kaboolian, "Quality Comes to the Public Sector," in *The Quality Movement and Organization Theory*, edited by Robert E. Cole and W. Richard Scott (Thousand Oaks, Calif.: Sage, 2000), pp. 131–54.

39. Compared with firms, within government a smaller proportion of the workforce produces directly for identifiable people outside the organization. If TQM were to have meaning for procurement organizations, the definition of *customer* was important. "TQM defines the next process down the line as the 'customer' for each process. . . . Some customers are external to the organization, others are internal, as when the output of some organization members is passed on to others." J. Richard Hackman and Ruth Wageman, "Total Quality Management: Empirical, Conceptual, and Practical Issues," in Cole and Scott, *The Quality Movement and Organization Theory*, p. 25.

40. Steven Kelman, "The Grace Commission: How Much Waste in Government?" *Public Interest*, no. 78 (1985): 74–75.

41. Philip E. Crewson, "Public-Service Motivation: Building Empirical Evidence of Incidence and Effect," *Journal of Public Administration Research and Theory* 7, no. 4 (1997): 499–518; David J. Houston, "Public-Service Motivation: A Multivariate Test," *Journal of Public Administration Research and Theory* 10, no. 4 (2000): 713–27.

Chapter 4

1. Bryce Ryan and Neal C. Gross, "The Diffusion of Hybrid Seed Corn in Two Iowa Communities," *Rural Sociology* 8, no. 1 (1943): 15–24; James S. Coleman, Elihu Katz, and Herbert Menzel, "The Diffusion of Innovation among Physicians," *Sociometry* 20 (1957): 253–70; James S. Coleman, Elihu Katz, and Herbert Menzel, *Medical Innovation: A Diffusion Study* (New York: Bobbs-Merrill, 1966); Ronald Freedman and John Y. Takeshita, *Family Planning in Taiwan* (Princeton University Press, 1969).

2. See "Technical Footnotes."

3. Everett M. Rogers, *The Diffusion of Innovations*, 4th ed. (New York: Free Press, 1995), pp. 268–74.

4. Ibid., p. 263.

5. Cited ibid., p. 274.

6. Ibid., pp. 273–74, 197.

7. Ibid., p. 273.

8. In chapter 3, I use education partly in this way to predict interest in job autonomy.

9. Rogers, *The Diffusion of Innovations,* p. 273.

10. Idealism, a potential early-adopter trait particularly relevant to organizational or political situations, is not discussed in Rogers. Nor is rebelliousness.

11. For examples, see John P. Kotter, *A Force for Change: How Leadership Differs from Management* (New York: Free Press, 1990), chap. 5; Jeffrey Pfeffer, "Management as Symbolic Action," in *Research in Organizational Behavior,* edited by L. L. Cummings and Barry M. Staw, vol. 3 (Greenwich, Conn.: JAI Press, 1981), pp. 1–52.

12. As quoted in Jeffrey Pfeffer, *Managing with Power* (Boston: Harvard Business School Press, 1992), p. 284.

13. The dependent variable in the first model took four values, two each for change vanguard members and early recruits, based on whether one answered "strongly disagree" or "disagree somewhat" to the question about one's initial attitude to reform, and to the question (discussed in chapter 3) about timing of support or opposition to procurement reform. If the response to the timing question was 1 ("waiting for a long time") and the initial attitude 5, then the respondent took the value 4 on this model; if the initial attitude was 4, then respondent value was 3. If the answer on the timing question was 2 through 10 and the initial attitude 5, then the respondent attitude was 2; if timing was 2 through 10 and initial attitude was 4, then it was 1. The dependent variable in the second model took five values, based on the five possible responses to initial attitude, but subtracting from the sample those in the change vanguard. Creating models in which the dependent variable took four and five values allowed use of ordinary least-squares regression.

14. Because of the modest sample size in the model predicting change vanguard membership, I eliminated nonsignificant variables so as not to bias the model excessively against reporting statistically significant results. For other models in this study, with larger sample sizes, this practice was not followed. However, as an exception I followed the same practice in the second model, to allow results to be more comparable, even though this model had a larger sample size. There are sources of bias in the coefficients because several variables, including the dependent variables, use recall questions and also because of sample attrition. These biases suggest that results must be interpreted with some caution, although in some cases biases make results conservative, that is, they are biased against reporting significant findings, and the size of reported effects is underestimated. See "The Impact of Sample Attrition and Retrospective Recall Bias on Frequency Distributions and Coefficients Discussed in Chapter Three," 2005 (ksghome.harvard.edu/~skelman/MS/SampleAttrition. pdf). I would like to thank my colleague Robert Jensen for helping me think through these issues. I also received valuable advice from my colleagues Suzanne Cooper and Sue Dynarski.

15. This was tested using an interaction effect between job level and idealism (or trust) in explaining change vanguard membership. To test for an interaction between two predictor variables means examining whether the relationship between one of the predictor variables and the dependent variable is greater at some values of the other predictor than at other values of that variable. To illustrate, imagine that high school boys with lots of math ability were encouraged to go as far as they could in developing math skills, while girls with the same ability were discouraged. A simple model with math grades as the dependent variable, and math ability and gender as predictors, might show a modest relationship between ability and grades and a negative one between gender and grades. The phenomenon is easier to understand if an interaction between ability and gender is used, which would show a different relationship between ability and grades for boys and girls. For people in the lowest job category, purchasing agent (2 percent of the sample in this model), there were small negative relationships between these variables and change vanguard membership.

16. The calculations are somewhat complicated, because interpretation of standardized coefficients is not straightforward where interaction effects are involved. Using nonstandardized coefficients, the impact on the dependent variable of moving from the lowest to highest possible value of most-respected co-worker attitude was 1.32 units. At the highest job level, the impact of moving from lowest to highest trust was 1.44 units. For idealism, it was .44 unit, corresponding to a nonstandardized coefficient of .12, a fairly large effect size in this model. These results suggest that both idealism and job level had an impact through a respondent's general ideology and not just through "diffusion of innovation" impacts on idealism-related willingness to support lost causes or the ability (related to education or job level) to conceive of an alternate world that does not already exist. The reason is that the impact of ideology provides a plausible story of why there should be an interaction effect between these variables, while there is no plausible story for why support of lost causes and job level should have a multiplicative effect, though such an interaction might exist in terms of the ability to conceive of an alternate world. The same is the case for interactions involving job level and the ideology variables. This does not mean that diffusion-of-innovation paths exerted no influence, only that it is likely that the path through general ideology did.

17. The strong power of trust and idealism in explaining change vanguard membership does not prove this directly (ideological criticisms might, in principle, have involved problems other than failure to focus on better value entirely, for example, simply an ideological criticism of distrust per se).

18. It would be plausible to believe that providing good customer service, as total quality management preached, might have been the ideological critique of change vanguard members. However, neither question designed to measure the impact of discontent with poor customer service (the questions about timeliness

and about an important part of one's job being to get program officials to obey the rules) explained membership in the change vanguard, though both explained becoming an early recruit.

19. To say that $p = .05$ means that the result is statistically significant at the .05 level, that is, that there is a 5 percent probability the result owes to chance. These numbers are for respondents who stated they would have said in 1992 that the system was broken and who also expressed a positive initial reaction to "reinventing government." If a less restrictive definition is used, including all respondents who stated they would have said the system was broken, the percentages become somewhat less dramatic—24 percent versus 10 percent ($N = 77$, $p = .09$ for two-tailed test).

20. Data are available for only four of the local office heads who had been in the change vanguard at the time reform began and were still in their organizations at the time of the survey.

21. See "Technical Footnotes." A source of ambiguity in the evidence is that the variable in the regression model measuring prereform dissatisfaction with contractor performance did not significantly relate to change vanguard membership ($p = .84$), nor was it significant in the early-recruit model, though it is possible that this question may turn out to have been measuring other phenomena than discontent with the failure of the traditional system to focus on best value. The interaction of this variable with job level was not significant either ($p = .88$). One possibility is that many respondents interpreted the question as mainly about their attitudes toward contractors, in which case there would have been noise from the answers of advocates of the traditional system who shared the system's hostility toward contractors and who would have been less likely to join the change vanguard. Another possibility is that the wording of the question ("We end up getting . . . ") encouraged people to answer it partly or mostly in the context of a judgment of their own personal contracting skills rather than thinking about characteristics of the system, in which case the result would partly measure confidence in one's own contracting or supervisory skills. (The question about timely service, which did not predict change vanguard membership but did predict being an early recruit, had a similar "we" wording, but respondents may well have blamed timeliness problems on "the system.") However, at a minimum this negative result does not provide evidence for the contention that change vanguard members were driven by discontent with the failure of the traditional system to focus on better value from contracting, and it may provide evidence against that view.

22. Note that this variable measures the extent to which the respondent reported being "driven to succeed at my job." One may schematically think of two ways to succeed—by working hard and successfully and by gaining the favor of one's superiors. In the models predicting support for job autonomy, being driven to succeed was related to wanting more autonomy; here, the element of working hard and successfully comes to the fore (gaining the favor of

one's bosses would be less relevant). The same is the case for the role of the drive to succeed in the models explaining successful reform experience that are presented in chapter 8. In this model, dealing with attitudes and not job behavior, the element of pleasing one's superiors comes to the fore, as it does in explaining reform attitude five years into the change effort (see chapter 8).

23. That this scale showed the effects it did is noteworthy, given how far removed questions in the scale were from procurement: based on these results, people who like to explore a new city on their own were more likely to be change vanguard members than those who did not.

24. See "Technical Footnotes."

25. It would not have been the positive association between education and job levels and support for job autonomy, since these were already controlled for in the model. See also "Technical Footnotes." At the lowest level of idealism (assuming a mean sample value for trust, which also interacted with job level), the nonstandardized coefficient in this model for job level was .18, meaning that higher job level was associated with *lower* likelihood of being in the change vanguard. This is consistent with the view that selection or gratefulness effects tended on their own to decrease discontent with the status quo, absent idealism.

26. The results show an ideology-related impact of idealism. We cannot tell from the data whether any of the impact of idealism on change vanguard membership also involved willingness to take on lost causes.

27. As noted later in this chapter, working for the Defense Logistics Agency was associated with being in the change vanguard, and the local office head of one of the two Defense Logistics Agency buying offices in the sample was a strong member of the change vanguard, who also actually introduced more changes in his office before procurement reform than any other local office head in the sample, so possibly this leader had an influence on people.

28. Note that the supervisor attitude question did not specifically measure supervisor membership in the change vanguard, just overall reform attitude.

29. Neither trust in others nor idealism was significant either as a main effect nor interacting with job level ($p = .77$ and .99 for main effects, respectively; .58 and .93 for interactions).

30. Nor were interactions between job level and either variable ($p = .58$ and $p = .25$, respectively) significant.

31. There are other possible explanations for this lack of observed relationship, however. See "Technical Footnotes."

32. At the lowest job level, the (nonstandardized) coefficient for education was only .01, while at the highest it was .27. The nonstandardized coefficient (on a similar five-point scale) for collective self-efficacy was .25.

33. Any impact of the selection effect, however, would still have been present.

34. Rebelliousness, unexpectedly, was a significant predictor in the early-recruit model in the *opposite* direction from in the change vanguard model:

here, it predicted being a skeptic or a fence-sitter. At the time change got unleashed, it would appear that rebels showed hostility against an effort supported by the (new) systemwide leadership and the local leadership now promoting its prochange views. I discuss this further in "Technical Footnotes."

35. Over the longer run, one's most-respected co-worker had a strong positive influence on reform attitudes; evangelism probably became tempered, and continuation of reform probably reduced any resentment over lobbying. Another possibility is that the previous workgroup variable only measured lesser conformity pressures from an antichange workgroup, not positive proselytizing by change vanguard members. See also "Technical Footnotes."

36. It was significant, with modest effect size, in explaining change vanguard membership, but these people had presumably decided to break with the system before the organization experienced its crisis; as suggested earlier, the positive impact may have reflected the influence of a very strong change vanguard member who headed one of the two Defense Logistics Agency offices in the sample.

37. Steven Kelman, "Downsizing, Competition, and Organizational Change in Government: Is Necessity the Mother of Invention?" unpublished, Harvard University, 2005.

38. Cynicism is not the same as rebelliousness, which was already in the model.

39. One indication of such greater cynicism is the difference between Defense Department and civilian agency respondents on a question about initial reaction to reinventing government. The mean value on the question, "My initial reaction to the National Performance Review was very enthusiastic," was 2.92 for civilian agency and 3.22 for Defense Department respondents. However, caution is in order regarding this difference owing to possible reverse causation.

40. Simon Schama, *Citizens* (New York: Knopf, 1989), p. 319.

41. Steven Kelman, *Push Comes to Shove: The Escalation of Student Protest* (Boston: Houghton Mifflin, 1970).

42. See "Technical Footnotes."

43. See, for example, William H. Starbuck and Frances J. Milliken, "Executives' Perceptual Filters: What They Notice and How They Make Sense," in *The Executive Effect,* edited by Donald C. Hambrick (Greenwich, Conn.: JAI Press, 1988), pp. 35–65; Jeffrey Pfeffer, *Competitive Advantage through People* (Harvard Business School Press, 1994), pp. 185–87.

44. However, I present evidence in a different context in chapter 8 that people's views on procurement policy did not seem to play much of a role in promotion decisions.

45. The first-order correlation between job level and venturesomeness or risk tolerance was .12, meaning that lower-level people were less venturesome.

46. Everett M. Rogers, *The Diffusion of Innovations*, 4th ed. (New York: Free Press, 1995), chap. 8.

47. Ibid., p. 295.

48. The word *enthusiast* (and, of course, the word *evangelist*) suggests change vanguard membership. However, the next response alternative was "initially a skeptic, but was brought around and became an enthusiast and evangelist." (Making an exact distinction in the question wording between change vanguard and early recruit would have been infeasible.)

49. Supervisors were separated from nonsupervisors because it was assumed that supervisors would get more requests. See also "Technical Footnotes."

50. Since the extent of requests for advice was reported as of the time of the survey and was not a recall question, it is possible that a person might have become a more frequent source of advice since the beginning of procurement reform because he or she was a reform advocate. The model therefore included the variable measuring overall attitude toward reform as a control. The model also included as controls demographic and other personality characteristics (job tenure, age, sociability) that might be associated with being a source of advice.

51. A higher number for the dependent variable represented being a greater source of advice.

52. Neither venturesomeness nor education, controlling for the other variables, was significant.

53. Bernard M. Bass, *Stogdill's Handbook of Leadership*, rev. ed. (New York: Free Press, 1981), chap. 20.

54. Another aspect of formal authority—the ability to influence the nature of the work environment for people on the front lines—also affects the ability of formal leaders to increase successful experience with reform and the extent of behavior change, themes to which I return in later chapters.

55. These are the questions discussed in chapter 3, where respondents were asked to recall how good a job their office had done five years earlier in providing timely service to program officials and in getting contractors who performed well. There, I discuss my concern that the question on contractor quality did not, in fact, measure what I had intended it to measure. Also, these results may present an unduly optimistic view, because the questions asked the extent to which "we" accomplished something—for example, "We generally get procurements or mods accomplished in a timely manner"—such that negative responses might have implied self-criticism.

56. Note the caveat that this was not a retrospective question but asked about current attitude.

57. I did not pose a question in the Frontline Survey asking whether people initially saw streamlining as what reform was "about" (though perhaps I should have) because I thought virtually all respondents would agree.

58. Since this is not the only time I draw on the literature of social revolution to help explain phenomena involving change in the procurement system, a word is in order for those who might find it unusual to draw analogies between mun-

dane changes in a large government bureaucracy and events as momentous as the French and Russian Revolutions and the collapse of communism in Eastern Europe. My answer would be that occurrences with different consequences may show similar patterns of causation. The epidemiology of the spread of a disease within a community may be similar for the common cold and bubonic plague. One might therefore learn something about the epidemiology of plague by studying the epidemiology of the cold, without implying plague and colds are similar in their effects.

59. V. I. Lenin, *What Is to Be Done?* (Moscow: Foreign Language Publishing House, 1952; originally published 1902), p. 203.

60. Michael Walzer, *Radical Principles* (New York: Basic Books, 1980), pp. 204–05.

61. Lenin, *What Is to Be Done?* p. 204.

62. See "Technical Footnotes."

63. See "Technical Footnotes."

64. In these societies, presumably the "interaction effect" between idealism and education would be even more powerful, since most of the educated were wealthy children who, absent idealism, would have a strong self-interest in supporting the status quo, somewhat analogous to the self-interest of those with higher education or job level in the traditional procurement system.

Chapter 5

1. Both this and the personal account in chapter 9 are adapted from, and to some extent expand on, Steven Kelman, "White House-Initiated Management Change: Implementing Federal Procurement Reform," in *The Managerial Presidency,* edited by James P. Pfiffner, 2nd ed. (College Station: Texas A&M Press, 1997), pp. 239–64.

2. Robert D. Behn, "Management by Groping Along," *Journal of Policy Analysis and Management* 7, no. 4 (1988): 643–63; Olivia Golden, "Innovation in Public Sector Human Services Programs: The Implications of Innovation by 'Groping Along,'" *Journal of Policy Analysis and Management* 9, no. 2 (1990): 219–48.

3. Looking back at footnotes for the case studies in my book, I see I interviewed only five contracting people. Of these, one, as noted in the book, did not behave like a "typical" contracting person. That, in fact, was one in five—eerily close to the proportion in the change vanguard as of 1993—but the similarity was easy to attribute to noise with a small number of interviews. Steven Kelman, *Procurement and Public Management: The Fear of Discretion and the Quality of Government Performance* (Washington: AEI Press, 1990), p. 116.

4. No "hints" were given, so respondents had to recall, on their own, information they had given five or more years earlier.

5. Included were only those who had earlier described the traditional system as broken or "not broken but with significant problems."

6. Furthermore, this question asked about overall reactions to reinventing government, which prominently included a call to downsize the federal workforce in general and the procurement workforce in particular, not just the procurement reforms.

7. These differences are likely to be understated. A large proportion of the sample did not answer this question, reflecting unease on their parts (as career civil servants) in answering what could appear to be a "political" question. More important, however, the percentage that did not answer the question varied widely across initial reaction categories, from 22 percent of change vanguard respondents to 44 percent of the strongest initial opponents. Thus failure to respond to this question correlated strongly with a hostile initial reaction to reform, suggesting that with data on this question from all respondents, the differences would have been even more dramatic.

8. I did not inquire about such details, mostly because I felt that people would be reluctant to talk about such a sensitive topic. Moreover, in the significant number of cases in which the local office head was a member of the change vanguard, probably little overt contention took place.

9. For local office heads enthusiastic about reform, authorization may have been all that was required to get reform initiated. The political process may not have been complicated: the boss may simply have set change in motion.

10. The evidence presented in chapter 4 is that early supporters were more willing than others to expose themselves to the risk of failure. In any event, controlling for a person's risk tolerance, lowering expected negative consequences of failure increases risks a person is willing to take.

11. In addition to the obvious reasons top-level support increased optimism by raising the visibility of the issue, the announcement of change increased the chances of achieving success when new practices were attempted by easing communication across organizations trying reform about pitfalls or "lessons learned," making people more optimistic they could succeed.

12. David Snow and colleagues, writing in the social movement literature tradition, refer to this as "value amplification," by which they mean "the identification, idealization, and elevation of one or more values, presumed basic to prospective constituents but which have not inspired collective action." David A. Snow, E. Burke Rochford, Steven K. Worden, and Robert D. Benford, "Frame Alignment Processes, Micromobilization, and Movement Participation," *American Sociological Review* 51, no. 4 (1986): 464–81, 469.

13. Martha Derthick makes a similar argument about how federal grants to state governments influence local behavior. Derthick seeks to explain a puzzle: When the federal government gives grants, it establishes conditions for receiving them but virtually never enforces these conditions by withholding aid to a recal-

262 NOTES TO PAGES 95–98

citrant state. Nonetheless, Derthick discovered that, for the impact of grants for Massachusetts public assistance programs, federal policies produced major state policy changes. Derthick explains this by arguing that grants provided an opportunity for local political forces who wanted the changes the federal government sought anyway. Martha Derthick, *The Influence of Federal Grants: Public Assistance in Massachusetts* (Harvard University Press, 1970), pp. 201–02. This also commonly occurs in Japanese politics, where advocates of a policy change—in the area of trade or foreign policy, for example—use "outside pressure" from the United States to increase support for change the advocates favor anyway.

14. See "Technical Footnotes."

Chapter 6

1. Rosabeth Moss Kanter, *The Change Masters* (New York: Simon and Schuster, 1983), pp. 99, 201, 101. More than thirty years ago, Neal Crasilneck Gross, Joseph B. Giacquinta, and Marilyn Bernstein issued a plea to treat resistance to change among organizational members as a variable, which should be the subject of research: "We would contend that in many organizations the empirical reality is that a number of their members are exposed to irritating problems and needless strain, and consequently would welcome innovations that appeared to offer solutions to their difficulties. . . . Researchers would be well advised not to treat the degree to which members of an organization are initially resistant to change as 'an organizational given,' but as a matter requiring empirical examination." Neal Crasilneck Gross, Joseph B. Giacquinta, and Marilyn Bernstein, *Implementing Organizational Innovations: A Sociological Analysis of Planned Educational Change* (New York: Basic Books, 1971), p. 204. This article, however, has essentially been ignored. I have located four other works suggesting the unleashing-politics path. First, in a study of organizational change at Imperial Chemical Industries in Britain, Andrew Pettigrew suggests that variations in successful change in different divisions initiated by outside change experts were partly owing to differences in existing receptivity to change in the units. But a good deal of Pettigrew's discussion relates to different levels of threat units faced from their external market environment, and he presents the most receptive environments merely as more willing to accept change, not as including people actively looking for an opportunity to initiate a change process. Andrew Pettigrew, *The Awakening Giant* (Oxford, U.K.: Basil Blackwell, 1985), chaps. 11, 12. See also Andrew Pettigrew, Ewan Ferlie, and Lorne McKee, *Shaping Strategic Change: Making Change in Large Organizations* (London: Sage Publications, 1992), chap. 2. Second, there is a short observation in an article by Jean Bartunek about organizational change in an order of nuns that came to see its mission as including promotion of social justice. At the end of the article, Bartunek asks (while noting the answer is "beyond the scope of

this paper") why papal statements in support of social justice became the occasion for initiating major change in the order she studied while in other orders the same statements had no such effect. The answer, she speculates, "is that some order members had a particularly strong interest in social justice work . . . before the period described in the case began." Jean M. Bartunek, "Changing Interpretive Schemes and Organizational Restructuring: The Example of a Religious Order," *Administrative Science Quarterly* 29, no. 3 (1984): 355–72, 368. The pope's statements gave them an opportunity to set in motion a process they would have supported even without these statements. Third, the study that perhaps comes closest to the argument presented here is the discussion by McNulty and Ferlie of business process reengineering at a British hospital. There were significant differences in the success of the initiative across different units of the hospital, and these differences resulted from the presence of a constituency with its own change agenda in some units, an agenda resonating with that of advocates of reengineering in the hospital's senior leadership. However, for reasons discussed later, the authors present their findings as an example of organizational change *failure*, not success. Terry McNulty and Ewan Ferlie, *Reengineering Health Care* (Oxford University Press, 2002). Finally, after I developed this theory there appeared an article that, in a theoretical presentation, has some features in common with the theory presented here. Myeong-Gu Seo and W. E. Douglas Creed, "Institutional Contradictions, Praxis, and Institutional Change: A Dialectical Perspective," *Academy of Management Review* 27, no. 2 (2002): 222–47. Additionally, some discussions have applied, though usually not using these words, a natural selection approach to organizational change, but generally in the context of change in corporate strategy, not frontline change. The best known of these appear in writings on intraorganizational politics. They discuss the role of the external environment in precipitating change, but the perspective is different: the basic idea is that market changes favor one faction over another and that, as times change, organizational winners change. Jeffrey Pfeffer, *Managing with Power* (Boston: Harvard Business School Press, 1992), pp. 304–06; see also Royston Greenwood and C. R. Hinings, "Understanding Radical Organizational Change: Bringing Together the Old and the New Institutionalism," *Academy of Management Review* 21, no. 4 (1996): 1022–54. Other discussions in the literature on strategy change suggesting natural selection appear to talk about variation of opinion rather than simply variations in organizational interest. Henry Mintzberg and Alexandra McHugh, "Strategy Formation in an Adhocracy," *Administrative Science Quarterly* 30, no. 2 (1985): 160–97; R. A. Burgelman, "A Process Model of Strategic Business Exit: Implications for an Evolutionary Perspective on Strategy," in "Evolutionary Perspectives on Strategy," special issue, *Strategic Management Journal* 17 (Summer 1996): 193–214. Although these approaches have some similarities with what I have discussed, the selection force I present is top leadership consciously seeking change, rather than impersonal (market) forces in the environment.

2. Quoted in Peter Hennessy, *Whitehall* (London: Secker and Warburg, 1989), p. 596.

3. See "Technical Footnotes."

4. David A. Snow and Robert D. Benford, "Ideology, Frame Resonance, and Participant Mobilization," *International Social Movement Research* 1 (1988): 197–217, 199.

5. See Graham Allison and Philip Zelikow, *Essence of Decision: Explaining the Cuban Missile Crisis*, 2nd ed. (New York: Longman, 1999), p. 299. Students of political advocacy also use the general term *framing* to refer to this phenomenon. Messages congruent with existing knowledge structures are also more likely to make an impact than incongruent ones. Shelley E. Taylor and Jennifer Crocker, "Schematic Bases of Social Information Processing," in *Social Cognition: The Ontario Symposium*, edited by E. Tory Higgins, C. Peter Herman, and Mark P. Zanna, vol. 1 (Hillsdale, N.J.: Lawrence Erlbaum, 1981), p. 98.

6. Saul D Alinsky, *Rules for Radicals* (New York: Vintage Books, 1971), pp. 108, 127; see also Elizabeth S. Clemens, "Organizational Form as Frame: Collective Identity and Political Strategy in the American Labor Movement," in *Comparative Perspectives on Social Movements: Opportunities, Mobilizing Structures, and Cultural Framings*, edited by Doug McAdam, John McCarthy, and Mayer Zald (Cambridge University Press, 1996), p. 214.

7. Richard Fletcher, *The Barbarian Conversion: From Paganism to Christianity* (New York: Henry Holt, 1997), pp. 253–54, 265–66.

8. Ibid., p. 273.

9. David A. Snow, E. Burke Rochford, Steven K. Worden, and Robert D. Benford, "Frame Alignment Processes, Micromobilization, and Movement Participation," *American Sociological Review* 51 (July 1986): 464–81.

10. Ibid., pp. 472–73.

11. What occurred is similar to what the literature on innovation refers to as the "re-invention" of an innovation as it is implemented (Rogers, *The Diffusion of Innovations*, pp. 174–80). This involves either customizing the innovation to fit local circumstances or picking for implementation a few features from the many the innovation included. Rogers finds that reinvention is common, though he does not discuss the mechanism for generating it noted here. (Reasons he cites include consciously changing the innovation to adapt to specifics of local conditions or of learning as one proceeds and the simple pride of developing a "homegrown" version of the innovation.)

12. Since members of the coalition were not necessarily aware they had different agendas, this should be distinguished from a conventional view of political coalitions suggesting that groups consciously aware of differences choose to band together to increase their joint political strength.

13. Andrew Van de Ven, Douglas Polley, Raghu Garud, and Sankaran Venkataraman, *The Innovation Journey* (Oxford University Press, 1999), p. 57.

14. Paul E. Berman, *Federal Programs Supporting Educational Change: Factors Affecting Implementation and Continuation* (Santa Monica, Calif.: Rand, 1977).

15. Armen A. Alchian and Harold Demsetz, "Production, Information Costs, and Economic Organization," *American Economic Review* 62, no. 5 (1972): 777–95. Bizarrely, this phrase, "to shirk," is claimed to be value neutral. Similarly, Douglas McGregor classically, if inelegantly, refers to "Theory X" of employee motivation. Theory X starts with the assumption that "the average human being has an inherent dislike of work and will avoid it if he can," so "most people must be coerced, controlled, directed, threatened with punishment to get them to put forth adequate effort toward the achievement of organizational objectives." Douglas McGregor, *The Human Side of Enterprise* (New York: McGraw-Hill, 1960).

16. This is consistent with most literature on job design, which argues that giving people more autonomy tends not only to make them happier with work but also to improve performance, as people work harder and come up with better ideas.

17. Charles L. Schultze, *The Public Use of Private Interest* (Brookings, 1977).

18. These ranged from introduction of credit cards for small purchases through simplified procedures for small buys and for the purchase of commercial items, as well as various changes to streamline operation of the competitive process for larger procurements.

19. McNulty and Ferlie, *Reengineering Health Care*.

Chapter 7

1. Many, for example, feature prominently in one of the most influential modern books on organizational behavior, Karl Weick's *The Social Psychology of Organizing* (New York: McGraw-Hill, 1979).

2. John P. Kotter, *Leading Change* (Harvard Business School Press, 1996), chap. 8, p. 123; see also Karl E. Weick, "Small Wins: Redefining the Scale of Social Problems," *American Psychologist* 39, no. 2 (1984): 40–49.

3. Michael Hammer and Steven A. Stanton, *The Reengineering Revolution* (New York: HarperBusiness, 1995), p. 129; Kotter, *Leading Change*, pp. 155–57.

4. Hammer and Stanton, *Reengineering Revolution,* pp. 129, 133.

5. In both cases, an "agree" response reflected a negative reaction to the change, "disagree" a positive one. These percentages may all be skewed in favor of reform support by recall bias, but there is no reason to believe they would be differentially skewed, so differences are certainly meaningful.

6. One question directed respondents to "recall the first change that took place in this office since 1993 that you associated in your mind with the idea of

'acquisition reform'" and then asked, "What was the experience with the change?" Sixty-five percent of those with good experiences volunteered a reason that the experience had been positive.

7. Percentages include only respondents who reported a positive experience and provided a reason the experience had been positive. Of the modest number reporting negative first experience, 30 percent stated as the reason that they had been told the change would make their jobs easier, but it had not.

8. The dependent variable was the score on the procurement-reform feeling thermometer.

9. First, the model included a control for the respondent's initial attitude, since this might affect both how successful one regarded one's experiences as having been and the dependent variable. Second, the percentage of the total variance in responses to the dependent variable explained by predictor variables is measured by the statistic R^2. The R^2 number presented here excludes the distortion and initial attitude variables. Third, arguing that substantive experience influenced attitudes suggests people concluded at t that, say, reform had empowered them and then, at $t + 1$, decided therefore they liked reform. However, these data come from a survey at one point in time, so the direction of causation might be the opposite, from reform support to good experience. In such cases, a respondent would be engaging in perceptual confirmation. The model therefore also included a control variable to measure distortion, developed, from other questions in the Frontline Survey, as follows: One question asked respondents, "What's your best guess about the proportion of your co-workers (at your office) whom you would regard as supportive of acquisition reform?" Since these data are available by workgroup, the proportion of co-workers who actually were supporters is known (that is, the percentage for whom the value of the feeling-thermometer variable measuring reform support was greater than 50). To form the distortion variable, the *actual* percentage of supportive co-workers was subtracted from respondent *perception* of co-worker support. (The categories on the survey question were "almost everyone," "about two-thirds," "about half," "about one-third," and "very few." To make these calculations, "almost everyone" was assumed to be 90 percent, and "very few" was assumed to be 20 percent.) The result could be a positive number (respondent overestimated co-worker support for reform), a negative number (respondent underestimated), or zero (respondent estimated correctly). To determine a respondent's value for distortion, if there was a positive value from this calculation and the respondent's own score for reform support was greater than 50, the value for distortion was equal to the calculated number. The same was the case if there was a negative value from the calculation and the respondent's own score for reform support was less than or equal to 50. If the value from the calculation was zero, or if the respondent overestimated support and was himself or herself critical of reform, or underestimated support while being personally supportive,

the value was set at zero; it was also set at zero if the respondent gave the response alternative "don't know" to the question about co-worker support. This variable thus measured the extent to which, if one was positive toward reform, one overestimated reform support among co-workers, and, if negative, one underestimated it. The higher the value the more a reform supporter engaged in perceptual confirmation. The lower the value, the more a critic engaged in it. Values around zero show a low degree of perceptual confirmation. With variables in a model subject to perceptual confirmation, including the distortion variable controlled for this. The distortion variable is included in a number of the other models presented here, where there are variables subject to perceptual confirmation. See also "Technical Footnotes."

10. To compute the effect size of each variable, one may multiply the coefficient by four. This represents by how many units (on a scale of 0 to 100) the predicted value of reform support increased if the respondent moved from "strongly disagree" to "strongly agree" on the experience variable.

11. All mean values except for the too-close-to-contractors question were reverse coded, so a higher value reflected more successful experience.

12. Overall mean values were positive toward reform-related experiences even in situations where only a minority agreed with the statement, because many respondents checked "mixed feelings."

13. This is a rough approximation. If positive feedback mechanisms themselves promoted successful experience, beyond the "inherent" nature of those experiences, this would mean that the role of positive feedback in explaining consolidation of support for change is understated: part of any impact of successful experience on change support derived from the role of positive feedback in contributing to successful experience. This would mean that the approach presented here underestimates the impact of positive feedback mechanisms. On the other hand, this approach exaggerates the effect of positive feedback. First, it in effect attributes everything not explained by good experience in these two areas (including measurement error) to positive feedback Second, it assumes that sources of successful experience less important in explaining initial discontent, such as experiencing reform as helping the government select best-value contractors, did not help explain development of proreform attitudes.

14. Robert Jervis, *System Effects: Complexity in Political and Social Life* (Princeton University Press, 1997), p. 125, and, generally, chap. 4.

15. Thomas C. Schelling, *Micromotives and Macrobehavior* (New York: Norton, 1978), chap. 4; Everett M. Rogers, *Diffusion of Innovations*, 4th ed. (New York: Free Press, 1995), pp. 257–61.

16. Negative feedback gets short shrift in the literature on the diffusion of innovation; for example, the literature notes the impact of the good experience of early adopters in encouraging diffusion, without noting possible counterinfluence of negative early experience. However, that diffusion of innovation is not

immediately self-sustaining suggests the presence early on of negative feedback forces holding diffusion back.

17. Frank J. Andress, "The Learning Curve as a Production Tool," *Harvard Business Review* 32, no. 1 (1954): 87–97; Roger W. Schmenner, *Production/ Operations Management*, 5th ed. (Englewood Cliffs, N.J.: Prentice-Hall, 1993), pp. 462–66.

18. Albert Bandura, *Social Foundations of Thought and Action* (Englewood-Cliffs, N.J.: Prentice-Hall, 1986), p. 49.

19. Amy Edmondson, "Psychological Safety and Learning Behavior in Work Teams," *Administrative Science Quarterly* 44 (1999): 350–83.

20. One can easily imagine, though, that unsympathetic co-workers or supervisors might create a climate of psychological danger for trying out the change, thus to a limited extent generating negative feedback.

21. Robert K. Merton, *Social Theory and Social Structure* (New York: Free Press, 1968), pp. 421–36. See also "Technical Footnotes."

22. Robert Rosenthal and Lenore Jacobson, *Pygmalion in the Classroom* (New York: Holt, Rinehart and Winston, 1968).

23. Russell A. Jones, *Self-Fulfilling Prophecies: Social, Psychological, and Physiological Effects of Expectancies* (Hillsdale, N.J.: Lawrence Erlbaum, 1977), p. 108. See also "Technical Footnotes."

24. Jones, *Self-Fulfilling Prophecies*, chap. 7.

25. Ibid., pp. 167–68; see also W. Peter Archibald, "Alternative Explanations for Self-Fulfilling Prophecy," *Psychological Bulletin* 81, no. 1 (1974): 74–84, 78.

26. Albert S. King, "Expectation Effects in Organizational Change," *Administrative Science Quarterly* 19, no. 2 (1974): 221–30.

27. Charles A. O'Reilly III and David F. Caldwell, "Informational Influence as a Determinant of Perceived Task Characteristics and Job Satisfaction," *Journal of Applied Psychology* 64, no. 2 (1979): 157–63, 161.

28. If perceptual confirmation simply meant that going-in attitude was reflected in coming-out attitude, then it would not change one's attitude, it would only stabilize it. However, perceptual confirmation can change the quality of one's perceived experience from what it otherwise would have been, influencing attitude indirectly.

29. Leon Festinger, *A Theory of Cognitive Dissonance* (Stanford University Press, 1962).

30. See "Technical Footnotes."

31. See "Technical Footnotes."

32. Jack W. Brehm and Arthur R. Cohen. *Explorations in Cognitive Dissonance* (New York: Wiley, 1962); Robert A. Wicklund and Jack W. Brehm, *Perspectives on Cognitive Dissonance* (Hillsdale, N.J.: Lawrence Erlbaum, 1976); John J. Sherwood, James W. Barron, and H. Gordon Finch, "Cognitive Dissonance: Theory and Research," in *Experimental Social Psychology*, edited by

Charles Graham McClintock (Holt, Rinehart and Winston, 1972) present good summaries of this literature.

33. Sherwood, Barron, and Finch, "Cognitive Dissonance," p. 84.

34. Joel Foxman and Robert C. Radtke, "Negative Expectancy and the Choice of an Aversive Task," *Journal of Personality and Social Psychology* 15, no. 2 (1970): 253–57; Ronald Comer and James D. Laird, "Choosing to Suffer as a Consequence of Expecting to Suffer: Why Do People Do It?" *Journal of Personality and Social Psychology* 32, no. 1 (1975): 92–101.

35 See "Technical Footnotes."

36. Lee Ross and Richard E. Nisbett, *The Person and the Situation: Perspectives on Social Psychology* (New York: McGraw-Hill, 1991), p. 50.

37. Robert B. Cialdini, J. T. Cacioppo, Rodney Bassett, and J. A. Miller, "Low-Ball Procedure for Producing Compliance: Commitment Then Cost," *Journal of Personality and Social Psychology* 36, no. 2 (1978): 463–76, 465. The difference between foot-in-the-door and lowballing is that in the former case an individual is willing to undertake larger actions having already undertaken smaller ones, while in the latter the individual is willing to continue to undertake a given action despite increased cost. Although these have many similarities, foot-in-the-door is probably more relevant to the study of organizational change.

38. Jonathan L. Freedman and Scott C. Fraser, "Compliance without Pressure: The Foot-in-the-Door Technique," *Journal of Personality and Social Psychology* 4, no. 1 (1966): 195–202.

39. Experiments have also shown an impact from lowballing. Subjects who had been asked to participate in an experiment at seven in the morning were about half as likely to agree to participate as those who initially agreed and were then assigned that time. Cialdini and others, "Low-Ball Procedure for Producing Compliance," p. 465. The difference in the percentage who actually showed up was even greater. See also "Technical Footnotes."

40. Simon Schama, *Citizens* (New York: Knopf, 1989), pp. 123–31.

41. Jervis, *System Effects*, p. 53.

42. Theodore Newcomb's pioneering sociological study examines the effect of social influence on making students at Bennington College more liberal while at school. Theodore M. Newcomb, *Personality and Social Change* (New York: Dryden, 1943). Leon Festinger and his colleagues conducted a corresponding pioneering social-psychological study at a married-student housing complex at MIT, showing high levels of intragroup uniformity in attitudes regarding and degree of activity in a tenants' association for student renters. Leon Festinger, Stanley Schacker, and Kurt Bach, *Social Pressures in Informal Groups* (New York: Harper, 1950). Both George Homans and Festinger present early summaries and interpretations of this literature. George C. Homans, *The Human Group* (Harcourt, Brace, and World, 1950); Leon Festinger, "A Theory of Social

Comparison Processes," *Human Relations* 7 (1954): 117–40. For a more detailed discussion in the context of procurement reform, see Steven Kelman, "Social Influence on Spread of Employee Support for an Organizational Change in Government: Conformity, Information, Persuasion?" Cambridge, Mass., 2005.

43. Or, alternatively, a majority of individuals in the group.

44. Elisabeth Noelle-Neumann, *The Spiral of Silence*, 2nd ed. (University of Chicago Press, 1993), chap. 2.

45. Georg Simmel, "Fashion," *American Journal of Sociology* 62 (1957): 541–58, 543 (originally published 1904).

46. Ronald S. Burt, "Social Contagion and Innovation: Cohesion versus Structural Equivalence," *American Journal of Sociology* 92, no. 6 (1987): 1287–1335, 1289; see also Sushil Bikhchandani, David Hirshleifer, and Ivo Welch, "A Theory of Fads, Fashion, Custom, and Cultural Change as Informational Cascades," *Journal of Political Economy* 100, no. 5 (1992): 992–1017; and Robert Axelrod, *The Complexity of Cooperation* (Princeton University Press, 1997), pp. 58–59.

47. A large literature in social psychology examines the importance of persuasive arguments made in groups in explaining attitude shifts among individuals in the group, compared with the effects of conformity. Eugene Bernstein and Amiram Vinokur, "Testing Two Classes of Theories about Group-Induced Shifts in Individual Choice," *Journal of Experimental Social Psychology* 9, no. 2 (1973): 123–37; Eugene Bernstein and Amiram Vinokur, "Persuasive Argumentation and Social Comparison as Determinants of Attitude Polarization," *Journal of Experimental Social Psychology* 13, no. 4 (1977), pp. 315–32.

48. Steven Kelman, *Push Comes to Shove: The Escalation of Student Protest* (Boston: Houghton Mifflin, 1970).

49. Kristen Luker, *Abortion and the Politics of Motherhood* (University of California Press, 1984), chap. 6.

50. As quoted in Jervis, *System Effects*, p. 166.

51. See "Technical Footnotes."

52. A. P. MacDonald, "Internal-External Locus of Control," in *Measures of Social Psychological Attitudes* (Ann Arbor, Mich.: Survey Research Center, 1973).

53. See "Technical Footnotes."

54. This fact is discussed in a different context in chapter 4. In modeling participation in the reform coalition, this is noted as a source of possible error in estimates for various predictor variables.

55. In the case of debureaucratizing change, they might be more supportive because they are on average younger and more educated than people already in the organization.

56. Why might such asymmetries occur? The example of why operation of the self-fulfilling prophecy may demonstrate change consolidation–promoting

asymmetry serves as an illustration. One reason is positive illusions: if people think they are better at doing things than they in fact are, this creates a built-in bias toward people's generally acting in ways making it more likely they will perform well, over and above positive and negative performance expectations growing out of the circumstances of individual situations (such as one's initial attitude toward procurement reform). A second reason applies specifically to experience in organizations: if supervisors organize change activities, they will most likely limit the ability of subordinates with negative expectations to behave in ways (say, by being slothful or sloppy) causing experience to be negative. Asymmetries might also occur regarding the differential impact of proreform and antireform supervisors (or other local leaders) on individual attitudes. If systemwide leadership is pushing a change, critical local leaders are likely to be less vocal in opposition than are supportive ones in support, creating potential for net positive feedback even absent majority support.

57. Since perceptual confirmation has not operated earlier in the organization's life, the way mean workgroup attitude operated to influence reform support even before the change process had began, one cannot benefit from perceptual confirmation's becoming "less negative" the way one can in the case of mean workgroup attitude.

Chapter 8

1. The rules included ones making it more difficult for the government to use credit cards for very small buys, procedures used in awarding contracts of less than $100,000, and rules imposed on companies selling commercial items.

2. *Federal Acquisition Regulation* 1.102(d) (www.acqnet.gov/far/load-mainre.html).

3. No variable, from the Frontline Survey or otherwise, allowed testing for the impact of the learning curve on successful experience with reform over time, so no empirical test of this influence was possible. The considerable research on operation of the learning curve, however, allows us to assume that it was a source of positive feedback.

4. The sample included employees who had started working in government contracting in 1994 or later, the time when people might have begun having a first experience with reform. See also "Technical Footnotes."

5. This statement was chosen because it was the overall experience variable with the largest effect size in the earlier regression explaining change support. It was possible that a regression predicting empowerment might reflect factors related to empowerment specifically, rather than to having had successful experience with reform generally. For this reason, the same model was also run with two other overall experience variables (whether reform made the respondent's job easier and whether reform made it easier for the government to get the best value). Generally, results were very similar. Where there are differences, they are

noted in the text or in footnotes. The overall experience model—and also the current reform support model to be presented later in this chapter—gives a net cumulative impact of a variable for the entire period of the change process but makes it impossible to test whether the impact of a mechanism was different at the end of the process versus the middle or toward the beginning.

6. See "Technical Footnotes."

7. And the result was just barely statistically significant ($p = .10$).

8. The mean value for supervisor reform attitude, based on subordinate report, was somewhat more proreform than neutral value (3.1, just above "somewhat supportive"), which is consistent with self-reports of supervisors in the Frontline Survey sample presented in chapter 4. This was also the case for local office head attitude, where 69 percent were in the reform coalition (see chapter 4). (The percentage with the most proreform value in this model was just under half, but this included only change vanguard members.) For most-respected co-worker, 41 percent were described by the respondent as "an early enthusiast." It is a bit hard from the wording of this question to determine whether a majority were in the reform coalition; a cautious view would be that there was probably not quite a majority.

9. See "Technical Footnotes."

10. There was no asymmetry; the quadratic terms were insignificant ($p = .42$ and $p = .92$, respectively). The quadratic term for mission impact was also insignificant ($p = .70$).

11. These self-reports may reflect positive illusions.

12. There was an extremely small negative relationship between education and successful experience at the highest job level and between job level and successful experience at the highest education level.

13. See "Technical Footnotes."

14. This controls both for initial attitudes toward the substance of reform and for perceptual confirmation.

15. The quadratic term was not significant ($p = .53$).

16. However, if one assumes current-attitude bias recalling initial expectation, the actual mean value was below 3.0, so the self-fulfilling prophecy did not on balance promote successful experience at the very beginning of the change process.

17. Perceptual confirmation did not have an asymmetric effect (the p value of the quadratic term was .92).

18. Actually, the highest level of self-confidence was associated with a decline in successful experience, compared with the next-highest levels. This is a puzzling result, explained perhaps by elements of reality (those with the highest self-confidence may get cocky and stumble) and perhaps by artifacts of responses to the questions (these individuals may set a higher bar for success, depressing self-reported scores on successful experience). This same result appeared in the burden-reduction model, where the effect of self-confidence was also asymmetric.

Quadratic terms for being driven to succeed and impact on mission were insignificant ($p = .43$ and $p = .75$, respectively). For a discussion of how the net effect of nonlinear variables was calculated, see "Technical Footnotes."

19. See "Technical Footnotes."

20. This result is consistent with the finding, presented in chapter 9, that respondents in offices whose local office heads worked to "deepen" the understanding of frontline employees to go beyond streamlining also were less likely to report that reform was about taking initiative on the front lines rather than leadership reform directives.

21. See "Technical Footnotes."

22. As measured by its standardized coefficient in a model, not shown here, without interactions.

23. Moving from an expectation rating of 4 to a 5 rating was associated with a very large .32-unit more successful experience, while moving from expectation 2 to 1 did not decrease successful experience at all (actually, there was a slight .02-unit increase). See also "Technical Footnotes."

24. The p values were .33 and .17, respectively.

25. The sample mean was –0.74—less than one unit, on a scale from –100 to +100.

26. The mean sample value (reverse coded) for liking change more over time was 3.71 (compared with 3.20 for believing reform had been empowering), with 62 percent agreeing (compared with 43 percent for reform being empowering).

27. See "Technical Footnotes."

28. With as-time-goes-by support included in the model, the p value for burden reduction (.12) actually fell just short of significance.

29. This argument does not require respondents to be conscious of the operation of these mechanisms. The survey questions asked opinions on various questions; it is the regression analysis that controls for experience-related effects and suggests that something beyond those effects helps explain reform attitude. Since one can hardly ask people direct questions to detect the existence of nonconscious psychological phenomena, the use of this variable in this way provides an unobtrusive test for the impact of these mechanisms.

30. A unique variance analysis involves putting all the other variables in the model, adding the variable of interest at the end, and examining the change in R^2.

31. R^2 changed from .32 to .33, removing the control variables. This is a very conservative test, because it assigns all covariance between as-time-goes-by support and other variables to the other variables, a particularly big problem here because of the (not surprisingly) high correlations among the variables. Using the same method, empowerment, the substantive experience variable with the largest effect size, accounted for unique variance of only 2 percent. See also "Technical Footnotes."

32. See "Technical Footnotes." Except for the three variables discussed in the text, none of the other variables tested showed evidence of asymmetry. P values

for quadratic terms for most-respected co-worker, supervisor, deference, career-enhancement perception, same message, and proreform office prestige were .17, .65, .26, .87, .95, and .18, respectively.

33. This is the coefficient when mean workgroup attitude is run as a main effect only, without interactions or a quadratic term (not shown in the table).

34. Actual sample values for mean workgroup attitude ranged from 35 to 95. The table shows 10-unit increments in mean workgroup attitude starting with the lowest sample value, proceeding to a 10-unit increment around the sample mean value for this variable, and ending with the highest sample value. See also "Technical Footnotes."

35. At the sample mean value for within-workgroup consensus.

36. The low, medium, and high values for within-workgroup consensus were chosen as 10, 20, and 25. See also "Technical Footnotes."

37. See "Technical Footnotes."

38. See "Technical Footnotes."

39. Except for the impact of systemwide procurement leadership at the highest respondent deference level. See also "Technical Footnotes."

40. Steven Kelman, "Social Influence on Spread of Employee Support for an Organizational Change in Government: Conformity, Information, Persuasion?" Cambridge, Mass., 2005. These mechanisms generated only positive feedback, with no countervailing negative feedback.

41. Supervisors disproportionately were initial reform supporters (see chapter 4); by the time of the survey, the vast majority supported reform. Forty-five percent reported that their immediate supervisor was "enthusiastic" about reform, 45 percent "somewhat supportive," and only 10 percent "somewhat skeptical" or "critical."

42. For systemwide leader influence, moving (for a most-deferent respondent) from minimum to maximum influence produced a very large 12.0-unit increase in the reform support scale of 1 to 100, while for the influence of the local office head, similar movement produced a 5.2-unit increase. By contrast, a movement from minimum to maximum value for most-respected co-worker influence produced a 9.4-unit increase in reform support. See also "Technical Footnotes."

43. For systemwide leader attitude, the crossover in values for the deference scale—the point at which systemwide leaders started promoting individual reform support—was 2.01 (on a scale of 1 to 5). For local office heads, it was 2.31. Ninety-four percent of the sample for whom systemwide leaders promoted reform support had values for deference; for local office heads, it was 90 percent of the sample.

44. An alternative view, following the discussion in chapter 4 of routes for systemwide leader influence, is that this difference across the three levels of leadership is explained by leader roles in providing reassurance or cover vis-à-vis the

wider political system. Systemwide leaders would be in the best position to pro-vide this, followed by local office heads, with first-line supervisors last. Since there is no reason to believe the impact of this alternative leader role would vary with respondent deference, visioning would be expected to account for at least part of leader influence. However, the possibility that the reassurance or cover role of leaders explains part of these results cannot be excluded.

45. $P = .19$, though the sign of the coefficient was in the predicted direction. Nor was the interaction between training and expectation significant ($p = .25$).

46. The p value for the second was .45. The p value for the career-enhancing variable was .13, just short of significance, but the sign was in the opposite direction (the more one thought reform support was career enhancing, the lower one's support). If the relationship here was real, it would appear to involve reverse causation: reform skeptics may have mocked the reform support of oth-ers as occurring because showing support for reform was career enhancing.

47. There was an effect, of very modest size and falling somewhat short of significance ($p = .16$), going in the opposite (nonironic) direction: respondents with an internal locus of control were more likely to support reform, a policy seeking to give them greater control over their destinies.

48. Indeed, at the highest value for being driven to succeed, reform support was actually very slightly lower (a little less than 1 unit) than at the next-highest value. Those really sensitive to what needed to be done to curry favor seem to have hedged their bets about the long-term future of the reform effort.

49. $P = .39$. The quadratic term was also insignificant ($p = .36$). The correla-tion between mean workgroup support for reform and mean workgroup first experience was .42, so good workgroup first experience had an impact on work-group attitude, which in turn exerted social influence on individual attitude. This model was run on the whole sample; however, running it only with respon-dents who had started working in government procurement before 1995 pro-duced the same results.

50. All but three of the nineteen offices studied experienced decreases in the size of their procurement workforce from 1993 to 1998, ranging from 40 per-cent to 6 percent. Two small offices, both in civilian agencies, increased the size of their procurement workforce, by 5 and 29 percent, and another civilian agency saw no change in workforce size.

51. That is, those who were at their jobs when reform started and were still around at the time of the survey.

52. See "Technical Footnotes."

53. See "Technical Footnotes."

54. At least those who were still in their jobs five years later, again making this a conservative test.

55. This was for respondents who had stayed in the same buying office (so people who got a new supervisor only because they had switched to a new office

were excluded). Subordinates who agreed with this statement (N = 100) reported a higher mean reform attitude of the new supervisor—3.7, on a scale of 1 to 4—while the mean supervisor attitude reported by subordinates who disagreed with the statement or had mixed feelings (N = 471) was 3.2. respectively. Of course, a subordinate might have felt that the new supervisor had gotten the job because of reform support even if in reality support reform had played no role in the selection decision.

56. Robert Jervis, *System Effects: Complexity in Political and Social Life* (Princeton University Press, 1997), pp. 126–27, 131–35.

57. What sticks out is what gets noticed. Susan T. Fiske and Shelley E. Taylor, *Social Cognition*, 2nd ed. (New York: McGraw-Hill, 1991), pp. 294–95.

58. Georg Simmel, "Fashion," *American Journal of Sociology* 62 (1957): 547–48 (originally published 1904); Jack W. Brehm, *A Theory of Psychological Reactance* (New York: Academic Press, 1966).

59. This is consistent with findings that people pay more attention to bad news than good. Joseph N. Cappella and Kathleen Hall Jamieson, *Spiral of Cynicism: The Press and the Public Good* (Oxford University Press, 1997).

Chapter 9

1. A careful reader may have noticed this regarding some of the mechanisms discussed in chapter 7. For example, foot-in-the-door refers to the effect of a small behavior change on the willingness to undertake a larger behavior change. But presumably this occurs because the small behavior change has an impact on a person's attitude toward the kind of change in question.

2. These factors influenced behavior change controlling for their indirect impact on behavior change through impact on attitude.

3. R. T. LaPiere, "Attitudes versus Actions," *Social Forces* 3 (1934): 230–37. Restaurants were far more likely to serve the couple than they had stated they would be in the letter.

4. For example, see Herbert Blumer, "Attitudes and the Social Act," *Social Problems* 3, no. 2 (1955): 59–65; Irwin Deutscher, "Words and Deeds: Social Science and Social Policy," *Social Problems* 13 (1966): 235–54; Allan W. Wicker, "Attitudes versus Actions: The Relationship of Verbal and Overt Behavioral Responses to Attitude Objects," *Journal of Social Issues* 25, no. 4 (1969): 41–78.

5. Deutscher, "Words and Deeds."

6. One-third of respondents in a survey asking whether a fictitious piece of legislation—the Public Affairs Act—should be repealed expressed either the view that it should be repealed or that it should not, without questioning whether it existed. Herbert Asher, *Polling and the Public: What Every Citizen Should Know* (Washington: CQ Press, 1992), pp. 21–22. See also "Technical Footnotes."

7. Philip E. Converse, "Attitudes and Non-Attitudes: Continuation of a Dialogue," in *The Quantitative Analysis of Social Problems,* edited by Edward R. Tufte (Reading, Mass.: Addison-Wesley, 1970), pp. 168–89.

8. Blumer, *Attitudes and the Social Act*, p. 6; Deutscher, "Words and Deeds," p. 248. See also "Technical Footnotes."

9. Richard J. Hill, "Attitudes and Behavior," in *Social Psychology: Sociological Perspectives,* edited by Morris Rosenberg and Ralph H. Turner (New York: Basic Books, 1981), p. 351.

10. Icek Ajzen, "The Directive Influence of Attitudes on Behavior," in *The Psychology of Action,* edited by Peter M. Gollwitzer and John A. Bargh (New York: Guilford Press, 1996), p. 385; see also Herbert C. Kelman, "Attitude and Behavior: A Social-Psychological Problem," in *Major Social Issues: A Multidisciplinary View,* edited by J. Milton Yinger and Stephen J. Cutler (New York: Free Press, 1978), pp. 412–20.

11. In a natural experiment involving Cornell University freshmen arriving on campus in the midst of a housing shortage, there was a dramatically greater link between attitudes toward the crisis and behavior in responding to the crisis (signing petitions, attending meetings) among freshmen who were assigned temporary housing than among those who had not been. Reported in Russell H. Fazio and Mark P. Zanna, "Direct Experience and Attitude-Behavior Consistency," in *Advances in Experimental Social Psychology*, edited by Leonard Berkowitz, vol. 14 (New York: Academic Press, 1981), pp. 166–68; see also Hill, "Attitudes and Behavior," p. 363; and Ajzen, "The Directive Influence of Attitudes on Behavior," p. 396. See also "Technical Footnotes."

12. Ajzen, "The Directive Influence of Attitudes on Behavior," p. 385.

13. See "Technical Footnotes."

14. One might also expect differences between how these factors exert influence. They promote successful experience by providing skills that make success more likely. For the extent of behavior change, they lower the cost of trying new behaviors.

15. Bibb Latane, Kipling Williams, and Stephen Harkins, "Many Hands Make Light the Work: The Causes and Consequences of Social Loafing," *Journal of Personality and Social Psychology* 37, no. 6 (1979): 822–32.

16. This is also a central tenet of behaviorist psychology, which studies the effects of "reinforcement" from a person's environment in encouraging the behavior that is reinforced.

17. See, generally, Edith Stokey and Richard Zeckhauser, *A Primer for Policy Analysis* (New York: Norton, 1978). Many studies in nonwork situations, including studies of how people react to incentive features of laws, tax regimes, and other public policies, suggest the ability of extrinsic rewards to shape behavior. For summaries of literature showing a positive impact of economic incentives on workplace production specifically, see Barry Gerhart, "Employee Com-

pensation: Research and Practice," in *Handbook of Industrial and Organizational Psychology*, edited by Marvin D. Dunnette and Leaetta M. Hough, 2nd ed., vol. 3 (Palo Alto, Calif.: Consulting Psychologists Press, 1990), pp. 522–30; and Candice Prendergast, "The Provision of Incentives in Firms," *Journal of Economic Literature* 37, no. 1 (1999): 16–17, 33–37. A shift to piece rates for workers installing auto windshields was calculated to be associated with a 35 percent increase in productivity, while a similar shift for department store sales clerks produced store-level productivity increases between 9 and 14 percent; increasing the top prize in golf tournaments and NASCAR races is associated with improvements in the average participant's golf score and the average speed at which race drivers drive. Judith Komacki and her colleagues present a general summary of behaviorist psychology studies that does not distinguish between money rewards and praise. Judith L. Komaki, Timothy Combs, and Stephen Schepman, "Motivational Implications of Reinforcement Theory," in *Motivation and Leadership at Work*, edited by Richard M. Steers, Lyman W. Porter, and Gregory A. Bigley, 6th ed. (New York: McGraw-Hill, 1996).

18. The literature deals just about exclusively with rewards. It would seem to make sense to broaden this to extrinsic incentives generally, which could include rewards and punishments.

19. Edward L. Deci and Richard M. Ryan, *Intrinsic Motivation and Self-Determination in Human Behavior* (New York: Plenum Press, 1985); Edward L. Deci, Richard Koestner, and Richard M. Ryan, "A Meta-Analytic Review of Experiments Examining the Effects of Extrinsic Rewards on Intrinsic Motivation," *Psychological Bulletin* 125, no. 6 (1999): 627–68. To use the language of the literature on attitude and behavior, the argument is that for the intrinsically motivated, extrinsic rewards undermine the propensity to translate a positive attitude into a corresponding behavior.

20. Rephrased into the language of attitude and behavior, intrinsic motivation is the propensity to act so as to reflect one's attitudes: positive attitude plus intrinsic motivation produce behavior reflecting one's attitudes.

21. Deci and Ryan, *Intrinsic Motivation and Self-Determination in Human Behavior*, pp. 44–48. This was separately determined to have been an activity the subjects liked.

22. Ibid., pp. 54–57. Note that many of the jobs examined in economic studies of productivity effects of economic incentives, such as windshield installers or sales clerks, provide little intrinsic motivation to those performing them. The empirical literature in economics also concludes that a substantial portion of the productivity effects of extrinsic rewards comes through a selection effect (that is, people believing ex ante that they will be below-average performers do not seek jobs with this reward structure in the first place, or they leave once such structures are introduced) rather than a motivation effect.

23. Bruno S. Frey and Reto Jegen, "Motivation Crowding Theory," *Journal of Economic Surveys* 15 (2001): 589–611.

24. The view of opposite effects is consistent with the findings of experiments reported in Uri Gneezy and Aldo Rustichini, "Pay Enough or Don't Pay at All," *Quarterly Journal of Economics* 115 (2000): 793–94. They find, for example, that small monetary payments per correct answer on an IQ test reduced the number of correct replies compared with giving no reward, but a larger payment increased the number of correct replies. In my example above, rewards are held constant while intrinsic motivation varies. In this experiment, it would appear that intrinsic motivation is held constant while rewards vary. See also "Technical Footnotes."

25. Deci, Koestner, and Ryan, "A Meta-Analytic Review of Experiments Examining the Effects of Extrinsic Rewards on Intrinsic Motivation," pp. 629–30, 638–39; Deci and Ryan, *Intrinsic Motivation and Self-Determination in Human Behavior*, pp. 91–93.

26. Thus rewarding people simply for engaging in an activity without requiring successful performance provides no information about competence and thus nothing to offset the impact of the loss of freedom. By contrast, rewarding people for meeting or exceeding a certain standard provides information about competence that balances the loss of control. Deci, Koestner, and Ryan, "A Meta-Analytic Review of Experiments Examining the Effects of Extrinsic Rewards on Intrinsic Motivation," pp. 628–29. The net effect of performance-contingent rewards on intrinsic motivation would then be theoretically indeterminate. Empirical studies generally show that, on balance, they reduce intrinsic motivation, that is, the control effect outweighs the competence-provision effect. Summarized ibid., pp. 643-45. See also "Technical Footnotes."

27. Deci, Koestner, and Ryan, "A Meta-Analytic Review of Experiments Examining the Effects of Extrinsic Rewards on Intrinsic Motivation," p. 638.

28. Bruno S. Frey and Felix Oberholzer-Gee, "The Cost of Price Incentives: An Empirical Analysis of Motivation Crowding Out," *American Economic Review* 87, no. 4 (1997): 746–55, 749, 753.

29. Richard M. Titmuss, *The Gift Relationship* (London: Allen and Unwin, 1970). It is also consistent with the finding in Merton's classic study of Kate Smith's marathon radio war-bond drive during World War II, where Smith mentioned nothing about bonds as a good investment, and where the study's survey results showed a majority opposed giving prizes to people who bought war bonds—buying war bonds to make money was not seen to be as valuable as buying war bonds to support the country. Robert K. Merton, *Mass Persuasion: The Social Psychology of a War Bond Drive* (New York: Harper and Brothers, 1946). For a discussion of the same phenomenon in a different context, see Steven Kelman, *Making Public Policy: A Hopeful View of American Government* (New York: Basic Books, 1997), chap. 10. See also "Technical Footnotes."

30. Gerald Zaltman, Jonny Holbeck, and Robert Duncan, *Innovations and Organizations* (New York: Wiley-Interscience, 1973), pp. 143–46; Robert B. Duncan, "The Ambidextrous Organization: Designing Dual Structures for Innovation," in *The Management of Organizational Design,* edited by Ralph H. Kilmann, L. R. Pandy, and D. P. Slevin (New York: North-Holland, 1976), pp. 177–79. One meta-analysis found "centralization" to be negatively related to implementation of innovations. Fariborz Damanpour, "Organizational Innovation: A Meta-Analysis of Effects of Determinants and Moderators," *Academy of Management Journal* 34, no. 3 (1991): 572. See also "Technical Footnotes."

31. These mechanisms were self-confidence, working late, being driven to succeed, believing reform support was career enhancing, and perceiving an external locus of control.

32. The behavior change variable was reverse coded, so a higher value implies more behavior change. See also "Technical Footnotes."

33. The numbers show the impact of a move from the minimum to the maximum value of the variable, expressed as a nonstandardized coefficient, on the four-point behavior change scale. (For mean workgroup attitude, the move is from a value of 50 to 70, which is the approximate range for most actual values this variable takes.) See also "Technical Footnotes."

34. Like a unique variance analysis, this attributes all covariance between the main-effects model and one including interactions to main effects.

35. The significant quadratic term for attitude in this model, and the various interactions in the model presented later in this chapter, make the impact of reform attitude hard to see, so to get an idea of the overall influence of attitude, controlling for other influences in the two models, calculations must be made without quadratic or interaction terms. Even then, it is not easy to estimate precisely how much attitudes affect behavior. For a discussion of how this range of estimates was determined, see "Technical Footnotes." A caution should also be noted. Based on findings in chapter 8, it is known that the link between reform attitude and reform-oriented behavior partly reflects the influence of behavior on attitude rather than the other way around. Attempts were made to correct for such simultaneity using a two-stage least-squares regression model, but it was not possible to develop appropriate instrumental variables to create such a model. I would especially like to acknowledge the assistance of my colleague Robert Jensen in helping determine whether it was feasible to develop a two-stage least-squares model. See also "Technical Footnotes."

36. Becoming very critical of reform (support moving from 30 to 20) was associated with a decrease in behavior change of only .07 unit, while increasing reform support from 80 to 90 with an increase of .18 unit.

37. As noted in other contexts, the drive-to-succeed variable has elements both of a performance-promoting personality trait (wanting to achieve) and of a personal benefit variable (wanting to gain the approval of one's bosses). The

effects of this variable are discussed below, in the context of personal-benefit variables.

38. P values for quadratic terms for self-confidence and working late were .66 and .28.

39. As noted later in this chapter, there was a significant interaction between reform support and job level in predicting behavior change, which is reported in the model. The standardized coefficient for job level as a main effect (not shown here) was .11, the largest for these variables.

40. P values for interactions of reform support with education, mission impact, and working late were .32, .30, and .32, respectively.

41. $P = .78$ and $p = .98$, respectively (the latter, not shown here, run as a main effect only). As is discussed later in this chapter, there were significant interactions involving workgroup attitude, standard deviation of workgroup attitude, and the individual's reform support, although even here the coefficients were small.

42. The suggestion would be that free-riding effects neutralized the positive impact from co-worker behavioral facilitation or other forms of influence. See also "Technical Footnotes."

43. Nor was the interaction with deference significant ($p = .30$).

44. Running this model without interactions (not shown here) to show average effect size, the standardized coefficient for supervisor attitude influence was .08.

45. Neither the interaction of training ($p = .43$) nor that of mere leader persistence ($p = .88$) with attitude was significant.

46. As noted earlier, the main effect of the attitude of the local office head was not significant; neither was the interaction with the respondent's reform attitude ($p = .79$).

47. Teresa M. Amabile, *Creativity in Context* (Boulder: Westview Press, 1996), pp. 107–19.

48. As in chapter 8, 10, 20, and 25 were chosen as low, medium, and high values for workgroup consensus.

49. An individual's most-respected co-worker was also a potential source of praise. However, the interaction between the attitude of the most-respected co-worker and respondent's attitude in predicting behavior change was insignificant ($p = .99$), just as the main effect had been.

50. An alternative explanation for this pattern of results involving supervisors and co-workers reported here would be that supporters do not need, or much benefit from, supervisor-provided incentives to undertake behavior change. Instead, "they'll do it anyway" because they like reform. As for critics, absent incentives, behavior will remain the same, while with them, some change occurs. (This might be called a "drag-along" effect.) However, several features of these results support an undermining effect as a better explanation for these results. Undermining suggests the possibility of a crossover where, at high levels

of reform support, people with proreform superiors might actually change behavior less than those with less-supportive ones; with drag-along effects, there is no reason for a negative relationship, only a reduced positive one. Failure to find a crossover would not imply that undermining was not the explanation for these results, since the undermining-effects hypothesis does not require crossover. But the crossover in the data—for all three external incentives variables—is inconsistent with a drag-along effect. Second, the presence of situations where co-worker praise is associated with more behavior impact on supporters than on critics, which was found with the triple interaction involving workgroup reform support, is consistent with undermining effects but not with drag-along effects. In situations where people receive praise from co-workers, the drag-along effect predicts the same results as for superiors—more behavior impact on critics. A final argument for drag-along effects as the explanation for these results would be that one could expect to see only small effects of extrinsic incentives on the reported behavior of those who were attitudinally proreform because, given that the highest-choice alternative in the survey for degree of behavior change was "significant impact," strong supporters would be expected to already have changed their behavior, as much as could be measured by the survey, without supervisor encouragement. The data suggest this is not a convincing proposition. Of respondents for whom reform support was 90 or higher, although 65 percent did give the highest possible response available for behavior change, 35 percent of those who were attitudinally extremely proreform could have indicated a response category within the bounds of alternatives presented showing greater behavior change than what they chose. See also "Technical Footnotes."

51. See "Technical Footnotes."

52. Those who strongly agreed that support for reform would enhance their careers changed their behavior more than those who agreed somewhat or had mixed feelings. But those who strongly disagreed changed their behavior more than those who disagreed somewhat or had mixed feelings. Explanations for this unexpected finding must be speculative: perhaps the small size of the sample (6 percent) who strongly disagreed were people who had already decided to change their behaviors a great deal and wanted to feel they were not the kind of people who would do so just to promote their personal careers. However, regardless of the explanation, the hypothesized negative feedback coming from respondents who strongly disagreed that reform support was career enhancing did not occur, leaving only the positive-feedback effect.

53. Run as a main effect only (not shown here), it was significant ($p = .01$), with a moderate effect size. Those driven to succeed may want to be seen as doing well at what they do. This might make them cautious about the number of changes they undertake and make them concentrate instead on doing well at what they do try, as long as they are seen as supportive of the general idea of

change (which may cause people not to notice that they are actually doing relatively less). Note that being driven to succeed was associated with less likelihood of joining the reform coalition before the change had become "politically correct" but greater attitudinal support later on—though even later on, those who most strongly agreed that they were driven to succeed at their jobs were slightly less proreform than those agreeing only somewhat, probably because these respondents wanted to hedge their bets against a future change of direction. All this suggests these respondents were strategic, in a self-serving way, in their approach. While the drive to succeed generally had a negative impact on behavior change, this impact may have been stronger at higher levels of reform support (though the interaction fell just short of significance). Also, people driven to succeed are more sensitive than others to extrinsic incentives. The interaction between reform support and the drive to succeed fell just short of significance ($p = .12$); even with the interaction, the crossover where the drive to succeed had a negative impact on behavior change was with reform support at 17, so that for virtually every respondent, there was a negative association. The possibly stronger negative relationship between being driven to succeed and behavior change among strong supporters of reform is consistent with the finding that extrinsic incentives have a negative impact on intrinsic motivation, which is present to a greater extent among strong supporters of reform. A quadratic term was insignificant ($p = .87$)

54. On net, believing that one lacked control was associated with slightly lower behavior change (a .05-unit decrease in the behavior-change scale of 1 to 4, compared with a hypothetical linear model with a neutral mean value) than believing that one was in control.

Chapter 10

1. See "Technical Footnotes."

2. Richard Fletcher, *The Barbarian Conversion: From Paganism to Christianity* (New York: Henry Holt, 1997). p. 273.

3. Ibid.

4. V. I. Lenin, *What Is to Be Done?* (Moscow: Foreign Language Publishing House, 1952; originally published in 1902), pp. 67–69. Lenin here quotes the German socialist leader Karl Kautsky.

5. The only example I have come across of a discussion in the organizational behavior literature of what I am calling deepening is an article on a change process at a Swedish hospital. The hospital director had an ambitious change program in mind, involving both quality improvement and cost reduction, but lacked support among doctors for the entire agenda. He chose to begin by emphasizing the need to achieve better treatment quality by organizing the hospital around organ-based "centers" rather than traditional specialties, which

corresponded to a desire for change widely felt within the hospital. But gradually the word "center" came to be "broadened" to include profit center as well, including the cost-reduction goal. Pia Lindell, Leif Melin, and Henrik J. Gahmberg, "Stability and Change in a Strategist's Thinking," in *Managerial and Organizational Cognition: Theory, Methods, and Research*, edited by Colin Eden and J. C. Spender (London: Sage, 1998), pp. 82–85, 84.

6. Richard L. Daft and Karl E. Weick, "Toward a Model of Organizations as Interpretation Systems," *Academy of Management Review* 9 (1984): 284–95; Dennis A. Gioia and Kuman Chittipeddi, "Sensemaking and Sensegiving in Strategic Change Initiation," *Strategic Management Journal* 12 (1991): 433–48. Existing attitudes of initial burden-reducers would indeed need to be unfrozen for deepening to occur, even if this did not apply more generally to initiating the change process, where people could get involved based on pre-existing attitudes.

7. Karl Weick, *Sensemaking in Organizations* (Thousand Oaks, Calif.: Sage, 1995), pp. 85–88. If the change effort itself is the source of turbulence, this is different from situations most authors have in mind in discussing sense-making moments, where the shock is typically exogenous.

8. See "Technical Footnotes."

9. See "Technical Footnotes."

10. Responses for the sample as a whole were remarkably similar.

11. Perhaps an exception was the goal of getting government to act "more like a business," a phrase reformers frequently used, almost as a catchphrase. I saw it as connected with better value, though it is hard to know how respondents regarded it.

12. As a further explanation, this additional statement was generally added, though it did not appear in the questionnaire: "Is there anything different going on in your head now compared to when reform started?"

13. One respondent (included in the 40 percent) reported having changed attitude to become more negative toward procurement reform than when it started.

14. To make interpretation more intuitive, responses were reverse coded.

15. The value could therefore range from −4.0 (strongly agreed five years ago, strongly disagree now) to +4.0 (strongly disagreed five years ago, strongly agree now).

16. These questions were part of a series of twenty-seven questions in the Frontline Survey about various features of the respondent's job and organization. Current attitude bias in answers to the recall question might reduce mean differences between the recalled period and now, making the estimates of change to be reported here conservative.

17. To make interpretation more intuitive, responses were reverse coded.

18. Except for the questions regarding change in innovation orientation and whether reform was about more than just burden reduction, it is impossible,

without knowing attitudes when reform began, to know to what extent support for better value represented deepening or merely continuation of earlier support. However, given that these respondents were initially preoccupied with personal burden reduction, it is plausible to presume they would not initially have been strong supporters of policies that they thought would increase their workloads. In fact, to the extent they might not have initially realized that these policies required more work, they might have become less supportive over time. Moreover, variance in factors hypothesized to cause deepening was associated with variance in current attitudes toward the better-value agenda. I argue below that this suggests deepening did occur.

19. Lyle E. Bourne Jr., *Human Conceptual Behavior* (Boston: Allyn and Bacon, 1966), p. 1.

20. Ibid., p. 2.

21. Susan T. Fiske and Shelley E. Taylor, *Social Cognition*, 2nd ed. (New York: McGraw-Hill, 1991), p. 105.

22. Jane E. Dutton and Susan E. Jackson, "Categorizing Strategic Issues: Links to Organizational Action," *Academy of Management Review* 12 (1987): 79.

23. Clifford Geertz, *The Interpretation of Cultures: Selected Essays* (New York: Basic Books, 1973), p. 232.

24. Edward L. Thorndike, "A Constant Error in Psychological Ratings," *Journal of Applied Psychology* 4 (1920): 25–29.

25. Richard E. Nisbett and Timothy DeCamp Wilson, "The Halo Effect: Evidence for Unconscious Alteration of Judgments," *Journal of Personality and Social Psychology* 35 (1977): 253. The halo effect involves judgments about different aspects of a single person. When we use information from a knowledge structure about a category of people, such as "Jews" or "construction workers," to make judgments about a person seen as a member of that category, this is generally referred to as stereotyping. Fiske and Taylor, *Social Cognition*, pp. 122–24.

26. Having a positively valenced category "procurement reform" is not the same as simply having a positive attitude toward reform, because people who are positive toward reform may differ in the extent to which they form categories.

27. There is certainly reason to treat responses to this question skeptically. Some argue that people are poor at understanding their own mental processes: in this view, verbal reports on mental processes involve "telling more than we can know." Richard E. Nisbett and Timothy DeCamp Wilson, "Telling More Than We Can Know: Verbal Reports on Mental Processes," *Psychological Review* 8 (1977): 231–59; a critique of that article is Eliot R. Smith and Frederick D. Miller, "Limits on Perception of Cognitive Processes: A Reply to Nisbett and Wilson," *Psychological Review* 85 (1978): 355–62. Certainly, if categorization, for example, were helping explain deepening, one would not expect to see

people be consciously aware of it. Nonetheless, I found many of these accounts interesting, and a number of determinants of deepening one might have expected to be present on theoretical grounds were found in these replies. However, frequency distributions should be seen only as suggestive.

28. See "Technical Footnotes."

29. Note the dependent variable measures current attitudes toward better value, not attitude change over time. How, then, can this model be used to make inferences about factors that might have produced deepening, that is, change over time? Variance in current attitudes might be caused by a number of factors. Among them, one is variance in the presence of deepening; this would produce variance in current attitudes by making the attitudes of some more supportive of better value over time, while not producing this in others. If variance in measures hypothesized to cause deepening is related to variance in current attitudes, one plausible explanation is that these factors produced deepening and that differential attitude change produced by deepening helps explain variance in current attitudes. In principle, something else about these factors, other than their having produced deepening, could be causing this; I have no candidate alternative accounts, however, for such relationships. See also "Technical Footnotes."

30. Small sample sizes make attainment of significance more difficult, making these results conservative. The not-just-burden-reduction and reform-about-innovation variables were reverse coded, so in all cases, a high value for the dependent variable means greater presence of deepening.

31. See "Technical Footnotes."

32. Local office heads' efforts to encourage deepening had a significant impact on the question of innovation-oriented change but in the opposite direction from that hypothesized: the more the local office head promoted deepening, the less likely the respondent was to perceive that reform was about taking local initiative rather than following an agenda coming from the top. This makes sense: in promoting deepening, local leaders *were* promoting a top-driven agenda, and the more they did so, the more likely were respondents to believe that reform was about a central agenda, rather than spontaneous local action.

33. First-line supervisors also had an influence on change in innovation orientation but in the opposite direction from that hypothesized. This question involved a comparison between a previous and a current situation; plausibly, proreform supervisors in the change vanguard had been encouraging people working for them to be innovative before reform was initiated, which would reduce the change over time.

34. Values for other predictor variables were kept at their weighted sample means. Some predictions are outside the range of values the variable can take.

35. This hypothetical regression line connected the points (job easier = 1, reform support = 100) and (job easier = 5, reform support = 0). Since there are only five actual values for the job-easier variable, this was in reality five points.

36. The deviation could be either positive or negative. For example, if a respondent had a made-job-easier value of 1 and a reform support value of 90, the deviation would be –10, since the value for reform support was 10 points lower than predicted if made-job-easier had fully predicted reform support.

37. An analogous regression line implying that reform attitude perfectly predicted categorization was created—the line connecting the points (reform support = 100, categorization = 0) and (reform attitude = 0, categorization = 6) (the maximum value categorization took in the sample).

38. That is, the respondent's reform support was greater than "expected," based on the response to the job-easier question.

39. That is, categorization was lower than it would have been based on the respondent's support for reform.

40. That is, the respondent's reform support was less than "expected," based on the response to the job-easier question.

41. See "Technical Footnotes."

42. In many cases, it would not have been possible to use the same variables to ask respondents the same questions about individual-level behavior. Thus it would have been impossible to ask to what extent an individual had personally participated in "less second-guessing of the judgments of contracting professionals," "more discretion for government contracting professionals," or "the credit card," for example, since these were worded as policies, not individual behaviors.

43. The workgroup was taken as the unit of observation rather than the individual respondent, since the question referred to how far the *office* had come. Mean responses were calculated at an office or unit level, depending on data availability, as with similar variables such as mean workgroup attitude toward reform.

44. See "Technical Footnotes."

45. The coefficient for burden reduction was somewhat short of statistical significance ($p = .16$), though the sample size was small.

46. Support for reform in general was measured, not support for the better-value agenda specifically, though it will be remembered that early supervisor supporters were disproportionately likely to support the better-value agenda.

Chapter 11

1. Steven Kelman, "Downsizing, Competition, and Organizational Change in Government: Is Necessity the Mother of Invention?" unpublished, Harvard University, 2005.

2. John P. Kotter, *Leading Change* (Harvard Business School Press, 1996), pp. 119, 122.

3. I was unable to test for impact of the learning curve.

288 NOTES TO PAGES 203–05

4. Thomas J. Peters and Robert H. Waterman Jr., *In Search of Excellence: Lessons from America's Best-Run Companies* (New York: Harper and Row, 1982), chap. 5.

5. In a public sector context, the bias for action came to be known as "management by groping along," based on a 1988 article and 1991 book by Robert Behn. Robert D. Behn, "Management by Groping Along," *Journal of Policy Analysis and Management* 7, no. 4 (1988): 643–63; Robert D. Behn, *Leadership Counts: Lessons for Public Managers from the Massachusetts Welfare, Training, and Employment Program* (Harvard University Press, 1991); see also Olivia Golden, "Innovation in Public Sector Human Services Programs: The Implications of Innovation by 'Groping Along,'" in *Innovation in American Government,* edited by Alan A. Altshuler and Robert D. Behn (Brookings, 1997), pp. 146–76.

6. This is separate from any direct impact of a consistent leader message on individual attitude or behavior.

7. For example, Kotter sees the ability to articulate a convincing vision of the ideas behind a change effort as "a central component of all great leadership" and key to the ability to achieve change. Kotter, *Leading Change*, p. 68, and, more generally, chap. 5.

8. Michael Hammer and Steven A. Stanton, *The Reengineering Revolution* (New York: HarperBusiness, 1995), pp. 36, 47–48.

9. Kotter, *Leading Change*, pp. 154–55.

10. Shelley A. Kirkpatrick and Edwin A. Locke, "Leadership: Do Traits Matter?" *Academy of Management Executive* 5, no. 2 (1991): 48–60, 51.

11. For example, Hammer and Stanton, *The Reengineering Revolution*, pp. 123–24.

12. Donald P. Warwick, *A Theory of Public Bureaucracy* (Harvard University Press, 1975), p. 68. Persistence is also recommended as necessary to persuade people of the necessity of change. Andrew Pettigrew, *The Awakening Giant: Continuity and Change in Imperial Chemical Industries* (Oxford, U.K.: Basil Blackwell, 1985), pp. 474–75.

13. A study of the tenure of presidential appointees during the 1970s and 1980s, other than commissioners of regulatory agencies, finds that the average appointee stayed on the job only 2.2 years Carl Brauer, "Tenure, Turnover, and Postgovernment Employment Trends of Presidential Appointees," in *The In-and-Outers: Presidential Appointees and Transient Government in Washington,* edited by G. Calvin Mackenzie (Johns Hopkins University Press, 1987), p. 175.

14. Robert T. Nakamura and Thomas W. Church, *Taming Regulation: Superfund and the Challenge of Regulatory Reform* (Brookings, 2003), p. 79.

15. This is a slight oversimplification, particularly for me, given my general responsibilities for government-wide procurement policy, but it is basically cor-

rect, and certainly both Preston and I defined our jobs as being "about" procurement reform.

16. Given that persistence is seen here as a system-level variable (that thus does not vary across our sample) and that we have only one case, how can we know persistence made a difference? The argument is partly a logical one. If it is true that some kinds of positive feedback increase with the mere passage of time and others turn positive in net effects only relatively later in a change process, then the longer an effort lasts, the greater the effects of positive feedback are likely to be, unless any decline in the impact of positive feedback mechanisms depending on mere initiation outweighs increased impact of other forms of positive feedback later on. Also, one may make casual empirical comparisons (such as the ones above) to situations where persistence was and was not present.

17. Robert Jervis, *System Effects: Complexity in Political and Social Life* (Princeton University Press, 1997), pp. 155–56; Paul David, *Technical Choice, Innovation, and Economic Growth* (Cambridge University Press, 1975).

18. Jervis, *System Effects*, p. 156.

19. Uri Gneezy and Aldo Rustichini, "Pay Enough or Don't Pay at All," *Quarterly Journal of Economics* 115, no. 3 (2000): 791–810.

20. Furthermore, some evidence suggests that government employees value extrinsic rewards less, which would mean the countervailing behavior impact of such rewards would be less per "unit" of incentive. See also "Technical Footnotes."

21. Amit Bordia and Anthony Cheesebrough, "Insights on the Federal Government's Human Capital Crisis: Reflections of Generation X," Harvard University, Kennedy School of Government, 2002, pp. 16–17.

22. Offices might consider establishing a new award, perhaps called the Good Soldier award, to recognize employees who have shown loyalty in working to implement management priorities—a reward for those not intrinsically motivated to follow such priorities. One should proceed with caution on this, because an organization should also want independent thinkers, willing to question management, but such an award might be helpful in some organizations (perhaps it could be paired with a Challenger of the Status Quo award for those who constructively shake things up).

23. It may be impossible, based on behavior alone, to distinguish between two individuals as to which is intrinsically motivated and which is not. Moreover, for an organization to fail to promote well-performing intrinsically motivated people would deprive it of opportunities to put the best people in higher-level jobs. Most important, a regime where high performers went unrewarded because they were intrinsically motivated while lower performers were rewarded to spur better behavior would create, and rightly so, devastating morale problems.

24. This is discussed in Edward L. Deci, R. Koestner, and R. M. Ryan, "A Meta-Analytic Review of Experiments Examining the Effects of Extrinsic

Rewards on Intrinsic Motivation," Psychological Bulletin 125, no. 6 (1999): 627–68, 629. So, for example, adding the phrase, "Keep up the good work," after telling an experimental subject that he or she had done well at a task caused feedback to be perceived as controlling and hence undermine intrinsic motivation.

25. Similarly, verbal comments should be made minimizing the hierarchical nature of the relationship between supervisor and employee, a relationship highlighting the controlling aspect of reward (for example, "When I say you've done a great job, I say it less as a supervisor and more as somebody who cares about the mission this organization needs to accomplish.")

26. Ference Marton and Shirley Booth, *Learning and Awareness* (Mahwah, N.J.: Lawrence Erlbaum, 1997), p. 142.

27. "Giddy with success" was a phrase Stalin employed regarding excesses during agricultural collectivization in the 1930s. One sees evidence of the operation of a giddy-with-success effect producing negative feedback in Hitler's decision to invade the Soviet Union (after military successes elsewhere) or in the Robespierrist period of the French Revolution. It is also sometimes argued that this problem is common to presidents, who, having gotten so far, come to believe they are "lucky" and that their risky decisions will turn out well. Giddiness from success may also result from positive illusions.

28. James G. March, *The Pursuit of Organizational Intelligence* (Oxford: Blackwell Business, 1999), p. 19.

29. Christopher Hood, *The Art of the State: Culture, Rhetoric, and Public Management* (Oxford University Press, 1998), p. 18. These considerations, of course, apply to life in general and not just to public management. Hood's account implies that all these conflicting considerations are created equal, so that ignoring one produces problems that are substantively as severe as ignoring another, creating a situation characterized by cycling, with no progress over time. If one believes conflicting considerations are not necessarily created equal, this conclusion would be too harsh.

30. Robert Simons, "Control in an Age of Empowerment," *Harvard Business Review* 73 (March 1995): 80–89. It is also almost always the case that when one tries something new, mistakes will occur as people experiment with an innovation; the danger, in these situations, writes James G. March, is that innovations will be abandoned "without spending enough time" learning how to do them right "to secure the gains from experience that are necessary to make [the innovation] fruitful." March, *The Pursuit of Organizational Intelligence*, p. 110. To be fair to ourselves, I worked just before leaving government to establish boundaries for acceptable behavior among agencies running newly developed streamlined procurement contracts, through what I called a Mayflower Compact that would establish self-government where no governance had existed before. My

successor also tried to get agencies running these contracts to enforce such boundaries. Both of us had difficulty gaining the attention of these agencies.

Appendix A

1. See "Technical Footnotes."

2. For a discussion of the low alpha coefficient, see "Technical Footnotes."

3. See "Technical Footnotes."

4. See "Technical Footnotes."

5. See "Technical Footnotes."

6. My intention in asking this question was to measure dissatisfaction with contractor performance quality generated by the traditional system. However, I believe that many respondents may have answered based on their hostility to contractors, a feature of the ideology of the traditional procurement system. For this reason, I am skeptical about results generated from tests involving this variable.

7. See "Technical Footnotes."

8. See "Technical Footnotes."

9. Arguments for why there might be a link between these variables and membership in the reform coalition are different from those for why there might be a link to supporting autonomy. With variables measuring desire for autonomy in this model, influences of variables also in the autonomy models control for impact on support for autonomy.

10. See "Technical Footnotes."

11. Respondents were asked to agree or disagree with the following statements: "These days you just can't trust most people"; "Most of the time people are pretty mean and selfish"; "If you really trust people, they'll almost always come through for you"; and "Most people really try to do the right thing" (alpha = .65). To reduce missing values, any respondent who answered at least one of these questions was given a value for the variable.

12. As with other variables, any result controls for the impact of venturesomeness on the desire for autonomy. One might imagine people strongly desiring autonomy but not if it required the upheaval of a change in organizational practices—they might like to be in an organization with lots of autonomy, but if they landed in one without it, they would not want to embark on a change process.

13. The views of top leaders, when reform was launched, did not vary; their support for change was a feature of the system to which all respondents were exposed. The strategy for dealing with this was to find something that does vary to capture the influence of something that does not. While top leader statements did not vary, the extent to which people listen to what top leaders say does. If

you did not listen to top leader statements, these leaders had no ability to influence you. For those who did listen, leader statements were potentially relevant. If leader actions did not affect even those who listened, listeners would not differ from nonlisteners; if they did, attitudes of listeners would differ. Another way of putting the same point is to note that if the top-leadership message had no influence, it would not matter how much a person listened to it. By seeing whether early recruits were more likely to listen to top leaders, I can see whether this (nonvarying) factor was influencing those whom it might influence.

14. The statements were, "Generally, I prefer to be by myself"; "I like spare time activities which allow me to get away from people"; "I would prefer a quiet evening at home to attending a social event"; "I only telephone friends when there is something important to discuss"; "I like eating alone"; "This is a good job for a loner"; "I would rather telephone a friend than read a magazine in my spare time"; "I like to talk with my colleagues on the job whenever I have the chance" (alpha = .61). The first seven questions were reverse coded, so a higher value means greater sociability. Respondents answering at least two questions were included in the scale.

15. Everett M. Rogers, *Diffusion of Innovations*, 4th ed. (New York: Free Press, 1995), p. 273.

16. See "Technical Footnotes."

17. It will be difficult to disentangle impacts on joining the change vanguard through early-adopter mechanisms and through ideological views about the traditional procurement system. The results presented below suggest there were impacts through ideology; they will not indicate whether there were additional "early-adopter" impacts.

18. See "Technical Footnotes."

19. See "Technical Footnotes."

20. See "Technical Footnotes."

21. See "Technical Footnotes."

22. See "Technical Footnotes."

23. See "Technical Footnotes."

24. See "Technical Footnotes."

25. After 1993 significant downsizing occurred among the procurement workforce as part of general efforts during the Clinton administration to reduce federal employment. In addition, a few other of the organizations in the sample became more subject to competition for gaining business from the customers of the system.

26. See "Technical Footnotes."

27. See "Technical Footnotes."

28. See "Technical Footnotes."

29. See "Technical Footnotes."

30. See "Technical Footnotes."

31. See "Technical Footnotes."

32. Basically, this is just looking at the idea that perceptual confirmation "distorts" a person's perceptions in a different light. An individual's value for this variable would be a function of the strength of any general psychological tendency causing perceptual confirmation, as well as what actual reality is like (actual reality establishes a natural limit on the gap between belief and reality that a person showing a high level of the tendency to perceptual confirmation can display). For a group, the mean value would also reflect the number of individuals who are prochange and antichange, since only prochange people can have positive values and only antichange people can have negative values. These phenomena act in opposite directions. Given all this, one would expect the mean sample value for this variable to fluctuate up and down in the course of a change process, as reality and the proportion of prochange and antichange people in the system changes. The coefficient for this variable should not be affected. See also "Technical Footnotes."

33. The "neutral" value for the variable must be determined deductively; the data themselves do not allow testing whether there is some level of the variable below which negative feedback takes place, that is, where experience is worse than it otherwise would have been if the characteristic were not operating at all. See also "Technical Footnotes."

34. See "Technical Footnotes."

35. A connection between initial attitude and initial experience might be due to support for underlying values behind reform, which influence both variables, rather than to the operation of a self-fulfilling prophecy.

36. See "Technical Footnotes."

37. Also, many Defense Department offices' initial experience with procurement reform involved milspec reform, which was harder to do than the initial changes tried in most civilian agencies.

38. See "Technical Footnotes."

39. The scale was additive; a respondent who had received no training in the format was coded 0, acquisition training generally coded 1, both general and reform-specific training coded 2, reform training specifically coded 3. The minimum value the scale could take was 0, the maximum was 12 (four kinds of training times three codes). Training was not included in the initial experience model since it was unlikely to have been important so early on. See also "Technical Footnotes."

40. The variables for supervisor or local office head attitude were also "updated" to reflect the time of the survey. Mean workgroup attitude was created by measuring the mean score for the procurement reform feeling-thermometer question for all other members of the respondent's workgroup (excluding the respondent) and assigning the value to each respondent in the group. See also "Technical Footnotes."

41. David Chan, "Functional Relations among Constructs in the Same Content Domain at Different Levels of Analysis: A Typology of Composition Models," *Journal of Applied Psychology* 83, no. 2 (1998): 236.

42. The lower the standard deviation, the less the variance among individuals around the group mean—and thus the more unified the group was in its reform attitude. The value of the standard deviation was assigned to each respondent in the workgroup.

43. The leader attitude questions controlled for influence through the content of what leaders were saying.

44. The opposite—nonironic—effect is also possible, whereby those believing they possessed greater control became more proreform. (In such cases, locus of control would not be an organizational feedback mechanism at all.)

45. See "Technical Footnotes."

46. See "Technical Footnotes."

47. To reduce the noise a bit, this variable was specified as the attitude of the supervisor the respondent had as of the beginning of reform, since proreform supervisors as of the beginning of reform were more likely to support the better-value agenda. See also "Technical Footnotes."

48. I also used the question about reform making it easier to select best-value contractors. This was problematic for a different reason, since it addressed only one feature of that agenda, namely, selection of contractors providing the best value (such as through the use of past performance in vendor selection), not other elements, such as experience with milspec reform or performance-based service contracting specifically, or innovativeness in general, making results with this specification conservative as well. Results with this variable (not shown here) were virtually identical; the few differences are noted.

49. The respondent was then directed to indicate, on a seven-point scale, whether he or she felt the idea was "not important" to procurement reform (1), "part, but not central" (4), or "central" (7).

50. In this case, the difference between personal opinion and centrality for past performance was 0, for milspec reform 2. With two variables in the denominator, the mean value of the differences would be 1.00. Nonresponses were excluded from the denominator.

51. Alternatively, the bit of available information may be that an idea is central to reform, and through categorization and subsequent knowledge structure-based information processing, the individual concludes the idea is a good one.

52. See "Technical Footnotes."

Appendix B

1. Laurence Lynn, "Public Management Research: The Triumph of Art over Science," *Journal of Policy Analysis and Management* 13, no. 2 (1994): 231–59;

see also Gary King, Robert O. Keohane, and Sidney Verba, *Designing Social Inquiry: Scientific Inference in Qualitative Research* (Harvard University Press, 1994).

2. Denise Rousseau, "Issues of Level in Organizational Research: Multi-Level and Cross-Level Perspectives," in *Research in Organizational Behavior,* edited by Barry M. Shaw and L. L. Cummings, vol. 7 (Westport, Conn.: JAI Press, 1985), pp. 1–37, 14; see also Blake E. Ashforth, "Climate Formation: Issues and Extensions," *Academy of Management Review* 10, no. 4 (1985): 837–47; William H. Glick, "Conceptualizing and Measuring Organizational and Psychological Climate: Pitfalls in Multilevel Research," *Academy of Management Review* 10, no. 3 (1985): 601–16; David Chan, "Functional Relations among Constructs in the Same Content Domain at Different Levels of Analysis: A Typography of Composition Models," *Journal of Applied Psychology* 83, no. 2 (1998): 234–46.

Index

Abramson, Mark, 84–85
Abstract thinking: by change vanguard members, 67–68; by early adopters, 61, 67–68; education levels and, 61, 71; job levels and, 61, 66, 71
Abuse: control as priority for Bush administration, 210–11; credit card use, 212; focus on control of, 14–15, 17–18, 54–55, 66, 210–11; during Iraq war, 211, 212; political attention, 212; rules meant to control, 14; scandals, 54, 211
Acquisition reform. *See* Procurement reform
Acquisition Reform Net, 140
Activating-the-discontented strategy, 6–7, 97; generalizability, 98–99; implications for theory and practice, 99–103; in procurement reform, 39; role of change vanguard, 132–33; size of reform coalition, 104–05
Affluence, autonomy and, 47, 51
Aiken, Michael, 27
Ajzen, Icek, 163
Alinsky, Saul, 101

As-time-goes-by support: as feedback mechanism, 123–27, 148–49; role in deepening, 186–87, 188–89, 193, 195, 208
Attitude changes: evidence, 3–4, 183–84; inducing as strategy for change, 6, 33, 40–41; link to behavior change, 160–63, 169, 171–72; role of successful experience, 117–18. *See also* Deepening
Autonomy, desire for: in bureaucracies, 43; of change vanguard, 65; explanatory models, 48–51; of leaders, 74; motivated, 46–47; principal-agent theory and, 105; of reform coalition members, 63–65, 78–79, 180; as source of discontent, 43, 45–51; sources, 46–51, 105

Bandura, Albert, 119
Behavior: consistency, 22–23; embedded, 23; influences on attitudes, 123, 125
Behavior change: determinants, 160; distinction from successful experience, 164; evidence, 198–200;